ECCLESIASTES/
LAMENTATIONS
A Commentary in the Wesleyan Tradition

Stephen J. Bennett

BEACON HILL PRESS
OF KANSAS CITY

Copyright 2010
by Stephen J. Bennett and Beacon Hill Press of Kansas City

ISBN 978-0-8341-2514-8

Printed in the United States of America

Cover Design: J.R. Caines
Interior Design: Sharon Page

Library of Congress Cataloging-in-Publication Data

Bennett, Stephen J., 1963-
  Ecclesiastes/Lamentations / Stephen J. Bennett.
     p. cm. — (New Beacon Bible commentary)
  Includes bibliographical references and index.
  ISBN 978-0-8341-2514-8 (pbk.. : alk. paper)
   1. Bible. O.T. Ecclesiastes—Commentaries. 2. Bible. O.T. Lamentations—Commentaries. I. Title.
  BS1475.53.B46 2010
  223'.807—dc22
                                                                2010004063

10 9 8 7 6 5 4 3 2 1

DEDICATION

ראה חיים עם־אשה אשר־אהבת Eccl 9:9

To Christi

COMMENTARY EDITORS

CONTENTS

GENERAL EDITORS' PREFACE

The purpose of the New Beacon Bible Commentary is to make available to pastors and students in the twenty-first century a biblical commentary that reflects the best scholarship in the Wesleyan theological tradition. The commentary project aims to make this scholarship accessible to a wider audience to assist them in their understanding and proclamation of Scripture as God's Word.

Writers of the volumes in this series not only are scholars within the Wesleyan theological tradition and experts in their field but also have special interest in the books assigned to them. Their task is to communicate clearly the critical consensus and the full range of other credible voices who have commented on the Scriptures. Though scholarship and scholarly contribution to the understanding of the Scriptures are key concerns of this series, it is not intended as an academic dialogue within the scholarly community. Commentators of this series constantly aim to demonstrate in their work the significance of the Bible as the church's book and the contemporary relevance and application of the biblical message. The project's overall goal is to make available to the church and for her service the fruits of the labors of scholars who are committed to their Christian faith.

The *New International Version* (NIV) is the reference version of the Bible used in this series; however, the focus of exegetical study and comments is the biblical text in its original language. When the commentary uses the NIV, it is printed in bold. The text printed in bold italics is the translation of the author. Commentators also refer to other translations where the text may be difficult or ambiguous.

The structure and organization of the commentaries in this series seeks to facilitate the study of the biblical text in a systematic and methodical way. Study of each biblical book begins with an **Introduction** section that gives an overview of authorship, date, provenance, audience, occasion, purpose, sociological/cultural issues, textual history, literary features, hermeneutical issues, and theological themes necessary to understand the book. This section also includes a brief outline of the book and a list of general works and standard commentaries.

The commentary section for each biblical book follows the outline of the book presented in the introduction. In some volumes, readers will find section **overviews** of large portions of scripture with general comments on their overall literary structure and other literary features. A consistent feature of the commentary is the paragraph-by-paragraph study of biblical texts. This section has three parts: **Behind the Text**, **In the Text**, and **From the Text**.

The goal of the ***Behind the Text*** section is to provide the reader with all the relevant information necessary to understand the text. This includes specific historical situations reflected in the text, the literary context of the text, sociological and cultural issues, and literary features of the text.

In the Text explores what the text says, following its verse-by-verse structure. This section includes a discussion of grammatical details, word studies, and the connectedness of the text to other biblical books/passages or other parts of the book being studied (the canonical relationship). This section provides transliterations of key words in Hebrew and Greek and their literal meanings. The goal here is to explain what the author would have meant and/or what the audience would have understood as the meaning of the text. This is the largest section of the commentary.

The ***From the Text*** section examines the text in relation to the following areas: theological significance, intertextuality, the history of interpretation, use of the Old Testament scriptures in the New Testament, interpretation in later church history, actualization, and application.

The commentary provides ***sidebars*** on topics of interest that are important but not necessarily part of an explanation of the biblical text. These topics are informational items and may cover archaeological, historical, literary, cultural, and theological matters that have relevance to the biblical text. Occasionally, longer detailed discussions of special topics are included as ***excurses.***

We offer this series with our hope and prayer that readers will find it a valuable resource for their understanding of God's Word and an indispensable tool for their critical engagement with the biblical texts.

Roger Hahn, Centennial Initiative General Editor

Alex Varughese, General Editor (Old Testament)

George Lyons, General Editor (New Testament)

ACKNOWLEDGMENTS

The irony of writing another commentary on the book that warns "of making many books there is no end" (Eccl 12:12) was lost on Pineda who, in A.D. 1620, wrote a folio commentary on Ecclesiastes that was 1,079 pages long (Ginsburg 1861, 123). And commentaries on Ecclesiastes continue to be published. My interest in Ecclesiastes goes back at least as far as high school days; I chose Eccl 12 as my selection when it was my turn to read before the class.

My study of Ecclesiastes for this commentary has made me increasingly aware of the ongoing relevance of this book to my own personal life. As my work progressed, I began to notice my children asking "are you busy?" without expecting to receive any attention from me ("busy" is a theme in Ecclesiastes, e.g., 1:13; 3:10). In everyday life, quotations from Ecclesiastes keep coming to me, and I am learning to be more content with the allotment that God has given me (Eccl 5:18). "I know that there is nothing better for men than to be happy and do good while they live" (Eccl 3:12).

Lamentations is also "a very modern book" (Provan 1991, 24). The book draws the reader into its questioning of God and yet shows a profound faith in the midst of such activity. The book was apparently written in response to a specific tragedy, and yet by giving expression to grief it continues to be helpful in bringing order to the chaos of any tragedy, personal or national.

The books by Seow (1997), Whybray (1989), and Ginsburg (1861) have been very influential on my thinking about Ecclesiastes. Provan's (1991) book has been very helpful for Lamentations. I would like to thank Roderick T. Leupp, Christi-An C. Bennett, and Alex Varughese (editor) for their careful reading of the manuscript and their many helpful suggestions. My students at Nyack College and Alliance Theological Seminary have also helped to refine my thinking as well as suggesting new interpretations. I am grateful to Nyack College for a sabbatical that allowed more time for writing. Taconic Retreat and Conference Center graciously provided a beautiful venue for concentrated periods of writing.

—Stephen J. Bennett

ABBREVIATIONS

With a few exceptions, these abbreviations follow those in *The SBL Handbook of Style* (Alexander 1999).

General

A.D.	anno Domini
ABD	*The Anchor Bible Dictionary*
ACCS	Ancient Christian Commentary on Scripture
B.C.	before Christ
BDF	Blass, Debrunner, Funk (1961)
BHQ	*Biblia Hebraica Quinta*
c.	century
ca.	circa
ch	chapter
chs	chapters
EDNT	*Exegetical Dictionary of the New Testament*, edited by Balz and Schneider (1990–93)
ed.	edited by
e.g.	*exempli gratia*, for example
esp.	especially
etc.	*et cetera*, and the rest
GKC	*Gesenius' Hebrew Grammar as Edited and Enlarged by the Late E. Kautzsch*
HALOT	*Hebrew and Aramaic Lexicon of the Old Testament*, edited by Koehler and Baumgartner (1994)
i.e.	*id est*, that is
ktl.	etc. (in Greek transliteration)
LXX	Septuagint (Greek translation of the OT)
MT	Masoretic Text (Hebrew OT)
n	note
n.d.	no date
NIDOTTE	*New International Dictionary of Old Testament Theology and Exegesis*
NT	New Testament
OT	Old Testament
s.v.	*sub verbo*, under the word
TDOT	*Theological Dictionary of the Old Testament*
TWOT	*Theological Wordbook of the Old Testament*
vol.	volume
v	verse
vv	verses

Modern English Versions

ESV	English Standard Version
KJV	King James Version
NASB	New American Standard Bible
NEB	New English Bible
NIV	New International Version
NJB	New Jerusalem Bible
NLT	New Living Translation
NRSV	New Revised Standard Version
RSV	Revised Standard Version

Print Conventions for Translations

Bold font	NIV (bold without quotation marks in the text under study; elsewhere in the regular font, with quotation marks and no further identification)
Bold italic font	Author's translation (without quotation marks)
Italic font	Author's literal rendering (without quotation marks)

Behind the Text:	Literary or historical background information average readers might not know from reading the biblical text alone
In the Text:	Comments on the biblical text, words, phrases, grammar, and so forth
From the Text:	The use of the text by later interpreters, contemporary relevance, theological and ethical implications of the text, with particular emphasis on Wesleyan concerns

Old Testament

Gen	Genesis
Exod	Exodus
Lev	Leviticus
Num	Numbers
Deut	Deuteronomy
Josh	Joshua
Judg	Judges
Ruth	Ruth
1—2 Sam	1—2 Samuel
1—2 Kgs	1—2 Kings
1—2 Chr	1—2 Chronicles
Ezra	Ezra
Neh	Nehemiah
Esth	Esther
Job	Job
Ps/Pss	Psalm/Psalms
Prov	Proverbs
Eccl	Ecclesiastes
Song	Song of Songs / Song of Solomon
Isa	Isaiah
Jer	Jeremiah
Lam	Lamentations
Ezek	Ezekiel

Dan	Daniel
Hos	Hosea
Joel	Joel
Amos	Amos
Obad	Obadiah
Jonah	Jonah
Mic	Micah
Nah	Nahum
Hab	Habakkuk
Zeph	Zephaniah
Hag	Haggai
Zech	Zechariah
Mal	Malachi

(Note: Chapter and verse numbering in the MT and LXX often differ compared to those in English Bibles. To avoid confusion, all biblical references follow the chapter and verse numbering in English translations, even when the text in the MT and LXX is under discussion.)

New Testament

Matt	Matthew
Mark	Mark
Luke	Luke
John	John
Acts	Acts
Rom	Romans
1—2 Cor	1—2 Corinthians
Gal	Galatians
Eph	Ephesians
Phil	Philippians
Col	Colossians
1—2 Thess	1—2 Thessalonians
1—2 Tim	1—2 Timothy
Titus	Titus
Phlm	Philemon
Heb	Hebrews
Jas	James
1—2 Pet	1—2 Peter
1—2—3 John	1—2—3 John
Jude	Jude
Rev	Revelation

Greek Transliteration

Greek	Letter	English
α	alpha	a
β	bēta	b
γ	gamma	g
γ	gamma nasal	n (before γ, κ, ξ, χ)
δ	delta	d
ε	epsilon	e
ζ	zēta	z
η	ēta	ē
θ	thēta	th
ι	iōta	i
κ	kappa	k
λ	lambda	l
μ	my	m
ν	ny	n
ξ	xi	x
ο	omicron	o
π	pi	p
ρ	rhō	r
ρ	initial rhō	rh
σ/ς	sigma	s
τ	tau	t
υ	upsilon	y
υ	upsilon	u (in diphthongs: au, eu, ēu, ou, ui)
φ	phi	ph
χ	chi	ch
ψ	psi	ps
ω	ōmega	ō
`	rough breathing	h (before initial vowels or diphthongs)

Hebrew Consonant Transliteration

Hebrew/Aramaic	Letter	English
א	alef	’
ב	bet	b
ג	gimel	g
ד	dalet	d
ה	he	h
ו	vav	v or w
ז	zayin	z
ח	khet	ḥ
ט	tet	ṭ
י	yod	y
ך/כ	kaf	k
ל	lamed	l
ם/מ	mem	m
ן/נ	nun	n
ס	samek	s
ע	ayin	‘
ף/פ	pe	p
ץ/צ	tsade	ṣ
ק	qof	q
ר	resh	r
שׂ	sin	ś
שׁ	shin	š
ת	tav	t

ECCLESIASTES

BIBLIOGRAPHY FOR ECCLESIASTES

Archer, Gleason L. 1964. *A Survey of Old Testament Introduction*. Chicago: Moody.

Baldwin, Joyce G. 1978. "Is There Pseudonymity in the Old Testament?" *Themelios* 4/1:6-12.

Barbour, Jennifer. 2008. "'You Do Not Know What Disaster May Happen in the Land': The City-Lament Mode in Qoheleth 12:1-8." A paper delivered at the Annual Meeting of the Society of Biblical Literature. Boston, Nov 24.

Barolín, Darío. 2001. "Eclesiastés 8:1-8: Consejos para leer entre líneas." *Cuadernos de Teología* 20:7-22.

Bartholomew, Craig G. 1999. "Qoheleth in the Canon? Current Trends in the Interpretation of Ecclesiastes." *Themelios* 24/3 (May): 4-20.

_____. 2009. *Ecclesiastes*. Grand Rapids: Baker.

Barton, George A. 1908. *The Book of Ecclesiastes*. International Critical Commentary. Edinburgh: T & T Clark.

Berger, Benjamin Lyle. 2001. "Qohelet and the Exigencies of the Absurd." *Biblical Interpretation* 9/2:141-79.

Berlin, Adele. 2002. *Lamentations: A Commentary*. Old Testament Library. Louisville, Ky.: Westminster/John Knox.

Blenkinsopp, Joseph. 1995. "Ecclesiastes 3:1-15: Another Interpretation." *Journal for the Study of the Old Testament* 66:55-64.

Bonhoeffer, Dietrich. 1997. *Letters and Papers from Prison*. New York: Simon and Schuster.

Briant, Pierre. 2002. *From Cyrus to Alexander: A History of the Persian Empire*. Winona Lake, Ind.: Eisenbrauns.

Brown, Dee. 1970. *Bury My Heart at Wounded Knee*. Repr. New York: Henry Holt, 1991.

Brown, William P. 2000. *Ecclesiastes*. Interpretation. Louisville, Ky.: John Knox.

_____. 2007. "Calvin and Qoheleth Meet After a Hard Day's Night" in *Reformed Theology*. Ed. Wallace M. Alston and Michael Welker. Grand Rapids: Eerdmans.

Bruce, F. F. 1952. "The Wisdom Literature of the Bible: The Book of Ecclesiastes." *The Bible Student* 23/4 (Oct): 144-48.

Brunschwig, J., et al. 2000. *Greek Thought*. London: Belknap.

Buhlmann, Alain. 2000. "The Difficulty of Thinking in Greek and Speaking in Hebrew (Qoheleth 3.18; 4.13-16; 5.8)." *Journal for the Study of the Old Testament* 90:101-8.

Bullock, C. Hassell. 1988. *Introduction to the Old Testament Poetic Books*. Chicago: Moody.

Callen, Barry L., and Richard P. Thompson. 2004. *Reading the Bible in Wesleyan Ways*. Kansas City: Beacon Hill Press of Kansas City.

Camus, Albert. 1967. *Lyrical and Critical Essays*. London: Hamilton.

Christianson, Eric S. 2007. *Ecclesiastes Through the Centuries*. Malden, Mass.: Blackwell.

Clarke, Adam. 1813. *The Holy Bible Containing the Old and New Testaments*. New York: Carlton and Porter.

Cohen, Abraham. 1946. *The Five Megilloth*. Hindhead, Surrey: Soncino.

_____, trans. 1983. *Midrash Rabbah: Ecclesiastes*. London: Soncino.

Coogan, Michael David, ed. 2001. *Oxford History of the Biblical World*. Oxford: Oxford University Press.

Cook, F. C. 1875. *The Holy Bible with an Explanatory and Critical Commentary*. London: John Murray.

Crenshaw, James L. 1987. *Ecclesiastes: A Commentary*. Old Testament Library. Philadelphia: Westminster.

Dahood, Mitchell. 1952. "Canaanite-Phoenician Influence in Qoheleth." *Biblica* 33:191-221.

_____. 1966. "The Phoenician Background of Qoheleth." *Biblica* 47:264-82.

Davis, Ellen F. 2000. *Proverbs, Ecclesiastes, and the Song of Songs*. Westminster Bible Companion. Louisville, Ky.: Westminster/John Knox.

Delitzsch, Franz. 1875. *Commentary on the Song of Songs and Ecclesiastes*. Repr. Grand Rapids: Eerdmans, 1982.

Driver, G. R. 1954. "Problems and Solutions," *Vetus Testamentum* 4/3:225-45.

Driver, Samuel Rolles. 1897. *An Introduction to the Literature of the Old Testament*. Repr. Cleveland: Meridian, 1956.

Eaton, Michael A. 1983. *Ecclesiastes: An Introduction and Commentary.* Downers Grove, Ill.: Inter-Varsity Press.

Elwell, Walter A., and Philip W. Comfort, eds. 2001. *Tyndale Bible Dictionary.* Wheaton, Ill.: Tyndale House.

Epstein, I., ed. 1959. *The Babylonian Talmud.* 43 vols. New York: Rebecca Bennet Publications.

Faulkner, R. O. 1973. *The Literature of Ancient Egypt.* New Haven, Conn.: Yale University Press.

Felleman, Hazel. 1936. *The Best Loved Poems of the American People.* New York: Doubleday.

Fox, Michael V. 1999. *A Time to Tear Down and a Time to Build Up.* Grand Rapids: Eerdmans.

Fredericks, Daniel C. 1988. *Qoheleth's Language: Re-evaluating Its Nature and Date.* Lewiston, N.Y.: Edwin Mellen.

Gammie, John G. 1989. *Holiness in Israel.* Minneapolis: Fortress.

Garrett, Duane A. 1993. *Proverbs, Ecclesiastes, Song of Songs.* Nashville: Broadman.

Gault, Brian P. 2008. "A Reexamination of 'Eternity' in Ecclesiastes 3:11." *Bibliotheca Sacra* 165 (Jan-Mar): 39-57.

Ginsberg, H. L. 1951. "Koheleth 12:4 in the Light of Ugaritic." *Syria* 33:99-101.

Ginsburg, Christian. 1861. *The Book of Ecclesiastes: Translated from the Original Hebrew with a Commentary, Historical and Critical.* Repr. New York: Ktav Publishing, 1970.

Gordis, Robert. 1968. *Koheleth—The Man and His World.* New York: Schocken.

Gropp, Douglas M. 1993. "The Origin and Development of the Aramaic *Šalliṭ* Clause." *Journal of Near Eastern Studies* 52/1:31-36.

Harper, A. F. 1967. "Ecclesiastes," in *Beacon Bible Commentary.* Ed. A. F. Harper. Kansas City: Beacon Hill Press of Kansas City.

Harrison, R. K. 1969. *Introduction to the Old Testament.* Grand Rapids: Eerdmans.

Healey, John F. 2001. *The Religion of the Nabataeans.* Leiden: Brill.

Hubbard, David A. 1991. *Ecclesiastes, Song of Solomon.* Communicator's Commentary. Dallas: Word.

Isaksson, Bo. 1987. *Studies in the Language of Qoheleth.* Uppsala: Uppsala University.

Japhet, Sara, and Robert B. Salters, eds. 1985. *Rashbam on Qoheleth.* Leiden: Brill.

Jarick, John. 2000. "The Hebrew Book of Changes: Reflections on *Hakkōl Hebel* and *Lakkōl Zēmān* in Ecclesiastes." *Journal for the Study of the Old Testament* 90:79-99.

Johnson, Raymond Eugene. 1986. "The Rhetorical Question as a Literary Device in Ecclesiastes." Southern Baptist Theological Seminary Ph.D. Dissertation.

Johnson, Samuel. 1810. *The Works of the English Poets from Chaucer to Cowper,* vol. 2. London: J. Johnson.

Kinlaw, Dennis F. 1968. "Ecclesiastes and Song of Solomon," in *Wesleyan Bible Commentary.* Ed. Charles W. Carter. Grand Rapids: Eerdmans.

Kovacs, Maureen Gallery. 1989. *The Epic of Gilgamesh.* Stanford, Calif.: Stanford University Press.

Kraus, Matthew. 2001. "Christian, Jews, and Pagans in Dialogue: Jerome on Ecclesiastes 12:1-7." *Hebrew Union College Annual* 70-71 (1999-2000): 183-231.

Krüger, Thomas. 2004. *Qoheleth: A Commentary.* Hermeneia. Minneapolis: Fortress.

Leith, Mary Joan Winn. 1998. "Israel Among the Nations: The Persian Period," in *Oxford History of the Biblical World.* New York: Oxford University Press.

Leppert, Richard D. 1996. *Art and the Committed Eye.* Boulder, Colo.: Westview.

Lichtheim, Miriam. 1975. *Ancient Egyptian Literature,* vol. 1. *The Old and Middle Kingdoms.* Berkeley: University of California.

_____. 2006. *Ancient Egyptian Literature,* vol. 2. *The New Kingdom.* Berkeley: University of California.

Loader, J. A. 1979. *Polar Structures in the Book of Qohelet.* New York: de Gruyter.

Lohfink, Norbert. 2003. *Qoheleth.* Minneapolis: Fortress.

Longman, Tremper. 1991. *Fictional Akkadian Autobiography: A Generic and Comparative Study.* Winona Lake, Ind.: Eisenbrauns.

_____. 1997. *The Book of Ecclesiastes.* New International Commentary on the Old Testament. Grand Rapids: Eerdmans.

Machinist, Peter. 1995. "Fate, *Miqreh,* and Reason: Some Reflections on Qohelet and Biblical Thought," in *Solving Riddles and Untying Knots.* Jonas C. Greenfield, et al. Winona Lake, Ind.: Eisenbrauns.

Marvin, F. R. 1902. *The Last Words (Real and Traditional) of Distinguished Men and Women.* New York: Revell.

Matthews, Victor H. 1991. *Manners and Customs in the Bible.* Peabody, Mass.: Hendrickson.

Matthews, Victor H., and Don C. Benjamin. 2006. *Old Testament Parallels: Laws and Stories from the Ancient Near East.* New York: Paulist.

Miller, Douglas B. 2002. *Symbol and Rhetoric in Ecclesiastes: The Place of* Hebel *in Qohelet's Work.* Atlanta: Society of Biblical Literature.

Moore, T. M. 2001. *Ecclesiastes: Ancient Wisdom When All Else Fails.* Downers Grove, Ill.: InterVarsity.

Murphy, Roland E. 1981. *Wisdom Literature.* Forms of Old Testament Literature. Grand Rapids: Eerdmans.

_____. 1992. *Ecclesiastes.* Word Biblical Commentary. Dallas: Word.

Newsom, Carol A. 1995. "Job and Ecclesiastes," in *Old Testament Interpretation: Past, Present, and Future.* Ed. James Luther Mays, David L. Petersen, and Kent Harold Richards. Nashville: Abingdon.

Ogden, Graham. 1987. *Qoheleth.* Sheffield: JSOT Press.

Peterson, Eugene H. 1980. *Five Smooth Stones for Pastoral Work.* Grand Rapids: Eerdmans.

Pritchard, James B., ed. 1969. *Ancient Near Eastern Texts Relating to the Old Testament.* Third Edition with Supplement. Princeton, N.J.: Princeton University Press.

Provan, Iain. 2001. *Ecclesiastes, Song of Songs.* NIV Application Commentary. Grand Rapids: Zondervan.

Rainey, Anson F., and R. Steven Notley. 2006. *The Sacred Bridge: Carta's Atlas of the Biblical World.* Jerusalem: Carta.

Redman, Matt and Beth Redman. 2000. Thankyou Music (PRS).

Russell, Bertrand. 2004. *History of Western Philosophy.* New York: Routledge.

Schoors, A. 1992. *The Preacher Sought to Find Pleasing Words: A Study of the Language of Qoheleth.* Leuven: Peeters.

Scott, R. B. Y. 1965. *Proverbs, Ecclesiastes: Introduction, Translation, and Notes.* Anchor Bible. New York: Doubleday.

Seow, C. L. 1997. *Ecclesiastes: A New Translation with Introduction and Commentary.* Anchor Bible. New York: Doubleday.

Simpson, William Kelly, ed. 1972. *The Literature of Ancient Egypt.* New Haven, Conn.: Yale University Press.

Spangenberg, Izak J. J. 1996. "Irony in the Book of Qohelet." *Journal for the Study of the Old Testament* 72:57-69.

Steinberg, Paul. 2007. *Celebrating the Jewish Year.* Philadelphia: Jewish Publication Society.

Towner, W. Sibley. 1997. "The Book of Ecclesiastes: Introduction, Commentary, and Reflections." *New Interpreter's Bible,* vol. 5. Nashville: Abingdon.

Ullendorff, Edward. 1962. "The Meaning of קהלת." *Vetus Testamentum* 12/2:215.

Unger, Merrill, F. 1957. *Unger's Bible Dictionary.* Chicago: Moody.

von Rad, Gerhard. 1965. *Old Testament Theology,* vol. 2. *The Theology of Israel's Prophetic Traditions.* New York: Harper and Row.

_____. 1972. *Wisdom in Israel.* Nashville: Abingdon.

Weeks, Stuart. 2008. "The Prologue of Ecclesiastes." A paper delivered at the Annual Meeting of the Society of Biblical Literature. Boston, Nov 24.

Whitley, Charles F. 1979. *Koheleth: His Language and Thought.* New York: de Gruyter.

Whybray, R. N. 1989. *Ecclesiastes.* New Century Bible Commentary. Grand Rapids: Eerdmans.

Wright, Addison G. 1980. "The Riddle of the Sphinx Revisited: Numerical Patterns in the Book of Qoheleth." *Catholic Biblical Quarterly* 42:38-51.

Wright, Charles Henry Hamilton. 1883. *The Book of Koheleth.* London: Hodder and Stoughton.

Wright, J. Robert. 2005. *Proverbs, Ecclesiastes, Song of Solomon.* Ancient Christian Commentary on Scripture. Downers Grove, Ill.: InterVarsity.

Youngblood, Ronald F. 1986. "Qoheleth's 'Dark House' (Eccl 12:5)." *Journal of the Evangelical Theological Society* 29/4 (Dec): 397-410.

INTRODUCTION
TO ECCLESIASTES

The title Ecclesiastes derives from the Hebrew *qōhelet*, which means someone who is a leader of an assembly or congregation (*ekklesia* in Greek). Most scholars today refer to the book by its Hebrew title Qoheleth. In the Hebrew Bible, this book is grouped with Esther, Lamentations, Ruth, and Song of Songs, and together these books are known as the Megilloth or the Five Festal Scrolls.

Ecclesiastes is one of the most interesting books in the Bible, in part because it is so different from the others, even from the other Wisdom books (Job, Proverbs, Song of Songs). Like the Wisdom books, Ecclesiastes largely ignores the history and law of ancient Israel, but it also challenges the accepted themes and theology of the wisdom tradition. This has led to puzzlement from general readers and a great diversity of interpretation from scholars. As such it is important to read the words of Qoheleth in the context of his argument as a whole, and also to acknowledge the possibility that other interpretations may also be correct. The purpose of this commentary is to present a viable (and hopefully helpful) interpretation of Ecclesiastes, while also including some of the diversity of interpretation that has gone before.

It seems that the paradoxes, enigmas, and contradictions of Ecclesiastes are purposefully presented to communicate a coherent message that attempts to get at the true meaning of life, while also recognizing the limitations of life in the OT context where there was no developed understanding of life after death. According to Qoheleth, meaning in life is limited by the leveling effect of death, by the sovereignty of God that limits human control, and possibly also by the threat of war, which was ever present in the Hellenistic and Persian periods. This makes striving for immortality in terms of wealth and renown a futile task but restores meaning to the simple pleasures of life (food, drink, relationships), which should be enjoyed as a gift from God. Thus the book advocates contentment over accumulation, wisdom over wealth, and portion over profit (see Theological Themes). The book recognizes that even wisdom has significant limitations. Everything in life may be limited, short-lived, incomprehensible, or even absurd, but there is good, and even joy, awaiting those who can accept this and live their lives under the sovereignty of God.

A. Authorship

The authorship of a biblical book has long been connected with the authority of the book (at least as far back as the rabbinic period; Berlin 2002, 31). Biblical authority for NT books was often connected with apostolic authority; thus challenges to an early date of a book have been seen as challenges to the authority of that book. This principle has been applied to OT books where authority was connected with a prophet or some other prominent figure whose credentials could be tested. In a world without printing presses, however, the production of biblical books was more of a drawn out process because copies had to be made by hand and therefore the community had more involvement in the writing. Thus the test of authorial authority is inadequate and is belied by the fact that many biblical books are anonymous, even though tradition may have ascribed authorship to most of these books. The authority of a biblical book, in the end, lies in the content of the book, which was recognized as inspired and canonical by the community of faith (Kinlaw 1968, 609).

The traditional view regards Solomon as the author of Ecclesiastes. This tradition goes back at least as far as the Talmud (ancient rabbinic writing). Solomonic authorship was not mentioned in the Jewish discussions at Jamnia (ca. A.D. 90), and the Septuagint (ancient Greek translation) does not translate 1:1 in a way that identifies Solomon, but translates *qōhelet* as *Ekklesiastou*, a member of the citizens' assembly (Christianson 2007, 89).

Ancient Views of Authorship

Views of authorship in the ancient world were different from modern concepts and for most of the OT period authors preferred to stay anonymous, which is apparently the aim of Qoheleth's enigmatic self-identification. There was no copyright law or financial gain for authorship and writers tended not to be very individualistic about their work. Any given book was considered community property and was likely to be a community product. Copying manuscripts by hand was expensive and if someone took the time and money to make a copy, then additions could be made that would make the book more valuable to the owner. As time went by, it became less likely that intentional changes would be made to books that were considered sacred scripture. One common addition that was often important was identifying the author of the book, or more specifically, the origin of the prophecy or sayings that are collected. So, most of the OT prophets have an editorial addition that identifies the prophets whose messages or biographical material have been recorded and collected. Likewise, various sages are identified as authors in the book of Proverbs (Solomon, Hezekiah as collector of Solomonic proverbs, Agur, and King Lemuel).

In the period between the OT and the NT, identifying authorship became more common and also led to the practice of attributing a book to a famous person of the distant past, such as Enoch, Abraham, or the twelve sons of Jacob. This practice, called pseudonymity, began in the third century B.C. (Baldwin 1978, 17).

The word *qōhelet* (NIV, "Teacher") could be a personal name but is more likely an identification of the title of the author (real or assumed). The word is unknown outside Ecclesiastes and has the form of a feminine noun, although it is always used with masculine verbs (if 7:27 is a scribal error).

Qoheleth is further identified as "son of David, king in Jerusalem," which is an obvious reference to Solomon, although 1:1 does not specifically mention Solomon's name. While the Hebrew word for "son" (*bēn*) can also mean descendant or disciple, the further qualifications "king in Jerusalem" (1:1) and "king over Israel" (1:12) narrow the scope down to Solomon alone. He was the only son of David who ruled in Jerusalem, although Absalom and Adonijah did rule briefly without David's consent. No other descendant of David ruled over *all* Israel except Rehoboam, the son of Solomon who succeeded his father only long enough to see the kingdom divided with Jeroboam becoming king of the northern tribes. Masoretic accents and the later references in 1:12—2:26 show that Qoheleth himself was king, not just the son of a king (although the latter is grammatically possible). Solomonic authorship is supported by Garrett (1993, 257-67), Archer (1964, 470), Unger (1957, 284), and Cohen (1946, 106).

There are, however, reasons to think that Solomon is not the author of Ecclesiastes. The book was probably written much later than Solomon's time (see the section on date below) and there are elements that do not seem to have come from Solomon, or even a king. The section on the author's reflection on life (1:12—2:26) seems to be loosely based on the description of Solomon in 1 Kgs 4 but does not correlate well with that of 1 Kgs 11. In Ecclesiastes the king is mindful of the limitations of wisdom, wealth, and pleasure, which had characterized his younger years. On the contrary, the portrait of Solomon in 1 Kgs 11 is one of a king who turned away from God in his old age and did evil, even succumbing to idolatry.

The Talmud explained this anomaly by taking the words "I, the Teacher, was king" (1:12) to mean that at some point Solomon ceased to be king, having been dethroned by Ashmedai, the prince of demons, as a punishment for his sins of idolatry, but that Solomon later repented (*Gittin* 68a).

The Solomonic authorship of Ecclesiastes was taken for granted for centuries but came under critical study in the seventeenth century. In 1644 Hugo Grotius raised the first serious challenge (Christianson 2007, 95). Driver noted a number of inconsistencies with authorship by Solomon, such as the place of judgment being filled by wickedness (3:16), the wrongs done by powerful oppressors (4:1), and corruption of rulers that hinders the appeal process (5:8) (1897, 441). Kings in ancient times did not write about themselves in a negative light. Archer argued that the arguments against royal authorship are not decisive (1964, 462-69). However, the book's perspective on kingship is suggestive of nonroyal authorship.

B. Date

Evidence for the date of a biblical book comes from a number of sources. The latest date a book could have been written (*terminus ante quem*) is the date of the oldest copy. Documents were written out by hand before the invention of the printing press, and none of the original documents of biblical books have survived, but only copies (of copies). The age of a copy can sometimes be determined by where it was found, or by writing style, since handwriting scripts changed over time. Sometimes carbon dating or the types of material that were used can assist in dating manuscripts. The oldest fragments of Ecclesiastes are from the Dead Sea Scrolls and are dated no earlier than 175 B.C. That means that Ecclesiastes most likely comes from a period earlier than the second century. Whitley's second century B.C. date is all but excluded by this evidence because it is highly unlikely that a relatively new book would have been accepted as authoritative so soon (1979, 148).

Clear allusions to Ecclesiastes in other writings would be the next evidence that could help with dating. There are similarities and differences between Ecclesiastes and the book of Sirach (dated to 175 B.C.). Some of these may be understood as allusions to or criticisms of Ecclesiastes. For example, Sirach agrees with Qoheleth that death is the final fate of all humanity. "Whether life lasts ten or a hundred or a thousand years, there are no questions asked in Hades" (Sirach 41:4; see Eccl 6:3-6; Krüger 2004, 28). Care must be taken in this approach because common ideas may have influenced both books; however, the Dead Sea Scrolls fragment supports a date for Ecclesiastes that is earlier than Sirach.

Historical references can provide a clue to dating. If a book mentions the fall of Jerusalem as a past fact, then it must have been written after that fact. Historical references in Ecclesiastes are few and not very helpful for dating, despite attempts to find plausible events in history that would be relevant (4:13-16; 8:2-4; 9:13-15; 10:16-17; Whybray 1989, 9). Nevertheless, Crenshaw, for example, has used "meager political data" to suggest a date for Ecclesiastes between 250 and 225 B.C. (1987, 50). He bases this on the apparent setting of the book in peaceful times (indicating a date before the Maccabean revolt, 164 B.C.), the attitude toward foreign rulers, and economic prosperity for Jews but restrictions under Antiochus IV. Whybray also argued for a Hellenistic date partly because of a perceived lack of evidence in Ecclesiastes of the conflict that raged in Palestine before 300 B.C. (1989, 11). However, Crenshaw's and Whybray's arguments for a lack of war in Ecclesiastes may be misplaced in light of the possible allusions to war or the results of war in the book (e.g., 3:1-8; 12:1-8).

In the absence of clear historical data, attempts are sometimes made to date a book by comparing the ideas contained in it with other contemporary literature. This method is vulnerable because it assumes that ideas develop in a linear fashion, and that all writers of a given time share the same ideas. Nevertheless, if historical data are not available, the known development of ideas can help to establish the date of a book or part of a book.

The development of thought has been a major factor in dating Ecclesiastes for Whybray, who dates the book to the Hellenistic period largely on the basis of connections with Greek thought such as a perception of God as hidden and remote, and Qoheleth's challenge of the doctrine of retribution (1989, 8). As Whybray acknowledges, Qoheleth is also greatly dependent on the religious and wisdom traditions of Israel, and some elements that are identified as Hellenistic can also be found to some degree in the Hebrew literature. For example, the book of Job (e.g., 2:3-5; 7:20) already offers some nuance to the doctrine of retribution. Similar philosophy could also be the result of similar experience. There are no other definitive indicators of direct Greek dependence, such as Greek words, in Ecclesiastes. As such, the development of thought cannot offer a precise dating for Ecclesiastes.

Linguistic evidence is something of a last resort for dating an ancient book as there is comparatively little evidence on the development of ancient languages. Often the book under consideration contributes to our knowledge of the language and so dating arguments are in danger of becoming circular. Neither is language development necessarily linear. Other factors may influence the use of linguistic innovations such as foreign influence, a colloquial tone, subject matter, and a conservative outlook. Despite this, the language of Qoheleth has been a major consideration in dating simply because of the lack of clear data from other sources, but also because the language differs markedly from the style of Hebrew employed in most of the Hebrew Bible. For this reason, Carol Newsom has identified the language of Ecclesiastes as one of the perennial problems of interpretation in current scholarship (1995, 184).

C. L. Seow has summarized linguistic arguments for dating under the headings orthography, foreign influences, and diction (1997, 11-21). Orthography refers to spelling, which changed over time as Hebrew scribes attempted to indicate vowel distinctions in the consonantal script. Ecclesiastes contains more of these vowel indicators (*matres lectiones*) than preexilic writings.

Foreign influence on the language of Ecclesiastes is seen in two Persian loanwords (2:5; 8:11), as well as significant Aramaic vocabulary and influence. Persian words are not found in any preexilic writings. Aramaic vocabulary is present in preexilic writings because Israel bordered the nation where that language originated (Syria), but exposure to Aramaic was greater after the exile and the postexilic biblical books reflect this. Seow attempts to refine the dating to the Persian period by means of nuances that are not found outside this period (1997, 14). For example, the word *šālaṭ* usually means "to have right, power" but in Ecclesiastes means "to have right of disposal," a meaning only found in the Persian period (e.g., Neh 5:15, but not Daniel; see Gropp 1993, 34). Along with other evidence for nuances found only in the Persian period, Seow's argument is persuasive, although Krüger rejects the opinion that *šālaṭ* never connotes (political) power in Ecclesiastes (verb, 2:19; 5:19; 6:2; 8:9; nouns, 7:19; 8:4, 8; 10:5) (2004, 36).

The category of diction refers to vocabulary and grammar. A common element used for dating is the choice of relative pronoun ("who," "which"). Preexilic books use the longer form (*'ăšer*) except for seven instances, while the shorter form (*še*) is common in many later works. Ecclesiastes accounts for half of the occurrences of the shorter form but also uses the longer form about as many times (this mixing of forms is unusual). The choice of relative pronoun could have been influenced by foreign vocabulary, a northern dialect, or colloquial speech, but taken together with other linguistic evidence is highly suggestive of a postexilic date. Seow found twenty-six expressions in Ecclesiastes that occur elsewhere only in postexilic texts (1997, 17-19), while the analysis of Schoors found thirty-four features that are typical of postexilic Hebrew (1992, 221).

Gleason Archer defended Solomonic authorship, mainly by rejecting a postexilic date for the language of Ecclesiastes. He argued that since the language is unique, it cannot be used to date the book to any period (1964, 462-69). However, as nineteenth-century German scholar Franz Delitzsch said in his famous quote, "If the Book of Koheleth were of old Solomonic origin, then there is no history of the Hebrew language" (1875, 190). Fredericks' arguments for an exilic or preexilic date for the language of Ecclesiastes depend on many possibilities for which evidence is lacking (1988, 262). For example, when Qoheleth shares vocabulary with postexilic documents but that vocabulary is lacking in preexilic texts, Fredericks appeals to the possibility that the words could have entered the language earlier than is shown by the literary evidence we have (Schoors 1992, 15). A preexilic date is also argued by M. Elyoenai, who sees the language as an early nonliterary popular language (1977, cited by Schoors 1992, 11). This argument is hypothetical because the nature of a nonliterary language cannot be known.

The book as a whole cannot be dated precisely on linguistic or other grounds. This is the position of Eaton, who does not attempt to date the book on the basis of language and leaves the matter undecided (1983, 19, 24). Isaksson's structuralist analysis also rejects the dating of Ecclesiastes on linguistic grounds (1987, 197).

Nevertheless, there are many elements of the language of Ecclesiastes that are unknown in the preexilic period, and linguistic arguments for a postexilic date for Ecclesiastes are compelling. The main choices within this time frame are the Persian period and the Hellenistic period. The arguments for a Persian date compiled by Seow are impressive and very precise (1997, 11-21). However, to some extent they argue from silence because if there were more data from the Hellenistic period they might reveal a more complex use of the language. Nevertheless, he has amassed a good amount of evidence. Arguments for a Hellenistic dating also tend to rely on silence, such as a perceived lack of evidence of war.

A majority of scholars support the Hellenistic dating, and yet the evidence does not exclude a Persian dating. Fortunately the social conditions for both periods are similar and Qoheleth's commercial interests apply to the monetary system that began in the Persian period and continued to develop in the Hellenistic period. So this commentary will attempt to interpret his message in relation to the postexilic era in general and the Persian period in particular.

C. Place of Origin

Linguistic evidence has been used to argue for a northern Israel provenance for Ecclesiastes (Dahood 1966, 264-82), but the linguistic features of the book are so unique and current knowledge of northern Hebrew so limited that this cannot be definitive. Jerusalem is mentioned in 1:1, but this probably does not give information about provenance since the verse was likely added by a later editor.

Palestine is favored as the provenance for Ecclesiastes because of elements in the book that fit better in that geographical location than other possibilities. These are references to reservoirs and wells (2:6; 12:6), leaky roofs (10:18), the temple (5:1; 8:10), farmers' attention to the wind (11:4), the three primary products of bread, wine, and oil (9:7-8), and also almond trees (12:5; Murphy 1992, xxii).

D. Audience, Occasion, Purpose

Standard Wisdom literature, such as found in the book of Proverbs, tends to be addressed to children who are being educated in skills for living (Prov 1:1-8). Ecclesiastes shares this tone to some extent (11:9; 12:12) but seems to target the older youth who has begun to see the limitations of the simplistic teaching addressed to children. This youth is developing abstract thinking and has noticed the complexities of life. Doing good does not seem to guarantee blessing from God. Qoheleth wants not only to identify with "the skepticism characteristic of youth" (Davis 2000, 161) but also to help the youth see that wisdom still has value and that God is still sovereign.

The doctrine of retribution is open to abuse in two directions. One is to work it backward and judge righteousness or wickedness by material wealth. The book of Job addresses this problem. The other is to use righteousness as a means to material wealth, as a kind of manipulation of God. Qoheleth rejects this approach and warns that wealth does not bring lasting satisfaction and can easily be lost (e.g., in a bad venture, 5:14). Instead, one's orientation in life should be the fear of God. Any material blessings that one does have should be enjoyed as a gift from God without endless striving for more. In a way this is Qoheleth's advice for coping in the postexilic world where money had become a commodity and wealth could easily be hoarded. He wanted to "subvert their preoccupation" with wealth (Seow 1997, 69).

The postexilic periods were times of great empires. Territories such as Palestine changed hands and were sometimes embroiled in foreign and domestic power struggles. The threat of war was often very real, and the results of war could be devastating. Qoheleth addressed the existential reality of death that everyone faces. He may also have been giving a warning about finding meaning in life in light of the possibility that war could sweep away life as it was known. Death could come unexpectedly or property could change hands unfairly with the arrival of a new regime.

E. Sociological and Cultural Issues

Ecclesiastes was written to a postexilic audience that lived in social systems very different from the earlier monarchies of Israel and Judah. The Babylonian, Persian, and Hellenistic emperors, some of whom called themselves "king of kings" (e.g., Darius I; Rainey and Notley 2006, 286), had a great deal of control over individual freedoms, especially through a system of provinces and governors (Matthews 1991, 151). This must have had a significant impact on Qoheleth's advice for conduct before the king, and especially his doctrine of the sovereignty of God.

Economic changes in the postexilic period reflected a growing move away from the agricultural economy of the preexilic monarchies to a monetary system. Nehemiah 5:3-5 indicates a continuation of agricultural activities, but these became complicated by heavy taxes that were often paid by mortgaging land and even enslaving family members. This is possible in a monetary economic system, and *kesep* became more than silver to be weighed out for every transaction; it became money. Official coins were hand-stamped from the sixth century on (Matthews 1991, 177). These coins bore the name of the province, "Yehuda." Large numbers of locally minted coins in small denominations dating to the fourth century B.C. have also been found in Israel; the Samaria papyri mention buying and selling and the use of money in the local economy, and for paying taxes (Leith 1998, 417). The arrival of money as a commodity to be hoarded was a target of Qoheleth's warnings about one's orientation in life (Eccl 5:13).

The economic system was fed by trade, which was increased through road building and maintenance, and also the development of shipping lanes (Neh 13:16). The new monetary system had great potential for economic advancement, and even slaves could engage in business deals. But those motivated by greed were vulnerable to great loss. Qoheleth addressed the new emphasis on trade in a warning about the failure of risky ventures (Eccl 5:14). These innovations in the Persian period were adopted and expanded in the Hellenistic period with the "introduction of Greek marketing techniques and fresh operating capital" (Matthews 1991, 194). Although the exact date of Ecclesiastes cannot be determined, the above analysis strongly suggests that the message of the book would have spoken to an audience in both Persian and Hellenistic periods.

F. Textual History and Composition

I. Text

The oldest complete copy of Ecclesiastes in Hebrew is the Leningrad Codex of the Masoretic text (A.D. 1008). Ecclesiastes is not in the older Aleppo Codex. Dead Sea Scroll fragments of the book (1:10-14; 5:14-18; 6:3-8; 6:12—7:6; 7:7-10, 19-20) have been dated from 175 B.C. to the mid-first century B.C. The Septuagint translation of Ecclesiastes differs from the Old Greek translations of other OT books. It has more in common with the literal translations of Aquila. Syriac and Latin translations also follow the Hebrew in most instances (Krüger 2004, 37-38).

2. Canon

Ecclesiastes is one of the books whose authority was challenged by the rabbinical school of Shammai. The Talmud records the dismissal of this challenge with recourse to the seventy-two elders famous for the translation of the Septuagint (Ginsburg 1861, 16).

3. Composition

The integrity of Ecclesiastes as entirely the work of a single author has been argued by such significant interpreters as Delitzsch (1875, 188, 200) and Fox (1999, 159). But most modern commentators see at least 1:1 and 12:9-14 as editorial additions. There are others who see major additions throughout the book by later editors of the book (D. C. Siegfried saw nine hands; Barton 1908, 28).

The third person narratives (1:1; 12:9-14) do seem to be editorial additions. Editorial additions are a common feature of OT prophetic books, as ancient scrolls tended not to have a cover page indicating author, title, and publication details. Whybray has made a compelling argument that the refrain "vanity of vanities" (KJV) found with variations at the beginning and end of the book (1:2; 12:8) is also an editorial addition (1989, 35; Barton 1908, 69, disagrees). While the word *hebel* ("vanity") is found thirty-eight times throughout the book, it is not an absolute declaration (apart from 1:2 and 12:8), but a response to specific circumstances or observations.

G. Literary Features

I. Genre

The three dominant literary forms of Ecclesiastes are reflection, instruction, and sayings, in that order. In reflections, the author uses personal thoughts and observations to make conclusions about a truth. The reflection in 1:12—2:26 has the form of a royal autobiography. Von Rad assigned the form "Royal Testament" to the whole book (1972, 226). However, not all the reflection is from a royal perspective. While the autobiographical tone pervades the book, the royal perspective does not. Some aspects of Qoheleth's reflection comprise a kind of dialogue with received wisdom or proverbs (e.g., Prov 11:19; Eccl 3:16), but the book as a whole is more complex than the diatribe of the Hellenistic period (Murphy 1992, xxxi).

Instructions are a common element of wisdom teaching and both positive (7:14) and negative (7:21) instructions are included in Ecclesiastes. Qoheleth instructs his audience on how to approach God (5:1-7) and how to behave before kings (8:2-6).

The specific sayings are not known outside Ecclesiastes, so some could be authored by Qoheleth but some could nevertheless be quotes of sayings that were well-known at the time. At times he seems to quote a known saying or perspective for the purpose of refuting or nuancing it (7:1) or to quote a saying sarcastically (10:19).

Other literary forms in Ecclesiastes are example stories (9:13-16), questions (some rhetorical, 1:3; see Johnson 1986, 1-304), woe oracles (4:10), and didactic poems (1:4-11).

The genre of Ecclesiastes as a whole is as elusive as the justice and wisdom about which Qoheleth writes (3:16; 7:24). Since the different literary forms in the book all have the purpose of instruction in the tradition of the wisdom teachers, perhaps an appropriate designation for the book as a whole would be "didactic collection." Reflections, instructions, and sayings are collected to make a point about how to respond to the complexities of life.

2. Linguistic Style

The language of Ecclesiastes is unique in the OT and all Hebrew literature. There is a baffling use of the personal pronoun that other books normally use only for emphasis (because it is inherent in the Hebrew finite verb). Another puzzling linguistic feature is the alternation between the two relative pronouns *še* and *'ăšer* (see the section on Date). Qoheleth makes little use of the *waw*-consecutive, a common verbal construction in Hebrew, but this may be explained by a lack of narrative in Ecclesiastes. Participles are a common feature in Ecclesiastes, a form that the OT makes little use of but which became more popular in postbiblical Hebrew.

3. Literary Style

The autobiographical style (except in chs 11—12, which move to direct address) yields a heavy use of personal pronouns in the book. The NIV translates with "I" eighty-three times (thirty-eight in the royal autobiography), which includes first person use of the finite verb but not the redundant use of the personal pronoun in the book (which would add another twenty-three occurrences).

Qoheleth also favors key words and phrases, repetition, wordplays, alliteration, chiasm (A, B, C, B', A' structure), and comparisons (see commentary for examples). Repetition is so important that Qoheleth's favorite words make up 20 percent of the book (Murphy 1981, 130, citing Loretz).

Qoheleth also uses much rare or unique vocabulary. Some words are found in no other biblical book (*hapax legomena*), and some are found in no other Hebrew literature. Many are Aramaic or their form is influenced by Aramaic. These features could be explained by date, dialect, or place of origin. But Qoheleth could be using the features of Aramaic, the *lingua franca* of his time, to give the flavor of the new commercial systems which that language served (suggested by Charles Eapen in a student seminar, Alliance Theological

Seminary, 2009; there are also a large number of commercial terms in Ecclesiastes). Likewise the grammatical anomalies (such as the mixture of relative pronouns) could be intended to disorient the reader in order to mirror the disorienting effect of the enigmas of life.

4. Structure

Many scholars see no discernible structure in Ecclesiastes (see Newsom 1995, 187). Others see a carefully composed structure based on form rather than content (such as A. G. Wright, 1980). Ginsburg analyzed the book into four major sections plus prologue and epilogue (1:1-10; 1:11—2:26; 3:1—5:20; 6:1—8:15; 8:15—12:7; 12:8-14) (1861, 17-21). Seow also analyzes the body of the book into four sections: Reflection: Everything Is Ephemeral and Unreliable (1:2—4:16); Ethics: Coping with Uncertainty (5:1—6:9); Reflection: Everything Is Elusive (6:10—8:17); Ethics: Coping with Risks and Death (9:1—12:8) (1997, 46-47). Such analysis requires reduction of diverse themes under simplified headings, and Qoheleth's habit of recycling themes tends to defy identification of this kind of structure.

There are, however, indications that some kind of intentional structure is present in the book as a whole, particularly with the editorial additions. Ecclesiastes begins with a title (1:1) then the theme, "vanity of vanities" (1:2 KJV). Likewise the book ends with a (nearly identical) repetition of the theme (12:8) and an epilogue (12:9-14). The body of the book does not contain the theme as stated in 1:2 and 12:8, but one of the usual variations occurs at 6:9 ("this also is vanity and a chasing after wind" [NRSV]), which coincidentally is preceded by 1,491 words and followed by 1,491 words. This is also just before the Masoretes' midpoint verse (6:10), which begins the second set of 111 verses (Seow 1997, 45, citing D. N. Freedman). The unit before this midpoint deals with the limitations of wealth (5:10—6:9) and the unit following deals with the limitations of wisdom (6:10—7:14). This has led some to seek a chiasm for the whole book (Lohfink 2003, 8), but this is difficult to identify (Krüger 2004, 8). Although key themes are repeated throughout the book, they do not seem to be arranged in a chiasm, or any other obvious overarching structure. Barbour observes that both the royal autobiography (1:12—2:26) and the concluding imagery (12:1-8) share the motifs of houses, plants, servants, singers, gold and silver (2008). If the conclusion (12:1-8) is presenting imagery of the desolation of war, then its position in the book signals a reversal of the prosperity under Solomon, with which the book began (see comment on 12:1-8). This commentary analyzes the book into fourteen units, as follows:

Outline

    I. Vanity of Vanities (Title and Theme) (1:1-2)
    II. There Is No Profit from Toil (Prologue) (1:3—11)

Summary

The book of Ecclesiastes begins with a title identifying the book as the words of Qoheleth and the statement of a theme: "vanity of vanities; all is vanity" (1:1-2 KJV). The book is further introduced by a treatise on the unending activities of nature and humanity, and the lack of profit that an individual can leave behind in the light of this constancy (1:3-11). This is followed by an investigation set as an autobiographical reflection by Solomon, and this sets the tone for the whole book (1:12—2:26). In this introduction the king investigates pleasure, wealth, and wisdom but does not find lasting satisfaction in any of these. A poem on time follows, which emphasizes God's sovereignty in human affairs (3:1-8) and is followed by advice to enjoy life (3:9-22), as well as a warning of a time for judgment (3:15-17). Comparisons in ch 4 begin with despair (4:1-3) but also advise contentment (4:4-6), companionship (4:7-12), and wisdom (4:13-16). Chapter 5 begins by urging caution in speech (5:1-9) and also addresses the issues of oppression and justice (5:8-9). A chiasm follows, which shows that wealth brings no lasting satisfaction and advises contentment with whatever God has given (5:10—6:9). The limitation and value of wisdom is addressed in the next unit, also in a chiastic structure (6:10—7:14). Then Qoheleth addresses the elusiveness of judgment (7:15-18), righteousness (7:19-22), and wisdom (7:23-24) with a conclusion that judgment is nevertheless a coming reality, and that righteousness and wisdom are still superior to the alternatives (7:25-29). More advice to enjoy life follows despite the mysteries of an unpredictable world (8:1—9:12). Then Qoheleth discusses the limited benefits of wisdom, by giving examples, some involving kings (9:13—10:19). Generosity is urged (10:20—11:6) and then more advice to enjoy life follows, but in the knowledge that all deeds will be judged by God (11:7—12:7). This course of action should begin in youth before the storms of old age and death (or perhaps war) overtake. The editorial theme is repeated (12:8) and an epilogue commends the book to the reader as "pleasing words"

(NRSV) and adds advice to obey God's commandments since all action will be subject to his judgment (12:8-14).

H. Theological Themes

Ginsburg on the Theology of Ecclesiastes

The design of this book . . . is to gather together the desponding people of God from the various expediencies to which they have resorted, in consequence of the inexplicable difficulties and perplexities in the moral government of God, into the community of the Lord, by shewing them the utter insufficiency of all human efforts to obtain real happiness, which cannot be secured by wisdom, pleasure, industry, wealth, &c., but consists in the calm enjoyment of life, in the resignation to the dealings of Providence, in the service of God, and in the belief in a future state of retribution, when all the mysteries in the present course of the world shall be solved. (1861, 16-17)

1. Vanity of Vanities (*hăbēl hăbālîm hakkōl hābel*)

The most obvious theme of Ecclesiastes is "vanity of vanities" (KJV) ("Meaningless! Meaningless!" in the NIV) found in 1:2 and 12:8, and translating the word *hebel*, which is used thirty-eight times in the book. The traditional KJV translation "vanity" is derived from the Latin word for "empty," a nuance that is probably lost on most English readers today. The Hebrew word, which literally means *breath, vapor*, defies translation since Qoheleth uses it with a variety of nuances (although NIV always translates it as "meaningless" in Ecclesiastes, but uses nineteen different translations when the word is used elsewhere in the Bible. Fox always translates *hebel* as "absurd" [1999, 30]).

The ambiguity of the word seems to suit Qoheleth as he presents the enigmatic nature of life in his book, often using enigmatic language (hence Bartholomew's translation of *hebel* as "enigmatic" [2009, 93]). It is probable that many of his uses of *hebel* are intended to convey more than one nuance at a time (Scott 1965, 202). *Hebel* is often used in connection with the phrase "chasing after the wind" (1:14; 2:11, 17, 26; 4:4, 16; 6:9). This seems to imply a futile task or at least an unattainable goal. Other uses are coupled with the word "evil" (*raʿ*), suggesting that he dislikes these aspects of life (2:17; 4:8; 6:2). Some contexts seem to indicate the meaning of *hebel* as "brief, fleeting" (6:12; 9:9; 11:10; see Job 7:16; Pss 39:5, 6, 11; 144:4; Jas 4:14 [*atmis*]). The word *profit, gain* is an important theme in Ecclesiastes, and the lack of profit is sometimes connected with *hebel* (2:11; 6:11). Some activities in life are inconsequential. Another nuance that Qoheleth seems to have in mind is "incomprehensible" (2:15, 26; 3:19; 4:16; 5:10; 8:10, 14; see Job 35:16 where *hebel* is parallel with the phrase "without knowledge").

The meanings "futile," "unattainable," "evil," "fleeting," "profitless," "inconsequential," "ineffective," and "incomprehensible" are used in different contexts with varying certainty and sometimes with overlap. The blanket statements in 1:2 and 12:8 that suggest that life is always and only meaningless do not seem to catch the message of the book as a whole. There are certain things about life that are meaningless (like hoarding wealth, and envy), but other things (like wisdom and family) are to be valued and enjoyed, even though their value and potential for enjoyment may be limited by other factors such as their ultimate unattainability and their fleeting nature. Part of the key to enjoying life is the fear of God and accepting his sovereignty.

2. Sovereignty of God (*yad hāʾĕlōhîm*)

The sovereignty of God is a major theme in Ecclesiastes and is sometimes expressed in the phrase "the hand of God" (*yad hāʾĕlōhîm*, 2:24; 9:1). One of the incomprehensible (*hebel*) things about life is that human action (such as wisdom and righteousness) does not always lead to the predictable result (success in life). Qoheleth's answer to this is that everything happens in God's time (ch 3) and according to his will. Whatever one has in life is a gift from God, it is from his hand; it is not under human control. God, however, has every right to bring judgment on those who are wicked and no doubt will someday (8:6; 11:9; 12:14). God is not the "distant despot" (against Crenshaw 1987, 30, who uses the language of Pedersen) but like the kings described in Ecclesiastes, he can be unpredictable and he must be approached with reverence and obedience (5:1; 8:2; 10:20). God is mentioned thirty-nine times in Ecclesiastes, while *hebel* is mentioned thirty-eight times. This is probably coincidental but nevertheless suggestive of the priority God takes over the enigmas of life. Although it sometimes seems that justice and meaning are absent from the world, God is still in control and in the end, his judgment will prevail.

3. Limitations of Wisdom and Righteousness (*hokmâ and ṣedeq*)

Ecclesiastes stands in the tradition of Wisdom literature, which includes Proverbs, Job, Song of Songs, some psalms, and a wealth of literature outside the Bible (there is also evidence of influence on the NT). The place of Ecclesiastes among this literature is seen partly in the frequency of vocabulary from the root "wisdom" (fifty-three times) as well as related vocabulary (such as "to know"; thirty-six times) and other features of Wisdom literature such as proverbs or short sayings (Seow 1997, 67). The standard message of Wisdom literature to its young audience is that godly choices lead to success in life and these choices should be conducted on the foundation of the fear of the Lord (see the section on retribution below). The presentation of wisdom to young audiences is necessarily simplified, and Ecclesiastes seems to be moving beyond the simple answers to address an older audience who have begun to see the complexities of life. Wisdom (and its counterpart, righteousness) does not always achieve the expected results. At times Qoheleth makes this point with such strength that it seems wisdom is of no use whatsoever (1:18; 2:16; 6:8; 7:7, 16; 8:17; 10:1), but at other times the value of wisdom is expressed, even if its powers are limited and all humanity must ultimately come under the sovereignty of God (2:13, 14, 19, 26; 4:13; 7:5-6, 11, 12, 19; 8:1, 5; 9:10, 13, 15, 16, 17, 18; 10:10, 12; 12:11).

4. Doctrine of Retribution, and Limitations (*mišpāṭ*)

The covenant between God and Israel included consequences for compliance or noncompliance. These consequences are identified as blessings and curses for the nation and are listed in Deut 27—28. Wisdom literature has a more individual focus, and the consequences were not so much national as individual. The consequences in Deuteronomy are also more intimately tied to Yahweh (the LORD), whereas in Wisdom literature they tend to be almost automatic without mention of God's involvement (Seow 1997, 66). The consequences in Wisdom literature are sometimes known as the "doctrine of retribution" and can be summed up in a proverb: "you reap what you sow" (see Job 4:8; Prov 11:18; 22:8; Hos 8:7; 10:12; also, 1 Cor 9:11; Gal 6:7).

Such a doctrine is open to oversimplification, and while it is the standard premise of Wisdom literature as reflected in the book of Proverbs, there are challenges to the doctrine within Scripture (Prov 11:16; 13:23; 14:13; 21:31; Jer 12:13; Mic 6:15). The book of Job provides a significant challenge with the defense that righteousness cannot be gauged by material blessings (Job 1:8; 2:3; 23:10). Ecclesiastes at times seems to abandon the doctrine altogether (8:14; 9:2-3) but then also acknowledges some value to it (11:9; 12:14).

Ginsburg saw in Ecclesiastes an acknowledgment of the limitations of retribution in this life and hence the belief that justice would be served in the world to come, thus anticipating the NT position (1861, 27). Most of the OT does not predict an eschatological judgment, however, and the references to future judgment in Ecclesiastes can all be understood as referring to the retribution an individual will face in this life. Nevertheless it is possible that Ecclesiastes was participating in a growing belief in an eschatological judgment day that the NT later develops. However, the tone of Ecclesiastes seems to be lamenting the lack of timely judgment from God while holding onto the belief that God will nevertheless bring justice (in this life).

5. Profit and Portion (*yitrôn* and *ḥeleq*)

The standard Wisdom literature doctrine of retribution advises godly choices leading to success in life, but Qoheleth repeatedly challenges the profit (*yitrôn*) of basic human activities. This seems to be a direct challenge to the developing monetary economy in the Persian and Hellenistic periods. The doctrine of retribution could easily be abused as a means to gain excess wealth, but Qoheleth rejects this approach with a warning that the results of wisdom are uncertain and that the satisfaction of wealth is limited.

Instead of pursuing profit, Qoheleth recommends satisfaction with one's portion (*heleq*), which is the gift that God in his sovereignty has given to every person. This portion cannot be changed, and the key to happiness is contentment with this gift.

6. Wealth and Contentment (*kesep* and *rāʾâ ṭôb*)

Wealth is an important theme in Ecclesiastes and while Qoheleth sarcastically identifies money (*kesep*) as an answer for everything (10:19), he also warns against risky business ventures, the unreliability of wealth, and the inability of wealth to bring lasting satisfaction (5:10-14). Wealth should not be the orientation of one's life.

Instead, one should be content with the portion that God has given. Enjoyment or contentment is literally *see good* (*rāʾâ ṭôb*) and involves seeing the gifts that God has given as good, instead of striving or wishing for more (2:24; 3:12-13; 5:18-19; 9:7-9). There is no guarantee that more can be gained in this unreliable world, and even if it is, it does not bring lasting satisfaction or leave an indelible impression on the world. This is not a fatalistic perspective characterized by the phrase "eat, drink, and be merry, . . . for tomorrow we die" (Isa 22:13 NLT) but a deep conviction that God's gifts are good and their enjoyment should not be diminished by constant striving for more.

Qoheleth's interest in wealth is seen in his rich vocabulary of commercial terms such as "gain" (*yitrôn*), "lacking" (*hesrôn*), "scheme" (*hešbôn*), "possessions" (*nĕkasîm*), "money" (*kesep*), "wealth" (*ʿōšer*), "rich man" (*ʿašîr*), "treasure" (*sĕgullâ*), "return" (*śākār*), "inheritance" (*nahalâ*), "skill" (*kišrôn*), "income" (*tĕbûʾâ*), "wealth" (*hămôn*), "burden" (*ʿinyān*), "labor" (*ʿāmāl*), "consume" (*ʾōkēl*), "worker" (*ʿōbēd*), "reward" (*hēleq*) (Seow 1997, 22; see Dahood 1952, 221).

7. Ethics

Ecclesiastes, like other Wisdom literature, is very much focused on the plight of the individual and does not call for sweeping reforms to bring social justice. Perhaps reform was seen as less of a possibility in the empires of the postexilic period. When Qoheleth does call attention to the plight of the oppressed, it is only to show what a nuisance it is for the wise to observe oppression (4:1; 5:8; 7:7). Nevertheless Qoheleth gives advice on how to act before kings (8:2-4), and he also calls for generosity (11:1-2).

The call to obey God's commandments in the epilogue is not mentioned elsewhere in the book, even though wisdom and obedience to the Law often go together elsewhere (Pss 1; 119). The call to fear God is found elsewhere in Ecclesiastes, and this is a common Wisdom literature theme (5:7; 7:18; 8:12-13; 12:13; twenty occurrences in Proverbs).

I. Hermeneutical Issues

1. Diversity of Interpretation

There is such a great diversity of interpretation of the book of Ecclesiastes that any conclusions must be reached with caution. The apparent contradictions in the book allow some interpreters to focus on one side of the argument, and others to focus on the other. It is difficult to strike a balance of interpretation that accounts for the paradoxes and complexity of the text.

Crenshaw's interpretation stands at one end of the spectrum (1987, 23-24). He sees Qoheleth's "oppressive message" as "life is profitless; totally absurd." He argues that Qoheleth "discerns no moral order at all," a message that stands in stark contrast to the wisdom teaching of the book of Proverbs. He sees the references to divine judgment (order) as a disturbance of thought and syntax, that is, they are added by an orthodox scribe to counteract "Qohelet's shocking advice" (e.g., 11:9b). Calvin seemed to distrust Ecclesiastes and did not write a commentary on it, only quoting it a few times in his *Institutes* (Brown 2007, 76).

Seow stands at the other end of the spectrum. He sees Ecclesiastes as a unit (even the epilogue) and takes the tone of the message as one of joy (1997, 38-43). Luther shared this view of Ecclesiastes (Ginsburg 1861, 112).

The complexity of the text is to some extent a reflection of the complexity of life itself (Fox 1999, 3). While Crenshaw believes that Qoheleth sees life as "totally absurd," he is also able to say, "Like [Qoheleth], I observe a discrepancy between the vision of a just world, which I refuse to relinquish, and reality as I perceive it" (1987, 23, 53). Qoheleth spends a great deal of time criticizing wisdom and retribution but still refuses to relinquish that doctrine altogether. Rather, he attempts to nuance it so that it will not be taken as an absolute guarantee. Life is totally absurd if it is pursued with certain values, but under other conditions it has meaning, although it also has limitations.

Interpretation of the book also rests on one's understanding of key words and phrases such as *hebel* ("vanity," "meaningless") and "chasing after the wind." Both are metaphors and their meaning must be determined by the context in which they are used. "Chasing after the wind" is a waste of time because the wind cannot be caught. However, some pursuits (like the attempt to interpret Ecclesiastes!) are worthwhile, even though they may never end in a definitive resolution.

2. Dealing with Contradictions

Ecclesiastes is famous for its contradictions, and these have been explained in a number of ways: (1) the book is a collection of sayings by different authors, and no coherency should be expected; (2) an editor(s) has added moralistic glosses to ensure that the perceived unorthodoxy of Qoheleth is not allowed to have the final say; (3) Qoheleth has quoted various traditional Wisdom sayings with the purpose of refuting them, or nuancing them; (4) Qoheleth's contradictions are intentional as he attempts to provide a balanced picture of the complexities of life. It is the last of these that is the approach of this commentary, while acknowledging the presence of some quotations that Qoheleth often refutes or nuances. This approach takes the final form of the text seriously and makes sense of the book as it stands.

3. Interpretive History

Known interpretation of Ecclesiastes begins with Sirach, who apparently knew of Ecclesiastes and wrote in some sense in dialogue with Ecclesiastes. The Talmud also records rabbinical interpretations and especially the debate over whether the book "defiles the hands," that is, has the kind of authority that would require ritual washing. Literal interpretation gave way to allegorical by the fourth century A.D. in both Jewish and Christian circles. For example, the former saw a reference to the Torah in "eating and drinking" (e.g., 2:24), and the latter a reference to the Eucharist. Literal interpretation returned with the Reformation. Historical-critical interpretation (beginning with Grotius, A.D. 1644) began to abandon the epilogue as the interpretive key to the book and instead saw a collection of different opinions. This methodology reached its height around the turn of the twentieth century (e.g., Barton 1908), and during the twentieth century the trend has been back toward seeing the book as a unity (usually with the exception of the epilogue, but not always). Bartholomew catalogs a number of recent approaches to the interpretation of Ecclesiastes, namely canonical, literary, new critical, structuralist, dialogical, narrative-literary, poststructuralist, feminist, and psychoanalytic readings (1999, 7-13).

4. Wesleyan Interpretation

John Wesley wrote *Explanatory Notes on Ecclesiastes* and interpreted the book literally with the exception of the images in 12:1-6. He took the sovereignty of God in ch 3 seriously, explained 7:29 in terms of original sin, and took 7:20 to mean that no one is universally and perfectly good. He appreciated a paraphrase titled *Choheleth; or, the Preacher* written by a "Turkey Merchant" (Journal February 8, 1768). Wesley wrote in his journal (January 12, 1777) that the various parts of Ecclesiastes are "in so exquisite a manner connected together; all tending to prove that grand truth, — that there is no happiness out of God."

Thomas Coke wrote *A Commentary on the Holy Bible*, which contained Ecclesiastes in the third volume (1802). Ginsburg called it "mostly a reprint of the unfortunate Dr. [William] Dodd's work" and notes that it sees Ecclesiastes as an argument for the necessity of the afterlife (1861, 196).

Adam Clarke's 1813 commentary follows the contention of the Turkey Merchant that "the subject of the book is the chief or sovereign good, which man, as a rational and accountable being, should here propose to himself." He denies Solomonic authorship and notes the unique language of Ecclesiastes (Ginsburg 1861, 196-97).

Wesleyan commentaries of the book include works by Harper (*Beacon Bible Commentary*, 1967), Kinlaw (*Wesleyan Bible Commentary*, 1968), and Schultz (*Asbury Bible Commentary*, 1992).

J. Liturgical Use of Ecclesiastes

In Jewish tradition, Ecclesiastes is read at the end of the dry season during the Feast of Tabernacles (Sukkoth). In the Hebrew Bible Ecclesiastes is grouped with five scrolls that are read at different festivals. The reason that Ecclesiastes was chosen for this festival is not clear, but Christianson (2007, 31) suggests two possibilities: the other four festivals had scrolls associated with them and so Sukkoth and Ecclesiastes came together by default; and "Ecclesiastes reflects the transient, fragile and joyful moods of Sukkoth, which remembers the time in the wilderness of rootless wandering, unstable habitation . . . and the hope of a promised land." Lohfink suggests that the invitations to rejoice in Ecclesiastes led to its association with Sukkoth, which is known as "the season of our rejoicing" (2003, in Steinberg 2007, 165). Some think that Ecclesiastes provides a somber balance to the celebration of Sukkoth (Peterson 1980, 162). Another possibility is that Ecclesiastes was in some sense seen as a warning against orienting one's life around the harvest (i.e., wealth), since Sukkoth comes during the fruit harvest, which is the last summer harvest before the rainy season begins and the plowing and planting cycle continues.

COMMENTARY ON ECCLESIASTES

I. VANITY OF VANITIES (TITLE AND THEME) (1:1-2)

BEHIND THE TEXT

The opening sentence of Ecclesiastes is the superscript and functions as a kind of title page for the book. The first word or words of a Hebrew book are often used as the title, and so these are chosen carefully. The Hebrew title of Ecclesiastes is the second word, *qōhelet* (**Teacher**). Like the superscripts of other OT books, v 1 was probably added by an editor or scribe to identify the book.

The mention of the **son of David, king in Jerusalem** calls to mind Solomon in all his glory, but there are reasons to think that Ecclesiastes comes from a later time, the Persian or Hellenistic period (see Authorship and Date sections in the Introduction).

The first two verses of Ecclesiastes establish the editorial framework and theme for the book. Verse 1 is the title of the book and v 2 introduces the theme of the book. The phrase "vanity of vanities" (KJV) (*hăbēl hăbālîm*, **Meaningless! Meaningless!**) is a literary device indicating the greatest or best of something (e.g., Song of Songs). It also forms an inclusio with its counterpart in 12:8. Though v 2 sets the tone, the declaration of **Meaningless!** is not followed in an absolute sense by the rest of the book. Rather, this declaration is explained with examples from the complexity and, often, ambiguity of life.

The Words of the Teacher

Editorial titles for OT books or collections often begin with **the words of** x or a similar formula. The book of Proverbs begins with "The proverbs of Solomon" and also has collections introduced as "The sayings of Agur," "The sayings of King Lemuel," "Sayings of the wise," and "These are more proverbs of Solomon" (Prov 1:1; 30:1; 31:1; 22:17; 25:1). Prophetic books also use this formula, for example, "The words of Jeremiah" and "The words of Amos" (Jer 1:1; Amos 1:1). A similar formula is found in the Egyptian Wisdom literature called "instructions," for example, "The instruction of the Mayor and Vizier Ptahhotep" (Pritchard 1969, 412).

IN THE TEXT

A. Title (1:1)

■ **1** Verse 1 introduces the content of the book as **the words of the Teacher** (*qōhelet*). *Qōhelet* is a word unique to Ecclesiastes and derives from the noun *qāhāl*, which means "assembly, convocation" (BDB 874). Thus *qōhelet* is "convener [of an assembly]" or "collector (of sentences)" (BDB 875 [although the verb is never used for collecting objects]). BDB identifies this as a masculine noun, but it has a feminine noun ending, and it takes the masculine verb (except in 7:27, which could be a scribal error). Ginsburg explained the feminine form by suggesting that Solomon was the personification of wisdom, which is a feminine noun in Hebrew (1861, 7; so Augustine and others). However, there are other cases of an office using a feminine form, even though the holder of the office is male (*soferet*, scribe, Ezra 2:55), and also of males whose names have a feminine form (Alemeth, 1 Chr 7:8). Moore's translation is "the Worship Leader," which is based partly on Solomon's dedication of the temple in 1 Kgs 8 (2001, 17, 117). Leading worship is not a function of Qoheleth in Ecclesiastes. Another suggestion is "arguer," based on Aramaic vocabulary (Ullendorff 1962, 215).

The Septuagint translated *qōhelet* with the Greek word *Ekklesiastou* ("member of the political assembly"). The translation "Preacher" (ESV) is misleading because Qoheleth was not the preacher in a church or other religious gathering.

Instead of an office or function, *qōhelet* could be a pseudonym or a nickname (Lohfink 2003, 10). In one or two uses of the word, the article is used ("*the* Qoheleth," 12:8 and probably 7:27), which would be unusual for a personal name. However, Ecclesiastes also uses *qōhelet* as a personal name in 1:12 and 12:9-10. There is no son of David or any other known person with the name *qōhelet*, although the verbal form is used with Solomon as subject in 1 Kgs 8:1. Ginsburg thought that *qōhelet* was used in order to present Solomon as an ideal and not as the actual author (1861, 244-45).

This commentary will use "Qoheleth" to refer to the author of the book and "Ecclesiastes" to refer to the book as a whole.

The phrase **son of David, king in Jerusalem** clearly points to Solomon, even though it is not a reliable indicator of Solomonic authorship. Solomon was considered the father of wisdom in ancient Israel, and his request for wisdom in 1 Kgs 3:3-15 is well known. In the list of Solomon's accomplishments he is also credited with writing three thousand proverbs and one thousand and five songs (1 Kgs 4:32). He is connected with the book of Proverbs, Song of Songs, and the apocryphal book Wisdom of Solomon.

B. Theme (1:2)

■2 Verse 2 establishes the theme of the book with Qoheleth's declaration, **"Meaningless! Meaningless!"** The meaning of the Hebrew word underlying **meaningless** (*hebel*) is difficult to convey in English. The context must determine which meaning is intended in any given verse. In this thematic verse, the context is the book of Ecclesiastes as a whole, thus it carries the rich connotations of the different uses. These meanings can be summarized as futile, unattainable, evil, fleeting, profitless, inconsequential, ineffective, and incomprehensible (see Introduction).

The literal meaning of *hebel* is *breath, vapor*. Breath is not by nature meaningless. It is essential for life. It is, however, brief, and while it is satisfying to breathe, breathing must be a continuous activity if life is to be sustained. So an individual breath gives no lasting satisfaction, but there must be more. Likewise, breathing is not an end in itself but is merely a means to life. This is the nature of life. It is filled with good things that are, by their nature, temporary, and that may be satisfying but are not an end in themselves. The Hebrew word *hebel* is a suitable vehicle for this aspect of life, which Qoheleth wishes to convey. The pleasures and accomplishments of life are meaningful, but they do not provide ultimate meaning. That is to be found in relationship with God.

43

Hebel (Meaningless)

> The noun *hebel* is used thirty-eight times in Ecclesiastes and thirty-five times elsewhere in the OT. The literal meaning is *vapor, breath*, which is seen in Isa 57:13 where *hebel* is used in parallel with "wind." The wind or breath will carry the idols away. The figurative meaning is "vanity" in the sense of insubstantial or worthless (BDB 210), and thus refers to something that evaporates (Ginsburg 1861, 259). This is relevant in the case of idols that "will perish" (Jer 10:15). The books of Deuteronomy, Kings, and Jeremiah often use *hebel* with the meaning "worthless idols" (e.g., Deut 32:21; 1 Kgs 16:13; Jer 2:5). Isaiah denounced the military help of Egypt as *hebel* in the sense of "useless" (Isa 30:7). The word is also used in parallel with "nothing" (*tōhû*) in Isa 49:4. The name "Abel" is *hebel* in Hebrew and shows the meaning of "temporary" as his life was so short (having been murdered by his brother Cain). The same root is used as a verb five times (2 Kgs 17:15; Job 27:12; Ps 62:10; Jer 2:5; 23:16).

The phrase "vanity of vanities" (KJV) (*hăbēl hăbālîm*, **Meaningless! Meaningless!**) follows a Hebrew idiom that expresses the superlative. Other examples are "Song of Songs" (*the best song*), "heaven of heavens" (KJV) ("highest heaven," 1 Kgs 8:27), "servant of servants" (KJV) ("the lowest of slaves," Gen 9:25), and "holy of holies" (NASB) (the "Most Holy Place," Exod 26:33). The superlative nature of "vanity of vanities" seems out of place as the rest of the book uses this vocabulary for various aspects of life but not as a blanket assessment of life as a whole (except as an inclusio to the whole book in 12:8). This may be an indication that v 2 (and 12:8) was added by the final editor (so Rashbam; Japhet and Salters 1985, 92, 212). Another reason it seems to be an editorial addition is that Qoheleth is referred to in the third person.

Verse 2 also seems to indicate that the significance of what Qoheleth observes about life and nature is not limited to his generation. The Hebrew verb *ʾāmar* (**says**) is in the perfect, which is usually translated with the past tense. However, it can also refer to an event that is viewed as a whole, even though it may not be completed at the time of writing. The present tense translation **says** emphasizes the continuing relevance and validity of Qoheleth's conclusions (Crenshaw 1987, 58).

Verse 2 concludes with the phrase, **Everything is meaningless.** The Hebrew word *kōl* (*everything* or *all*) is found throughout the book, in about ninety-one verses out of the two hundred twenty-two verses of the book. The predominant use of this word in Qoheleth conveys a universal perspective and Qoheleth's concern with "all of life," as he reflects on the meaning of life (Towner 1997, 278).

Verse 2 serves not only as the theme or motto for the whole book but also as the opening statement for the introduction (1:3-11). This introduction does not use the word *hebel* but describes the continuous activity of nature, the lack of novelty, and the lack of remembrance. The author describes the activities in vv 3-11 as *hebel*, which in the context may be taken to mean "incomprehensible, ineffective." The impact of the alliteration in v 2 is striking. There is a preponderance of "h" and "l" sounds, not least because of the repetition of the word *hebel* (five times in eight words): *hăbēl hăbālîm ʾāmar qōhelet hăbēl hăbālîm hakkōl hăbēl.* The very sound of the sentence has a continuous and incomprehensible nature to it. This alliteration serves to emphasize the continuous nature and incomprehensibility of the activities described in vv 3-11.

FROM THE TEXT

For the author of Ecclesiastes Solomon is a prime example of someone who had great wisdom and wealth but who failed to grasp the real meaning of life. While the descriptions of Solomon's wisdom and wealth in 1 Kings are superlative, he ended his life away from God, entrapped by the very pleasures that were available to him because of his wisdom and wealth. Thus the example of Solomon serves as a dire warning to those who would make wisdom and wealth an end in themselves and thus risk losing the real meaning of life: a right relationship with God and contentment with whatever God in his sovereignty has apportioned to each one. However, for most people in ancient Israel, life on earth was not meaningless, though in their faith there was no clear development of the idea of an afterlife. The faithful in Israel were committed to living their life to the fullest in the here and now. Qoheleth does not say that life in the final analysis is "meaningless" or "absurd." While he viewed life as temporary and incomprehensible, he also regarded it as a gift from God that is to be valued and lived to the full. It is this perception of life that leads us to find contentment in Christ. This is what Paul seems to be saying when he writes: "I have learned to be content whatever the circumstances" (Phil 4:11; see also Phil 1:21-26). Living life to the full in submission to God is the antidote to despair and meaninglessness.

A picture of vanity: The still-life painting style known as "vanitas," from sixteenth- and seventeenth-century Northern Europe is often accompanied by the motto from Eccl 1:2 in Latin. The paintings are intended to convey the transient and fragile nature of life by means of symbols such as skulls, bubbles, musical instruments, and hourglasses (Leppert 1996, 57-58).

II. THERE IS NO PROFIT FROM TOIL (PROLOGUE) (1:3-11)

BEHIND THE TEXT

Verses 3-11 follow the thematic pronouncement that all is vanity (v 2). While that pronouncement may have been an editorial addition, and is certainly intended to function as the theme for the book as a whole, it also colors the reading of what immediately follows (1:3-11).

These verses form the introduction for the book and set the tone for the book as a whole. It is not immediately obvious just what that tone is. The topic at hand is the constant flow and insatiable nature of the environment and life (e.g., rivers flowing into the sea, v 7). Does this make life meaningless or meaningful? The opening and closing framework of the passage seems to suggest the former. There is no profit to human toil (v 2), and there will be no remembrance by future generations (v 11). The language used is also characterized by redundancy and helps to give emphasis to the meaningless nature of life. However, the lack of lasting profit does not mean that life cannot be enjoyed in a meaningful way, as Qoheleth will make explicit in later chapters.

Several important themes are introduced in this unit through the use of the words **gain, labor, under the sun,** and **remembrance.**

The observation that water flows to the sea but does not overflow the sea (v 7) led to the assumption in the ancient world that the water somehow made its way back to the beginning of the rivers, specifically by means of passages under the earth. The Targum of Ecclesiastes makes this explicit, "all the rivers and streams of water run and flow into the ocean, which surrounds the world like a ring, and the ocean is not full; and to the place where the rivers have run and flowed, thither they return again through the subterranean channels" (see Ginsburg 1861, 263).

Verses 3-11 may be labeled as a reflection poem. These verses convey the author's observations about various aspects of nature and human life. Literary devices include verb and noun forms that use the same root (v 3, **labor, toils,** *ʿāmal*), repetition (v 6), and rhetorical questions (vv 3, 8, 10). Repetition emphasizes the message that there is nothing new (v 9). Verses 3-11 can be outlined as follows:

No One Leaves a Surplus (1:3)
Nothing Changes (1:4-8)
Nothing Is New or Remembered (1:9-11)

IN THE TEXT

A. No One Leaves a Surplus (1:3)

■3 Qoheleth's rhetorical question, **What does man gain from all his labor at which he toils under the sun?** introduces an important theme: the lack of lasting profit for human activity during the short life span of each individual. Qoheleth uses the word **man** (*ʾādām*) in v 3 and elsewhere in the book in a generic sense, referring to all humanity (but see comment on 7:28). The endless toil without any gain is the lot of all humanity.

The profit or **gain** (*yitrôn*) is not the normal surplus that arises from business activity or employment. It is the extra gain that would allow someone to get ahead and to leave a surplus at the end of one's life (the root form *yātar* means "to remain over"). For example, a farmer's gain is a surplus that could be sold from a harvest after meeting the needs of his family and animals and seed for the following year. In a business venture, gain is a profit that would allow expansion of a business, and not just payment of employees and debts and purchase of replacement stock. The word is of Aramaic origin (Fredericks disagrees; 1988, 227) and occurs only in Ecclesiastes (1:3; 2:11, 13; 3:9; 5:9, 16; 7:12; 10:10, 11) but is common in postbiblical Hebrew (Ginsburg 1861, 260). This suggests a postexilic date for the book. Other words for "profit" occur throughout the OT (*yāʿal, sākan, ḥālaq, bāṣaʿ*), and the rhetorical question "what profit?" occurs nineteen times (e.g., Hab 2:18; Job 21:15; eight times in Ecclesiastes; Johnson 1986, 127-28).

Dialogue Between a Man and His Ba

Are you not a man? Indeed you are alive, but what do you profit? Yet you yearn for life like a man of wealth. (Faulkner 1973, 203)

The word **gain** signals a commercial interest in Ecclesiastes that is evidenced by a plethora of commercial terms and an interest in business ventures (e.g., 5:14). It is also one of four examples that Seow identified as occurring as economic terms in Egyptian Aramaic texts from the fifth century B.C. (but not before the fifth century; also "lacking," 1:15; "scheme," 7:25; "wealth," 6:2) (1997, 13).

In Ecclesiastes, **gain** or profit is used in contrast to "lot" or "portion." While there were young entrepreneurs in the developing economies of the postexilic era who oriented their lives around profit, Qoheleth advised contentment with one's portion. Wealth and wisdom would not be enough to control life in an incomprehensible and unpredictable (*hebel*) world. What is needed instead is submission to God's sovereignty, which leads to contentment with the portion that God has assigned to each one.

The profit in question is the result of **labor** (*ʿāmāl*). This **labor** is not the positive labor of a fulfilled worker. Its predominant use in Qoheleth indicates a unique emphasis of Qoheleth (twenty-two times out of fifty times in the Hebrew Bible). The term here connotes an unpleasant, arduous toil and is sometimes translated "trouble" (Jer 20:18; there are more neutral words for "work," *măʿăśeh*, *ʿăbôdâ*). It is intensified by the use of the same root for noun and verb: *all his toil at which he toils* (*běkol-ʿămālô šeyyaʿămōl*). The emphasis is thus on trouble, suffering and pain of hard labor, the destiny of humans reflected in the narrative in Gen 3 (Towner 1997, 280).

The phrase **which he toils under the sun** conveys special vocabulary in Qoheleth. The relative pronoun **which** (*še*) is not unusual in postexilic Hebrew, but Qoheleth's use is unusual because the author also uses a longer word with the same meaning (*ʾăšer*). Most biblical books use one or the other. There is no explanation for this mix, unless Qoheleth is trying to portray the enigmas of life by using enigmatic language.

The phrase **under the sun** is unique to Ecclesiastes in the OT (used twenty-nine times; Ecclesiastes accounts for thirty-five occurrences of the word **sun** out of a total of one hundred eighty-four in the OT). In English the connotation of **under the sun** may be negative, especially in the context of toil. Working under the hot sun is tiresome (Ps 121:6). But the sun also represents light and the source of life in the ancient world and was even an object of worship (Ps 84:11; Eccl 11:7). The preferred expression in the OT is "under heaven [sky]," which is also used by Qoheleth (1:13; 2:3; 3:1). It seems that **under the sun** refers to the realm of the living, whereas "under heaven [sky]" does not distinguish between mortal existence either in the land of the living, or in Sheol, the underworld. However, Qoheleth uses both phrases with no apparent difference in meaning. Qoheleth may also be emphasizing the universality of his observations (Hubbard 1991, 46).

Medieval Jewish interpreter Ibn Ezra saw in the phrase **under the sun** an allusion to revolving time, which is consistent with the usual interpretation of v 5 as an emphasis on the cycles of the sun (see Ginsburg 1861, 49). Verse 5, however, is more likely emphasizing continued and constant activity rather than cycles. **Under the sun** is used by some extrabiblical texts including Greek texts. This does not prove Greek influence, as it is also used in sixth and seventh century B.C. Phoenician and Elamite documents (Eaton 1983, 58). The particular focus of the phrase in v 3 is apparently the brevity of an individual life when compared with the constancy of nature. Individual life lasts "but a day" (i.e., one sun) while the earth remains for ages (v 4, ʿôlām).

Epic of Gilgamesh, 2000-1550 B.C.

Must I lay my head in the heart of the earth
that I may sleep through all the years?
Let mine eyes behold the sun
        That I may have my fill of the light!
Darkness withdraws when there is enough light.
May one who indeed is dead behold yet the radiance of the sun!
(Old Babylonian version; Pritchard 1969, 89)

What do humans gain from all their toil if they are merely surviving? This is like the proverbial boy who complained that he did not learn much at school, as evidenced by the fact that he had to go back again the next day! As the sun pants (šôʾēp) its way across the sky (1:5), so humans are stuck in an endless stream of events that they cannot fathom or control. The context is necessary to determine the expected response to this rhetorical question. A series of positive values from labor could be listed if v 2 had not already declared everything *hebel* and the following verses did not emphasize the constancy of nature. As it stands, the answer to the rhetorical question is "nothing." There is nothing to be gained from the toil of humanity. Once the human lifespan is over, the world will be the same as it ever was. No surplus will be left behind. This is an important theme in Ecclesiastes as it implies a lack of contentment with the portion that God has given. While there is a definite satisfaction in a hard day's work (5:12), there is dissatisfaction if that work is oriented around striving for excessive profit.

B. Nothing Changes (1:4-8)

■ **4** Verse 4 continues the theme of endless activity with the phrase **generations come and generations go,** or more literally, *a generation goes and a generation comes*. The verb **go** (*hālak*) is used elsewhere to refer to death, both in Ecclesiastes (3:20; 5:15) and other OT texts (Ps 39:13; Job 10:21; 14:20; 2 Sam 12:23). This is an important verb in this unit and helps to emphasize the ongoing nature of life. The participial form here (*hōlēk*), which emphasizes ongoing action, adds weight to this theme.

Even though individual human lives do not last long "under the sun," in the big picture there is a constancy of human life. One generation goes to the grave, while another comes into the world (Hebrew *bô'* can mean "come" or "enter"). The focus of the word **generation** (*dôr*) is on a group of people (household) rather than a time frame (it sometimes means "dwelling"; Isa 38:12 NRSV). It is the people who come and go, rather than the time that comes and goes. Ogden suggests that the emphasis could be on the generations of nature, rather than people (1987, 30).

While human generations go and come, **the earth remains forever.** The **earth** represents the first of the four elements that ancient philosophers discussed. The others—air, fire, and water—are subjects of the following verses (Ibn Ezra, see Ginsburg 1861, 261). **Forever** (*'ôlām*) does not have the timeless connotation in Hebrew that it does in English. *'Ôlām* means a long time, or an age, whether in the past or the future (ancient Hebrew thought tended to be more concrete than abstract).

This last line of v 4 is usually taken as a contrast between the permanence of the earth and the temporary nature of human life. But Fox seems to be right when he suggests that the emphasis is on the unchanging nature of humanity (i.e., the world) rather than the permanence of the earth (1999, 166). **Generations go** or walk (*hōlēk*), while **the earth remains** or stands (*'ōmādet*, Ginsburg 1861, 261; see Pss 104:5; 119:90). Whether going or standing, both human life and the earth itself (or the world, i.e., the population) remain essentially the same. So the conjunction (**but**) should probably be taken as "and/also."

Nevertheless, by alluding to death, Qoheleth has also marked the brevity of individual human life. It is precisely because of the continuous going and coming of human generations, that an individual human life can make little difference (or "profit") to the whole.

■ **5** Verse 5 now shows the unchanging nature of the sun's activity. If Qoheleth were interested in economy of words, then the wording "the sun rises and sets" would have been sufficient. The repetition of **sun** in the phrase adds to the poetic impact and helps to emphasize the endless nature of life, which is the subject of this unit.

There is an anomaly in the Hebrew of the first word of v 5, which is literally *and he rose* or *and he will rise* (Qal perfect, *wĕzāraḥ*). The other verbs in this verse are participles, emphasizing the continuous motion of the sun (even the other occurrence of **rises** is a participle, *zôrēaḥ*). Thus *wĕzāraḥ* is commonly translated as a participle (**rises**) with the assumption that the first two consonants of the word were reversed in a scribal error (called metathesis; *wzrḥ* instead of *zwrḥ*, suggested by BHS. The first two letters look similar in Hebrew, *waw* and *zayin*, ו and ז). However, the same result is possible by changing the vowels only, which has the advantage of preserving the consonants (*wĕzōrēaḥ*; Krüger 2004, 47).

The language of v 5 reflects the ancient view of the sun rising and setting. Modern usage retains this vocabulary, but we understand that the sun is stationary while the earth revolves around it. Ancient Hebrew culture did not understand this, but based its science on observation. **The sun sets** is literally *the sun enters*, that is, it enters the earth. Ancient cosmology explained the appearance of the sun back in the east each day with the assumption that it had traveled under the earth (through Sheol) to get back to its place.

The "hurrying" of the sun could be an analogy to the toil of humans. The sun is panting with exhaustion as it runs its meaningless course across the sky yet again, just as wild donkeys pant for air in exhaustion and starvation (Jer 14:6). The panting calls to mind the literal meaning of *hebel*, "breath." But the "hurrying" (*šô'ēp*, "panting" or "pressing") seems to be positive here, a panting of anticipation. So in Ps 19:5 the sun is pictured as a bridegroom who leaves his room and runs his course with joy, returning like a strong man.

Gordis thinks that the author conveys in v 5 the idea of the cycles of the sun as "monotonous, exhausting . . . , without joy or meaning" (1968, 206). But Weeks has suggested that the constant motion, and not the cyclical nature of the sun's movement, may be the focus here (2008). Thus the sun's activity remains unchanged by human toil, as does the earth (v 4).

■ **6** The subject of v 6 is delayed in the Hebrew so that the reader is lured into the assumption that it is still the sun that goes **to the south and turns to the north;** and goes **round and round** (see the Septuagint). At first glance this seems to be nonsense (the sun travels east to west, not north and south) and most interpreters see the wind as the subject. The problem is that the wind in Palestine usually blows from west to east (off the Mediterranean). The delayed subject has the effect of portraying both sun and wind going around. The word *turn* is used four times (*sōbēb*, **turns, round, round, course**), and *go* is used twice (*hôlēk*, **blows, goes**). The repetition of words seems to emphasize the continuous activity of the sun and wind. This also suggests that *sōbēb* and *sĕbibōtāyw* (**round and round; courses**) in v 6b should be translated in the usual sense of "turn," as the wind does not have predictable cycles (11:4-5) and the emphasis seems to be on the continued activity of the wind (Weeks 2008). It could be that Qoheleth wants to complete the four points of the compass to show the comprehensive nature of the activity of sun and wind.

The north-south movement of the sun was not problematic for ancient interpreters who either assumed that the sun makes it way back to the east each day by an unseen northerly route, or they interpreted v 6*a* as a reference to the sun's north-south movement over the course of the year (Weeks 2008). So it would seem that v 6*a* confirms that the mention of the sun in v 5 does not emphasize cycles, but varied, and especially continuous motion. Like the generations and the earth, the activity of the sun is constant and is not changed by the activities of humans as they strive for profit.

■ **7** The ongoing activity of sun and wind is matched by the **streams** in v 7. The cycle of evaporation and precipitation was a mystery in the ancient world. Aristophanes also puzzled over the fact that the sea does not increase its volume, despite being supplied by rivers (see Barton 1908, 74). Ancient Hebrews apparently believed that the earth was a disc floating on the sea and that this water (no longer salty) made its way up through the earth to replenish the streams and springs. This view is reflected in the medieval Jewish interpreter Rashi who quotes with approval the book Siphri, "they return by a submarine passage, and go again upon the earth into the sea, and come back again under the sea" (see Ginsburg 1861, 39).

However, the returning of the water may not be the issue in 1:7. The Hebrew literally reads *to the place (the sea) which the streams go, there they go again (or are returning to go)*. The emphasis is on the continual flow of the waters, not their returning or where they come from (so Hertzberg, cited by Gordis 1968, 207). Even though the word *šûb* usually means "return," in this context it means "again" (BDB 998a; Delitzsch 1875, 223; see 4:1, 7; 9:11).

Brown sees the cosmic activity in vv 4-7 as toilsome and purposeless (2000, 23). This is remarkable as the predictability of nature has been celebrated elsewhere in Scripture as an element of the divinely established order of the universe (Gen 1), as necessary to life since a departure could cause a disastrous flood (Gen 8:21-22), and as the product of God's wisdom (Prov 8:22-31). The sun does what it does every day because God created it that way (Gen 1:16-18); any departure would be chaos. The sea is not full because God has set boundaries for the sea that it may not cross (Gen 1:6-10; Prov 8:27). All this was declared good in Gen 1, and yet Qoheleth seems to find it boring. Bonaventura noticed this anomaly in the thirteenth century A.D. (Ginsburg 1861, 109).

It is believable that Qoheleth would challenge the received views of order in nature. His book challenges the common wisdom about moral order. But that does not seem to be his point in ch 1. The evidence reveals a positive, or at least neutral, view of the predictability of nature. His point is that human activity does not change the basic functions of the cosmos.

■ **8** Verse 8 extends the constancy in nature to the continuous nature of human activity. **All things** could also be translated *all words* (*haddĕbārîm*), and all other occurrences of *haddĕbārîm* in Ecclesiastes have the meaning **words,** not **things.** This translation (**words**) is relevant since the next clause is literally, *no one is able to speak* (**more than one can say**), and later in the verse the ear has **its fill of hearing** words.

The mention of **wearisome** (*yĕgē'îm*) seems at first to corroborate the interpretation of the monotonous repetition of nature in vv 4-7. All words have been overused. They have become weary ("feeble," Ginsburg 1861, 263) and have wearied those who listen, although Ibn Ezra rejected the transitive interpretation (see Ginsburg 1861, 51, 264). The adjective occurs only two other times (both intransitive; Deut 25:18; 2 Sam 17:2). The verb is intransitive when in the Qal conjugation and transitive when Piel (Eccl 10:15; Josh 7:3). Thus Delitzsch rejected the translation **words** and argued that the things mentioned earlier (generations, sun, wind, streams) are weary or in labor (1875, 224). This interpretation sees v 8*a* as a conclusion to the observations on nature, which are seen as an analogy to meaningless activity in the human realm.

It seems to be, however, that the observations from human activity are merely more evidence of constancy in life, of the inability of human activity to make a lasting impression on the world. Thus Weeks reads v 8*a* as a rhetorical question, supporting the assertions in the rest of v 8: "When all words are worn out, can one no longer speak?" (2008). The answer to this is yes. Speaking does not cease for all the weariness of the words, any more than seeing or hearing ceases. These activities are never ending (the NEB translates the second half of v 8 as a question, and the first half as a statement).

The eye has seen everything but is not satisfied, and the ear has heard everything but, like the sea, is not full. While the emphasis of this is on the constancy of the world, which is not changed by human profit, it also anticipates a theme later in the book; that is, the lack of human satisfaction (4:4; 5:10).

C. Nothing Is New or Remembered (1:9-11)

■ **9** Qoheleth continues his argument that nothing can be added to the world by following up the specific examples given in vv 3-8 with general statements: **What has been will be again, what has been done will be done again; there is nothing new under the sun.** With these claims, Qoheleth rejects the possibility that human effort can make a difference to the world.

Verse 9 introduces an uncommon linguistic feature involving the unusual relative pronoun *še* (see comment on 1:3). This is the combination *mah-šše-* (lit., *what which,* **what**) with the sense "that which." Usually *mâ* is an interrogative ("what?"). The combination is common in Ecclesiastes (1:9; 3:15, 22; 6:10; 7:24; 8:7; 10:14) and in the Mishnah. It is equivalent to the Aramaic expressions *māh-dî* and *māh-dî* (Dan 2:28-29).

■ **10** "There is nothing" (*ʾên kol*) of v 9 is matched by *there is something* (**is there anything,** *yēš dābār*) in v 10. **Look! This is something new** is a hypothetical quote that is denied. Anyone who says something is new is wrong. **It was here already, long ago** (since ancient time; lit., *for ages*, *lĕʿōlāmîm*). This ironic use of "there is" seems to be a subtle criticism of the wisdom tradition that often introduced a wisdom saying with this wording (eight times in Proverbs). Qoheleth has more criticisms of the wisdom tradition later in the book.

However, the denial of novelty in Qoheleth is not absolute. Qoheleth himself introduces novelty by writing his book and by using language that is unique or new to the literature of the OT. Verse 10 uses a unique word for **already** (*kĕbār*), which occurs only in Ecclesiastes (eight times). There are many other unique features to the language of Qoheleth.

The word **before** (*lĕpānēnû*) betrays the Hebrew concept of advancing time as it literally means *at the face*, or *in front of* (BDB 816b). Rather than marching ahead into the future, the Hebrew mind conceived of backing into the future, which is sensible since we can see what has been, but not what will be. Likewise the adverb *after* (i.e., what happens later or in the future, *ʾaḥar*, 4:16) literally means *back, behind (the part at the back)* (BDB 29b).

As the inability of humans to add profit to the world goes against the standard wisdom teaching, so the denial of novelty goes against biblical teaching elsewhere. God's actions throughout the history of Israel involved novelty, and prophets announced a new covenant (Jer 31:31-33), a new heart (Ezek 18:31), and a new exodus (Isa 43:5-6). But while Qoheleth is pessimistic about human ability to make a difference, he is more positive about the power of God and advocates human submission to his sovereignty (3:14).

■ **11** Qoheleth further dismisses the hypothetical claim of novelty (v 10) with the assertion in v 11 that anyone who claims there is something new simply does not remember the same phenomenon in the past.

The lack of memory relates to the *formers* (**men of old,** *lārîʾšōnîm*) and the *latters* (**those who are yet to come,** *lāʾaḥărōnîm*). This could refer to people, things, or time. In the flow of the argument, all three have been and will be forgotten. Ginsburg favored the interpretation of "people" as he saw the whole unit as a contrast between abiding nature and fleeting humanity (1861, 267). This is supported by the masculine form of *formers* and *latters*, which always applies to people, whereas the feminine form is used for things (Isa 42:9; 48:3, etc.). The toil of former generations has made no difference to the activities of nature or humanity. It is not even remembered.

No Profit from Toil

In this unit (1:3-11) Qoheleth invites his readers to reflect on the profit of labor, which is a preoccupation for human beings. Is there profit in one's toil? Can human effort add anything to the world? The answer is no. Human toil does not leave a surplus that makes a discernible difference to the world (v 3). Generations keep coming (v 4), the sun keeps shining (v 5), the wind keeps blowing (v 6), the streams keep flowing (v 7), mouths, eyes, and ears keep talking, seeing, and hearing (v 8), and things of the past continue into the future and there is nothing new (vv 9-10). Any perception to the contrary is simply a lack of memory, and current human achievements will not be remembered either (v 11).

This is a helpful corrective to human attempts to control outcomes, and even to control God. In the scheme of the world as a whole, human toil does not leave a surplus. Therefore it falls to people to accept God's sovereignty and be satisfied with the gifts he gives, without endless striving that will not make a lasting difference.

Satisfaction in life can only come by relinquishing control to God and his timing. This means enjoying life and even work, which comes to us as God's gracious gift and an opportunity to participate in God's creative work in the world through human agency. Paul invites the Colossians to approach their work "as working for the Lord" (Col 3:23), thus giving human activity meaning in Christ. Even suffering has meaning for those who are in Christ (1 Pet 4:13).

Qoheleth's call to contentment critiques those who would use the doctrine of retribution as a means to gain wealth and easy living. The idea that righteousness yields rewards for the individual is a major theme of the book of Proverbs. It is a valuable doctrine when addressing the young audience of Proverbs who need to know that their actions have consequences. But when it is taken to extremes it can lead to abuses such as the judgmental attitude of Job's counselors who assumed that his suffering was the result of sin (see also Prov 11:16; 13:23; 14:13; 21:31). It is also open to the abuse of being taken as a guarantee of a good life, which then becomes an inappropriate motivation for righteousness. This seems to be the abuse that Qoheleth attacks. Work is good, as is wisdom and righteousness, but the profit from work should not be an end in itself, nor should wisdom and righteousness be driven by selfish motives.

Novelty and Fame

Remembrance of the past was very important in Hebrew culture because immortality was achieved through memory (the OT does not develop a doctrine of resurrection to any great extent). Qoheleth challenged an overemphasis on one's reputation after death (7:1-2), as it seemed that past generations were soon forgotten. The NT addresses this deficiency in the resurrection. Immortality will not be through memory only.

Qoheleth's claim that nothing is new is remarkable to those of us who have seen rapid change in the modern age. It seems that in large part Ecclesiastes is written to an audience that had grown up with simplistic wisdom, and having matured, was tempted to abandon that wisdom in favor of new possibilities. Qoheleth concurs, to a point. But wisdom still has value even though it needs to be nuanced. In some ways this sentiment is echoed in Rudyard Kipling's 1919 poem "The Gods of the Copy Book Headings." The title refers to copy books used in the schools of his time. Proverbs were printed at the top of each page for the children to copy, thus learning traditional wisdom as they practiced handwriting. Kipling's poem notes a departure in his day from the traditional wisdom in favor of change that was to bring a better world. World War I (1914-19) left such hopes shattered, and the proverbial wisdom of the copy books suddenly seemed relevant again. Qoheleth might challenge such hopes and dreams with a proverb of his own, **There is nothing new under the sun** (1:9). Despite the rapid technological advances of the modern age, there is still value in the old wisdom, though it should not be oversimplified.

Vanity (hebel)

The reader is alerted to the theme of "vanity" (**meaningless,** *hebel*) by the editorial theme for the book in v 2, but the word *hebel* is not used in 1:3-11. The sense in which the activities of life and nature and the lack of novelty and remembrance of vv 3-11 are *hebel* is not immediately clear. Are they meaningless, temporary, or incomprehensible? It is the human toil that is temporary and inconsequential when juxtaposed with the activities of nature and even of humanity as a whole. This is not true in an absolute sense. As Towner notes, "Acts of courage, loving-kindness, and compassion" do make a difference in the world and represent a participation in "the eternal reality of the love of God" as revealed through Jesus Christ (1997, 294).

III. I WAS KING IN JERUSALEM (INTRODUCTION) (1:12—2:26)

BEHIND THE TEXT

Ecclesiastes 1:12, together with 1:1, draw the reader's mind to the magnificent King Solomon. Although the book was probably not written by Solomon, his famous wisdom and riches (1 Kgs 4, 10) set the stage for Qoheleth's argument that even the most wisdom and wealth possible cannot bring lasting satisfaction.

The prior units of the book established the theme of *hebel* and the constant nature of life. This unit gives an example of the great king Solomon, who might be expected to have the capability to fill his coffers and to experience wisdom to the fullest. However, even he was unable to find satisfaction in these pursuits, just as the rivers never fill the sea (1:7). His pursuit of satisfaction in these things amounted to a chasing of the wind, a task that is never complete (2:11; 1:6). The unit is followed by the topic of God's sovereignty and timing (3:1-22), which emphasizes the contrast between human striving for more, and acceptance of whatever God has given in his time (3:11).

59

Boasting Kings

In the ancient Akkadian document Epic of Gilgamesh, the hero is a king who had many accomplishments in his city of Uruk, including seeing, experiencing, and considering everything, even a long journey in search of immortality. He built the wall and sanctuary of his city of high-quality fired bricks and the document claims that his achievements were without equal and will not be matched by a future king (Pritchard 1969, 73). This forms part of the background for the boasting of the king in Eccl 1:12—2:26. Gilgamesh is also set in the context of a failed search for immortality, which resembles Qoheleth's affirmation of the finality of death (3:19; 9:2, 5-6, 10). Qoheleth may also be mocking the royal inscriptions that boasted of kings' accomplishments, such as the Phoenician Karatepe inscription (eighth century B.C.; Fox 1999, 154).

Royal Grant

The theme of "portion" or "reward" (*heleq*, 2:10, 19) seems to be related to the Persian system of property grants, which usually favored the king's relatives and friends. These grants came with the responsibility of collecting taxes but also allowed the recipient to keep some of these revenues. One Aramaic contract refers to this as "my portion from the king" (Seow 1997, 24). Other vocabulary from royal grants is also used in Ecclesiastes (see 5:18-20). The grants were not necessarily inherited by the recipient's heir. This makes sense of the concern in 6:2 that a stranger will inherit the fruit of one's toil. Qoheleth seems to apply this institution of the royal grant to humanity in general, which has received the gift of life from God as a kind of royal grant.

The genre of 1:12—2:26 is royal autobiography, a type of reflection. This genre is also known from other ancient documents, such as the Egyptian instructions of Amenemhet and Merikare (Pritchard 1969, 414-19; see also Longman 1991, 1-274; Longman 1997, 15-20). It also resembles the "grave biographies" recorded on the walls of Egyptian tombs. These contained a recitation of accomplishments, a collection of maxims, and exhortations to reflect on death (Davis 2000, 174). Literary devices include variations of the "better than" saying (2:13, 24) and metaphor (2:14). The word **heart** (*lēb*) is repeated fourteen times in this unit (forty-one times in the book) in the sense of "mind." English translations do not always convey the word with "heart" but often translate *lēb* as **myself** or **mind** (see 2:3). The repetition of the word **heart** shows the thoughtful and autobiographical nature of this unit and the book as a whole. Ecclesiastes 1:12—2:26 can be outlined as follows:

I Studied and Explored (1:12-18)
I Tested Pleasure and Wealth (2:1-11)
I Tested Wisdom (2:12-16)

I Began to Despair (2:17-23)
What to Do? Enjoy! (2:24-26)

IN THE TEXT

A. I Studied and Explored (1:12-18)

■ **12** Verse 12 begins with a self identification (**I, the Teacher, was king over Israel in Jerusalem**), which clearly identifies this unit as the royal autobiography. There are two forms of the first person pronoun (**I**) in Hebrew. Qoheleth consistently uses the shorter and later form *ʾănî* rather than *ʾānōkî*. The self-identification is similar to the editor's note in the superscript (1:1); the editor may have composed the superscript based on this verse. Verse 12 may be an imitation of other ancient royal texts, such as "I am Kilamuwa, the son of Hayya," "I am Yehaumilk, king of Byblos," and "I am Azitawadda, blessed by Baal" (Fox 1999, 170-71).

Qoheleth is also identified in v 1 as **king in Jerusalem.** The phrase **over Israel** narrows down the possibility of the identity of the king in v 12. "Son of David" in v 1 could mean any descendant of David, and **in Jerusalem** suggests the possibility of any of the kings of Judah. But **over Israel** can only apply to Saul, David, or Solomon, who were kings during the days of the united monarchy, or to those who reigned over the northern kingdom after the division of Solomon's kingdom in 922 B.C. The phrase "son of David" excludes the possibility of any of the northern kings because they did not belong to the Davidic house. Since Jerusalem was not the capital of Israel during the days of Saul, one could make the reasonable assumption that Solomon is the king intended by v 12.

This conclusion, however, does not mean that Solomon wrote Ecclesiastes, but that this royal autobiography is based on the life of Solomon and has lessons drawn from Solomon's experience. There is no indication in the book of Kings that Solomon had regrets at the end of his life. The author of Kings concludes the narrative of Solomon's kingship with a strong condemnation of his idolatry (1 Kgs 11:9-10).

The grammatical form of the words **was king** (*hāyîtî melek*) seems to indicate that the individual intended by v 12 was no longer king when Qoheleth wrote his work. This presented a problem for ancient rabbis because it implies that Solomon is not the author (the conclusion of Ginsburg; 1861, 245). Some rabbis dealt with this by supposing that Solomon was forced to give up his throne by a demon named Ashmedai (Talmud, *Gittin* 68a). Others interpreted *melek* (**king**) as "teacher" and so removed the claim of Solomonic authorship (Crenshaw 1987, 71). The choice of verb was probably affected by Qoheleth's literary device of writing in the voice of a king in the distant past. Otherwise, if the author were contemporary with Solomon, he could have used the imperfect or the participle (the latter is very common in Ecclesiastes).

■ **13** In v 13, the king that Qoheleth introduced in v 12 begins to recount his quest to seek and **explore . . . all that is done under heaven.** The idiom *I gave my heart* (**I devoted myself**) refers to concentrating the mind. Ancient Hebrews had no concept of the function of the brain and ascribed all thinking power to the heart (other organs were also believed to be involved in emotions: liver, kidney, bowels; see Isa 10:7; Judg 16:17; Job 12:3; Jer 11:20; Lam 1:20; 2:11). This was beginning to change by the time Daniel was written; Nebuchadnezzar and Daniel have visions in their heads (Dan 2:28; 4:5, 10, 13; 7:1, 15).

The task at hand is to **study** and **explore.** This studying and exploring will be done **by wisdom** (*ḥokmâ*). **Wisdom** is a key word in Ecclesiastes (occurring fifty-three times including verbal forms).

Ḥokmâ (Wisdom)

The emphasis of wisdom is not on intellectual ability but on prudence in the sense of making an appropriate judgment and choosing the best course of action. The literal meaning focuses on skill, and the word was used to describe the skill of the tabernacle builders (e.g., Exod 28:3). Thus, wisdom is life skills; not only knowing what to do, but doing it. This is the focus of Wisdom literature as a whole, which is primarily targeted toward young men who are learning to make wise choices in life—choices that will lead to prosperity and well-being.

Qoheleth resolved to research all deeds that are done **under heaven.** Qoheleth uses this expression three times in the book instead of his favored phrase **under the sun,** which also occurs in the next verse. **Under heaven** seems to be a more comprehensive term. In Hebrew, "heaven" is the same word as "sky" (*šāmayim*) and was understood as the dwelling place of God, not humans. In pagan thought all the gods, including sun, moon, and stars, were believed to live in the sky. **Under heaven,** therefore, refers to the realm of mortals, living and dead. "Under the sun" is more specifically the land of the living, excluding the dead in Sheol, who never see the sun. Qoheleth, however, does not seem to make a distinction between the two phrases. **Under heaven** may be used here for variety.

Before the lengthy account of the studying and exploring is given, the result is already expressed in the phrase **What a heavy burden God has laid on men!** This **heavy burden** is literally an *evil business* (*ʿinyan rāʿ*). *ʿInyan* is one of the many commercial terms used in Ecclesiastes and shows an interest in the developing commercial system of the period. The noun is only used in Ecclesiastes (1:13; 2:23, 26; 3:10; 4:8; 5:3, 14; 8:16) and also in postbiblical Hebrew (BDB 775b). The root for *ʿinyan* is shared by two other meanings, "afflicted" and "witness." This could give the phrase overtones of "evil affliction" or "evil witness," the latter of which was preferred by Ibn Ezra (see Ginsburg 1861, 53).

The business God has given humanity is *evil* (**heavy,** *rāʿ*), which has a broader meaning in Hebrew than in English. It can mean an evil nature but can also refer to calamity. Thus "evil" can come from God in the form of natural disaster or enemy attack (Job 2:10; Amos 3:6; Isa 45:7).

The sovereignty of God is expressed in the latter part of v 13. The business that humanity busies itself with is something that is given by God (**God has laid,** *nātan ʾĕlōhîm*). The verb *give* is used often in Ecclesiastes to express the sovereignty of God. Later Qoheleth will propose enjoyment of the lot that God has given (e.g., 3:12, 22; 8:15; 9:9; 11:8-9), but here the activity of humanity is characterized as an "evil business" (**heavy burden**).

The first mention of **God** in Ecclesiastes shows the Wisdom literature preference for the international and transcendent name for God, Elohim, rather than the more national and personal covenant name, Yahweh. This generalization fits with the emphasis of Ecclesiastes on God's sovereignty and transcendence, rather than personal interaction and covenant or national concerns.

■ **14** Verse 14 begins with the declaration **I have seen** (*rāʾîtî*), which is a key phrase for Qoheleth as well as the main method of gathering information in Wisdom literature. Wisdom teachers observed the world or received traditions from their wisdom teachers, unlike the prophets who heard directly from God or received revelation through visions and dreams. Qoheleth's activity of seeing is thus observing and studying the world to gain understanding and insight into the end result of all human activity and the way the world is structured.

Another key phrase is introduced in this verse, **a chasing after the wind.** The word for **chasing** (*rĕût*) comes from the verb for tending a flock of sheep (*rāʿah*). The Hebrew root forms of the verbs *to see* (*rāʾah*) and *to chase* (*rāʿah*) sound the same, which further emphasizes the connection between Qoheleth's seeing of human activity and chasing the wind. This metaphor seems to compare the human attempt to control the movement of the wind to the effort of a shepherd to control the movement of sheep. Both are futile and meaningless. A similar image is used in Hos 12:1 where Israel is said to feed on the wind (*rōʿeh rûaḥ*) and pursue the east wind. In Hosea's case, the meaningless pursuit is multiplying falsehood and violence and making a covenant with Assyria, only to be conquered by Egypt. Ibn Ezra observed the possibility that "feeding" is the sense in v 14 so that those who feed upon the wind are not satisfied (see Ginsburg 1861, 53, 270).

Chasing the wind is thus a metaphor for a futile task with an unattainable goal, similar to the English comparison to a dog chasing its tail. The wind can never be caught, and the difficulty of the endeavor is emphasized by the character of the wind as described in 1:6. It goes around and around and around. This comparison provides the nuance of *hebel* in this context. The activities that will be described are not merely fleeting or incomprehensible, they are futile and unattainable. The connection between **wind** and vanity (*hebel*) is also contained in the literal meaning of *hebel* (**meaningless**), which is *breath, vapor*. The Epic of Gilgamesh has a similar connection, "As for human beings, their days are numbered, and whatever they keep trying to achieve is but wind!" (Kovacs 1989, 20).

■ **15** In v 15 Qoheleth quotes a proverb that may have its background in Egyptian Wisdom literature, **What is twisted cannot be straightened; what is lacking cannot be counted.** The verb "straighten" (*litqōn*) is a Qal infinitive construct, giving the literal translation *what is crooked cannot straighten*, thus the suggested emendation from BHS to read it as passive (*lĕhittāqēn*, Niphal). This requires adding one consonant but is supported by the Septuagint. The word **lacking** (*ḥesrôn*) is used only here in the OT and is an economic term used in Egyptian Aramaic texts from the fifth century B.C. (and is not known before the fifth century B.C.; Seow 1997, 13). This is one of the examples of Aramaic vocabulary that suggests a postexilic date for Ecclesiastes.

 The sovereignty of God in this proverb is clearer in the parallel in 7:13, which comes in a list of proverbs. There it is specifically God who has made something crooked, and humanity is unable to straighten it. In the Egyptian context, the crooked was a simple person who could be straightened out by wisdom (*Instruction of Ani*; Seow 1997, 122). The way of wisdom is a straight path (see Prov 3:6). Here Qoheleth seems to be anticipating his argument that even wisdom is vanity. Humans cannot control outcomes, and the following verses will explain this with reference to the lack of satisfaction in pleasure, wealth, and wisdom. The differences between human expectation and experience are innumerable.

■ **16** Qoheleth continues the personification of his heart in v 16 where he speaks with it (**I thought to myself,** lit., *I spoke with my heart*). This is similar to a common phrase in English, "I said to myself."

 At this point Qoheleth begins to list his accomplishments in a résumé style. His greatness and increased wisdom are first on the list. The style here is typical of the boasts of Assyrian kings. The phrase **anyone who has ruled over Jerusalem before me** is part of the format of these boasts (Delitzsch 1875, 229). It is not meant to refer to King David, the only Israelite king to rule from Jerusalem before Solomon, or to Jebusite kings who may have ruled before the Israelites. Ginsburg saw this as an argument against Solomonic authorship since it emphasizes the hypothetical role of Solomon (1861, 247, 273). The key word *saw* is repeated in this verse, in the sense of **experienced.**

The combination of the related terms **wisdom and knowledge** is common in the Bible (e.g., Exod 35:31; Prov 1:7). **Knowledge** tends to be more cognitive but also includes skill (Exod 31:3), experience, and relationship (to know someone). **Wisdom** involves knowledge and skill (Isa 10:13) and emphasizes putting knowledge into practice in life choices. Both **knowledge** and **wisdom** are connected with the fear of Yahweh (Prov 1:7; Ps 111:10).

Delitzsch on Wisdom and Knowledge

In general, we may say that *chokma* is the fact of a powerful knowledge of the true and the right, and the property that arises out of this intellectual possession; but *dāăth* is knowledge penetrating into the depth of the essence of things, by which wisdom is acquired and in which wisdom establishes itself. (1875, 230)

■ **17** Verse 17 begins with a *waw*-consecutive (*wā'ettĕnâ*)—a grammatical form very common in Hebrew narrative but only used three times in Ecclesiastes (1:17; 4:1, 7; Whitley 1979, 1). This is partly because Ecclesiastes does not have much narrative and partly an element of the overall peculiarity of Qoheleth's language. According to Crenshaw, the *waw*-consecutive is employed here (v 17) to indicate a substantial period of observation and reflection (1987, 75). But it is not clear that this is the case, as conclusions are given before this verse and more explorations are recounted in the following chapter. The result of the search in v 17 is also a **chasing after the wind,** a phrase that uses the same root as 1:14 but a different noun form (*ra'yôn* instead of *rĕ'ût*).

Verse 16 ends with the claim that Qoheleth became great in "wisdom and knowledge." There are two infinitive forms in v 17 ("to know wisdom and to know madness" [NRSV]). The second form (*da'at*), which is the same as the first but without the preposition, however, also could be understood as a noun ("knowledge"); thus, it is possible to read the phrase as "to know wisdom and knowledge, madness and folly"). Ancient versions thus took the first infinitive to govern all four words (wisdom, knowledge, madness, folly; Septuagint, Aramaic, Latin). Modern translations, however, by taking both forms as infinitives, translate the phrase as "to know wisdom and to know madness and folly" (NRSV) (**to the understanding of wisdom, and also of madness and folly**).

The translation of v 17 poses other difficulties, especially in making sense of the words **madness and folly** (*hôlēlôt wĕsiklût*). The word translated **madness** (*hôlēlôt*) is used elsewhere only in Ecclesiastes (2:12; 7:25; 9:3; cognate in 10:13; verbal form in 2:2 and in other books). It comes from the root *hālal*, "to boast" (Qal) or "praise" (Piel). The word translated **folly** is misspelled in this sentence (*śiklût, sin* instead of *samek*), which actually relates it to a root meaning "prudent." The meaning **folly** is confirmed, however, by some manuscripts that have the correct spelling and by the combination of **madness** and **folly** elsewhere in Ecclesiastes (with the correct spelling, 2:12; 7:25; 10:13).

The confusion of Hebrew letters *sin* and *samek* was common in late Hebrew and Aramaic (Job 5:2; 6:2; 10:17; 17:7; Ezra 4:5; 5:12; Whitley 1979, 16).

Did Qoheleth, the wisdom teacher, really experience madness and folly? Or is he projecting this experience back to Solomon for the purpose of his argument? David pretends to be mad in 1 Sam 21:12-15, which could also be the case with Qoheleth. He tried on madness as part of his experiment but was not actually mad (see Ibn Ezra, in Ginsburg 1861, 54). Another possibility is that **madness and folly** are completely out of place here, because at this point the experiment is to experience wisdom (later he will consider madness and folly in 2:12). Ginsburg may have been right in his assessment that "the words (madness and folly) have crept into the text through the carelessness of a transcriber" (1861, 274). Although there is no textual evidence for this, it makes better sense in the context of Qoheleth's argument.

■ **18** The result of increasing wisdom is increasing **sorrow.** There is a literal side to this suffering, as corporal punishment was used in the wisdom schools. This is documented in Egyptian and Sumerian texts (Crenshaw 1987, 76). More significantly, the wise observer sees the complexity of life and carries the weight of this knowledge, unlike the fool in the English proverb, for whom "ignorance is bliss."

Repetition in this verse adds to the feel of continuous motion in the observation and application of wisdom, as it did in the description of the endless activities of nature (e.g., 1:6). There is also a coupling of **wisdom** and **knowledge** as in v 16, suggesting further that these two words belong together in v 17 (i.e., "knowledge" is a noun in 1:17, not a verb). **Sorrow** and **grief** are also paired in 2:23.

B. I Tested Pleasure and Wealth (2:1-11)

■ **1** A new paragraph is introduced in ch 2 with the phrase *I spoke in my heart* (**I thought in my heart**). This verb and preposition are different from those in the similar phrase in 1:16. In this case the verb for "spoke" is *ʾāmartî* (instead of *dibbartî*) and the preposition is **in** (*bĕ*, instead of "with," *ʿim*). Following the exploration of wisdom (1:16-18), the topic is now pleasure. Will pleasure be found to provide lasting satisfaction?

The verb **I will test** (*ʾănassĕkâ*) has an unusual spelling with the Hebrew letter *he* added to the suffix (also found in Gen 10:19; Jer 40:15; and Qumran texts). The Latin Vulgate took the *kaf* (of the suffix) as part of the verb, assuming the root *nsk*, "to pour out" (instead of *nsh*, "to test"), apparently with the idea of pouring out wine, which will be the topic in v 3 (Whitley 1979, 18).

The phrase **to find out what is good** is literally *see in good*, continuing the emphasis on the verb *to see* in this unit. The verb is an imperative and the phrase has the sense "enjoy yourself" (i.e., experience good; see 2:24; 3:13; 5:18; 7:14; 9:7; 11:7). Even before the pursuits of enjoyment are recounted, Qoheleth declares that this is *hebel*—it does not last or give lasting satisfaction. The pursuit of pleasure is profitless (Miller 2002, 108).

■ **2** Verse 2 declares that **laughter** is madness (**foolish,** *měhôlāl*). Laughter is often used in the sense of derision or mocking (Job 12:4; Jer 48:27). The indictment against joy (**pleasure,** *śimḥâ*) is not as strong as for **laughter,** but joy is still found to be of no use. Later in the book, joy is commended as a gift from God (2:26; 5:20).

Ginsburg took this verse as a direct address to laughter and pleasure, giving the sense, "To laughter I said (you are) mad, and to pleasure what (are you) doing?" (see Ginsburg 1861, 276). This has the advantage of taking the preposition "to" (*lě*) literally rather than supplying the unusual translation "of." The word **foolish** (*měhôlāl*) could be translated as "praiseworthy" as in the Talmud and Rashi, but this does not fit the context (Ginsburg 1861, 277, citing *Shabbat* 30:2).

The form of *this* (*zōh*) differs from the usual form (*zōt*) but is used occasionally elsewhere in the OT (Judg 18:4; 2 Kgs 6:19; Ezek 40:45). It resembles the later form used in postbiblical Hebrew (*zô*, see Hos 7:16; Ps 132:12; Murphy 1992, 16). This is another example of Qoheleth's unique use of language (see Introduction).

■ **3** Verse 3 carries the vocabulary and theme from the introduction into this unit with the statement **I tried** (lit., *I explored with my heart*; see 1:13). Throughout this journey into base pleasures of **wine** (representing all feasting) and flesh (*bāśār*, **myself**), Qoheleth notes that he remained guided by wisdom. This was merely an experiment; perhaps a warning to young people not to try this experiment themselves.

Cheering (*māšak*) literally means *to draw, lead, prolong.* Ecclesiastes is the only book that uses it with the sense "cheer" (and only once), apparently with the idea of drawing attention, or attracting, hence **cheering** (BDB 604). G. R. Driver suggested the sense "sustain" (with reference to Aramaic and Arabic), and he translated "to sustain my flesh with wine" (1954, 15). BHS suggests transposing letters and emending to give another word for "sustain," which occurs in Song 2:5 (*liśmôk*, instead of *limšôk*).

While wisdom was found to have no lasting value in 1:16-18, Qoheleth is careful to explain that his further experiment into pleasure and folly is not conducted without the restraint of wisdom (**my mind still guiding me with wisdom**).

The word **guiding** (*nōhēg*) is used in the OT for driving or leading animals (2 Kgs 4:24; Ps 78:52) but in later Hebrew with the meaning "behave, conduct oneself" (Whybray 1989, 53). This meaning seems to fit this context better (i.e., "my mind behaving with wisdom").

An apparent contradiction between **embracing folly** and being guided with wisdom, led to the suggested emendation of BHS to read "not embracing folly" (*l' 'hz* instead of *l'hz*). The whole argument in 1:12—2:26, however, is to show the folly of Solomon's "wisdom," and so **embracing folly** is not out of place here, and similar thoughts recur in Ecclesiastes (2:12). **Few days** is literally *number of days* (*mispar yĕmê*) and so does not necessarily emphasize that life is short.

Fourteen Days of Happiness

Fifty years have passed since I became Caliph. Riches, honors, pleasures—I have enjoyed all. In this long time of seeming happiness I have numbered the days on which I have been happy. Fourteen. (Ascribed to Abd Er-Rahman III; in Marvin 1902, 2)

■ **4** What follows is an impressive list of accomplishments reminiscent of the tone in the description of Solomon in 1 Kgs 3—11, although there are few correspondences in detail and some notable omissions. There is no mention in Ecclesiastes of building the temple, one of Solomon's greatest accomplishments; however, **houses** are mentioned, and "house" is one of the words used for "temple" in the OT (along with a Sumerian loanword, "palace," *hêkāl*; TDOT 3:382). Solomon did build **houses** in the sense of palaces and temples, not only for himself and Yahweh, but also for his wives and their gods (1 Kgs 6—7; 9:24; 11:7-8).

Vineyards were a common possession for a king. Ahab, king of Israel, coveted the vineyard of Naboth since it was adjacent to the palace (1 Kgs 21), and Solomon himself is mentioned in connection with a vineyard in Song 8:11-12.

■ **5** The accomplishments of the king in v 5—**gardens, parks,** and **trees**— are not specified as accomplishments of Solomon in 1 Kings, but kings in the ancient world were known for their parks. The Hanging Gardens of Babylon are a famous example. The **gardens** are not vegetable gardens but parks, and the Hebrew word (*gan*) derives from the verb "to guard," which was one of the functions of Adam in the Garden of Eden (Ginsburg 1861, 280). **Parks** (*pardēsîm*) is one of two Persian loanwords in Ecclesiastes that is important evidence that the book originated in the Persian period or later. The word is used in other postexilic books (Neh 2:8; Song 4:13) and was also borrowed by Greek in the form *paradeisos* (used to translate the Garden of Eden), from which the English word "paradise" comes (via Latin).

■ **6** Like gardens and parks, **reservoirs** were often built by kings. King Mesha of Moab boasted of this on the Moabite Stone (ninth century B.C.; Eaton

1983, 66). The reservoirs are a blessing and a necessity in a land where there is little or no rain in the dry season and few significant rivers for irrigation. The word for **reservoir** shares its spelling with "blessing" since receiving a blessing involved bending the knee, as did drinking at a reservoir (Ginsburg 1861, 282). There is a grammatical anomaly in this verse as the pronoun used for **reservoirs** is masculine, although the verb is feminine. This feature is seen elsewhere in Ecclesiastes (2:10; 10:9; 11:8; 12:1; Murphy 1992, 17). Linguistic anomalies are common in Ecclesiastes.

■ **7** The **male and female slaves** (ʿăbādîm ûšĕpāḥôt) are not supposed to portray Solomon as oppressive but were considered a symbol of status as well as luxury. The completely different economy of that time is reflected in the lack of distinction between "slave" and "servant" in the language. Hebrew has only one word for both, the literal meaning of which is *worker*. While slavery could be cruel, it was a varied institution that was taken for granted. No one ever called for the abolition of slavery or protested against it. Some slaves could even own their own slaves, such as Ziba, the slave of Saul, who owned twenty servants (2 Sam 19:17; ABD 6:58-65). Verse 7 includes Qoheleth's claim that he had **more herds and flocks than anyone in Jerusalem** before his time.

■ **8** The **gold** and **silver** that Qoheleth **amassed** was wealth that would be expected for **kings** and provincial leaders. **Provinces** (hammĕdînôt) could also mean "prefects" (from the root "to rule, judge"), which is attested in the Canaanite Ugaritic literature (*Anat* 2.15-16; Crenshaw 1987, 80). The article is out of place ("*the* provinces/prefects") but is typical of the unusual language in Ecclesiastes.

The **amassed silver and gold** in v 8 correlates with the accounts of Solomon's great wealth in silver and gold in 2 Chr 9:27 and 1 Kgs 10:14-25. In ancient Israel, precious metals were used in transactions, by weighing the metal and later through use of coins. This is a statement of great wealth that, like the other elements of this royal experiment, does not bring lasting satisfaction.

The Hebrew for **harem** (šiddâ wĕšiddôt) utilizes the singular and plural of the same word and thus has an unusual grammatical construction; the meaning of this word is not certain. Delitzsch interpreted the unusual grammar as an indication of a multitude of women (1875, 238-39). The translation **harem** or "concubine" is based on a possible connection with the word "breast" (šad) or "seize [a woman as plunder in war]" (šādad). Cognate languages Akkadian, Ugaritic, and Arabic have similar words for "woman" (Krüger 2004, 58). Ancient translators struggled with the meaning and rendered it as "steward" or "goblet" (Longman 1997, 92). From the overall context, the two most obvious omissions from the list of Solomon's activities here are horses and wives, but Ecclesiastes is not following the other biblical information about Solomon closely. The context of the verse is wealth but also singers. The theme of wealth is supported by Böttcher's reading (following Rashi) "chest and chests" in the sense of *"abundance of anything"* (Wright 1883, 330).

Rabbi Eleazar on Solomon's Wealth

If another had declared, *Vanity of vanities, saith Koheleth* (Eccl. 1, 2), I might have said that this man who had never owned two farthings in his life makes light of the wealth of the world and declares, *"Vanity of vanities"*; but for Solomon it was appropriate. (In Cohen 1983, 86)

■ **9** Verses 9-11 conclude the quest for pleasure with the conclusion that "everything is meaningless" (v 11), as the quest for wisdom was also "a chasing after the wind" (see 1:17). The wording of 2:9 is similar to 1:16 and 2:7. The mention of **anyone in Jerusalem before me** is the last explicit reference to the author as king, although this royal experiment continues to the end of ch 2, and the tone and first person reflection continues throughout the book. While Qoheleth is critical of wisdom in 1:16-18, in 2:9 he assures his audience that **wisdom stayed with** him during his experiment into pleasure. This contradiction shows that while he wishes to expose the limitations of wisdom, he does not wish to abandon it. He is still a wisdom teacher.

■ **10** The language of v 10 echoes the gift of wisdom to Solomon in 1 Kgs 3:5, where Solomon is told by God to "Ask for whatever you want me to give you." **My eyes desired** is literally *my eyes asked for.* Solomon was a king who was accustomed to getting what he wanted.

The pleasure that Qoheleth found in his toil was his **reward** (*helqî*). This word is also translated "portion" and is used of the land that was parceled out to the Israelites when Joshua entered the land. This is a key word in Ecclesiastes and may be contrasted with "profit" (*yitrôn;* see 1:3). In Ecclesiastes, "portion" is the lot in life that every human must accept according to the sovereignty of God. The echo of the land distribution by Joshua hints at a time in Israel's history when the economy was based on agriculture. If the system worked as intended, no one could accumulate excess profits because income was tied to land. The limited portion of land meant that crop production was limited, which in turn meant that profit was limited.

In the time when Ecclesiastes was probably written (Persian or Hellenistic period), this agricultural economy was gone, as was the family inheritance of land established by Joshua. The economy was based on money, and land ownership was controlled by the emperor and his representatives. In this economy one could make excessive profits (*yitrôn*), even without owning land. The whole premise of Qoheleth, however, is that an effort to gain excessive profit is vanity (1:3). There is no gain to (excessive) toil, but instead one should be content with the portion (*heleq*) God has given, which in this case is pleasure through one's toil.

One of the pleasures enjoyed in the royal experiment is wealth; the word *ʿāmāl* (**work** and **labor**) can also mean "wealth" (2:19; Ps 105:44). The king took delight in his **work,** that is, in the wealth he worked to accumulate; toil itself is not listed as one of the pleasures in 2:1-9.

Epicurus on Pleasure

Pleasure is the beginning and end of the blessed life. (In Russell 2004, 233)

■ **11** In v 11 Qoheleth *turned* (*ûpānîtî*, **surveyed**) to reflect on his experiment (see 2:20 and 4:1). Elsewhere the turning is "to see" something in life, as in v 12, but in v 11 there is an ellipsis. The turning is to consider what Qoheleth has done by his own **hands.** Verse 11 supplies the preliminary conclusion that pervades Ecclesiastes: **everything was meaningless, a chasing after the wind; nothing was gained under the sun.** The specific context of this meaninglessness is the pursuit of wisdom (1:13-18) and pleasure (2:1-11). Self-indulgence does not lead to lasting satisfaction (it is profitless), and wisdom cannot be relied upon to bring the expected results or happiness. Life is not that simple, even though the wisdom teachers of Proverbs had portrayed wisdom as the key to success in life, and that success as the motivation for wisdom and righteousness.

C. I Tested Wisdom (2:12-16)

■ **12** Verse 12 begins a new paragraph as the king has considered all deeds (1:13-15), wisdom (1:16-18), and pleasure (2:1-11), and now turns (*ûpānîtî*) to the subject of the inevitability of death, which means that the advantage of wisdom is limited (2:12-16).

The verb "to see" (**consider**) is used elsewhere in the sense "experience" (1:16). The king had experienced busyness, wisdom, and pleasure (1:13—2:11), and now he seems to step back and observe more philosophically. He ponders **wisdom, madness,** and **folly** in the light of the succession of kings. Like the kings of the royal inscriptions, the king in Ecclesiastes had claimed to be greater than all who ruled before him. If this is so, what claim can the next king make? The greatest king has already lived.

Though the words **madness and folly** seem to be an addition in 1:17, here in 2:12, these words are not out of place. Qoheleth is not *experiencing* **madness and folly** but merely assessing them and comparing them with wisdom, as the next verse shows.

English translations have supplied the verb "to do," as suggested by BHS, in the rhetorical question **What more can the king's successor do** (*meh hāʾādām šeyyābô ʾaḥărê hammelek*; lit., *What the man [do] who comes after the king?*). Delitzsch attempted a translation without supplying the verb: "For what is the man who might come after the king, him whom they have made so long ago!" (1875, 245). Verse 12 is one of the instances in Ecclesiastes where both relative pronouns (*še* and *'ăšer*) are used in the same verse. The result of this pronoun switching is a very strange sounding Hebrew, which may be the point of the complex word choice. The verse asks a puzzling question and uses puzzling Hebrew to do so.

■ **13** Nevertheless, Qoheleth concedes that wisdom is superior to folly, and not just a little better. The difference is as great as the difference between light and darkness (compare the English comparison, "Like night and day"). **Wisdom is better than folly** is literally, *there is profit belonging to wisdom* (*yēš yitrôn laḥokmâ*). This word for profit (*yitrôn*) is used only in Ecclesiastes and prior uses have been negative, there is no profit for labor (1:3; 2:11). Despite acknowledging the limitations of wisdom, Qoheleth now finds that there is profit in wisdom. Light and wisdom are connected elsewhere (Prov 6:23), and the Torah is also connected with light (Ps 119:105); however, the Torah is not an emphasis in Ecclesiastes, except in the editorial conclusion (12:13). Light is truth that guides actions in Ps 43:3. Wisdom also connects ignorance with darkness (see Job 38:19).

■ **14** A proverb is now quoted in v 14: **The wise man has eyes in his head, while the fool walks in darkness.** Open eyes are connected with wisdom elsewhere (Exod 23:8; Deut 16:19; Prov 20:13). Once again this emphasizes the huge chasm between wisdom and folly. It is the difference between having sight and being blind. But then Qoheleth dismisses the importance of this difference because both wise and fool will face **the same fate;** the underlying idea here is that both will die and will go to the same place. Sheol, the place of shades and darkness, is perhaps implied here as the fate of both wise and fool.

Fate (*miqreh*) is a key word in Ecclesiastes and is used only three times elsewhere in the OT (Ruth 2:3; 1 Sam 6:9; 20:26; it is used seven times in Ecclesiastes plus three times in the verbal form). In this verse it is used in the sense "event," but elsewhere in the book it has the sense of a chance happening. This is certainly beyond human control, but it could be interpreted as beyond divine control also. However, in the book as a whole, God's sovereignty is emphasized, and ch 3 especially argues God's control over every time and season of life. Perhaps Qoheleth intends a double meaning of chance, which is under God's providence, as the word is used in the "chance" happening of Ruth finding herself in the field of Boaz (Ruth 2:3). Qoheleth also utilizes the cognate verb **overtakes** (*qārâ*) in v 14.

■ **15** Verse 15 concludes that the universality of death is vanity (incomprehensible). The particle *'āz* in this verse has caused translation problems. **What then do I gain by being wise?** is literally, *Why was I wise then gain?* ("Why then have I been so very wise?" [NRSV]). The word **gain** (*yôtēr*) is related to the key word "profit" (*yitrôn*) and is itself used seven times in the book (2:15; 6:8, 11;

7:11, 16; 12:9, 12) and once outside Ecclesiastes (Esth 6:6). *Hebel* (**meaningless**) is used here in the sense "incomprehensible." It does not make sense that the wise and foolish should both meet the same end.

■ **16** Verse 16 echoes the movement of the opening poem (1:2-11), which began with the comprehensive statement of vanity and closed without the expected inclusio (another reference to vanity), but with the lament that nothing would be remembered. This is contrary to the wisdom of Prov 10:7 where "the memory of the righteous will be a blessing, but the name of the wicked will rot." In a culture that values honor and has little concept of a resurrection, the way one is remembered after death is very important. Yet Qoheleth is driven to exclaim, **Like the fool, the wise man too must die!** The shock of this statement is intensified by the use of **die** (*yāmût*), whereas euphemisms are used in the previous texts to describe death ("same fate," 2:14; "generations go," 1:4; "few days," 2:3).

D. I Began to Despair (2:17-23)

■ **17** The problem of death still occupies Qoheleth's attention in the next paragraph (2:17-23). The tone of v 17 is quite different from that of 2:1-11 where the king claimed to have found pleasure in his toil. Now the incomprehensible nature of life causes Qoheleth to declare that he hated life. Following the blunt mention of death as the final leveler (v 16), v 17 comes as another shock because wisdom teaching as a whole promoted the idea of long and prosperous life (Prov 3:16; 8:35). It is possible to take this statement at face value; that Qoheleth really does hate his meaningless life, but this statement is made in the context of the royal autobiography. The point is that Solomon's lifestyle did not lead to lasting satisfaction but represented a distortion of balanced wisdom teaching. Qoheleth has used shock value to great effect, getting the attention of his audience.

If Qoheleth had a hatred of life that was absolute, then the logical course of action would be suicide. This is never advocated in the book, which does not ask the question of Hamlet, "To be, or not to be." Qoheleth does not despair over life itself, but over an orientation to the pursuit of wealth and pleasure as an ultimate good. This does not lead to lasting satisfaction. Qoheleth laments the finality of death, but in the end this is to be accepted as the lot of all humanity, whether wise or foolish.

So high was the value of life in the biblical tradition that interpreters have found the statement that life is hateful to be unorthodox, and so the Targum, ancient versions, and church fathers have interpreted this as a hatred of sin (Ginsburg 1861, 294). This is unnecessary, however, because the life that is hated is not life itself but life lived in the futility of chasing wealth and pleasure. The nuance "futility" for *hebel* (**meaningless**) is signaled by the accompanying designation **chasing after the wind.**

Of the cold reality of life and death, Qoheleth said it **was grievous to me,** literally *evil upon me.* The preposition ʿ*āl* with **to** as its meaning here is a late development; its usual meaning is "upon" (Esth 3:9; 1 Chr 13:2). In a sense, the matter is also "upon" Qoheleth as a heavy burden, part of the burden that a wisdom teacher must bear (1:18; see Isa 1:14).

■ **18** Qoheleth laments that he will have to leave everything he has worked for to **the one who comes after** him. This statement is incomprehensible in the agricultural economy of ancient Israel. It was of utmost importance to have children who would carry on one's legacy, and to leave them with a "goodly heritage" (KJV; Ps 16:6; Jer 3:19). In Solomon's case, however, as Qoheleth would know, his son Rehoboam was a fool and lost the empire and even the nation. After Rehoboam's folly only the tribe of Judah was ruled by the Davidic kings.

In the time when Ecclesiastes was probably written (Persian or Hellenistic period) the issue of inheritance was completely different. Since land grants were made by the emperor or his representatives, a property owner did not always have the right to pass property on to the next generation (Seow 1997, 23). He literally did not know whether the future owner of his land would be wise or a fool (v 19). Ginsburg saw in this an implication that the king had no heir, thus an argument against Solomonic authorship (1861, 248).

■ **19** Qoheleth's abiding view of the value of wisdom is apparent in v 19 as he laments the possibility that his successor may be a **fool.** Qoheleth may be willing to expose the limitations of retribution and wisdom, but he was raised with the standard wisdom teaching and seems to wish that life could be that simple.

Who knows is usually used in the positive sense of anticipation that some good might come out of the situation (2 Sam 12:22; Joel 2:14; Jonah 3:9; Ps 90:11; Esth 4:14). For Qoheleth it is a rhetorical question with the foregone conclusion that the outcome will be negative (Eccl 2:19; 3:21; 6:12; 8:1; see Prov 24:22).

The verb *šālaṭ* (**control over**) is a key word in Ecclesiastes (2:19; 5:19; 6:2; 7:19; 8:4, 8, 9; 10:5). Elsewhere in the OT it occurs in late texts (Neh 5:15; Esth 9:1; Ps 119:133) and Aramaic (Dan 2:39; 3:27; 5:16; 6:24). This suggests a postexilic date for Ecclesiastes. The basic meaning is "to domineer, be master" (BDB 1020). Seow, who places Ecclesiastes in the fifth to fourth century B.C., argues that *šālaṭ* meant "to have the right of disposal" in the Persian period (1997, 14). This seems to be the meaning here in v 19; the issue is who will get the fruit of the king's work, and not who will rule over him. In later usage, however, this word seems to have gained the more general connotation "to rule" (Gropp 1993, 34; see also Krüger 2004, 36). The nuance of *hebel* (**meaningless**) in this verse is "incomprehensible."

■ **20** In v 20 Qoheleth "turns" again, but the vocabulary is different from 2:12 (NIV does not translate this word). This time the word is *sābab*, the same word that was used in 1:6 for the wind going around and around on its circuits. Perhaps Qoheleth has turned to consider so many things now that he is spinning like the wind! Indeed, the result of this turning is not another consideration but **despair over all** his **toilsome labor under the sun.**

■ **21** The collapse of inheritance laws is not only incomprehensible (*hebel*) but also a great evil (**great misfortune**). Thus the nuance of *hebel* (**meaningless**) here is "futile, evil, incomprehensible." The expected follow-up to **this too is meaningless** is "a chasing after the wind" (2:17), so the departure in this verse comes as a surprise to the reader. The first words of both phrases are similar, thus lulling the reader into thinking that the sentence will end with the same phrase (the usual *rĕʿût rûah* instead of *rāʿâ rabbâ*).

The word **skill** is unique to Ecclesiastes in this form (*kišrôn*), but variants occur in Esth 8:5 and Ps 68:6. Like many of the rare words in Ecclesiastes, it is common in Aramaic and postbiblical Hebrew.

■ **22-23** Verses 22 and 23 bring together vocabulary from the opening poem and from the beginning of the royal autobiography. **Toil** was the profitless activity of 1:3, and **work** is the same word used in the phrase "unhappy business" (ESV) in 1:13 (NIV: "heavy burden"). Qoheleth does not find rest from his toil even at night; perhaps the thought being expressed here is that the pain of toil during the day continues even into the night, and torments his mind to the extent that he cannot sleep. The tone of the final paragraph in this unit is negative as Qoheleth declares, "This is also vanity" (KJV) (*hebel*; futile, profitless, incomprehensible).

E. What to Do? Enjoy! (2:24-26)

■ **24-26** A balance to the optimism of 2:10 and the pessimism of 2:23 comes in the conclusion to this unit. Ecclesiastes 2:24-26 provides the balance, even though the final chorus will be, as always, "this is also vanity" (KJV). The sovereignty of God is incomprehensible but evident, and therefore a person should enjoy whatever God has given (see 3:12, 22; 5:18; 8:15; 9:7-9). True enjoyment comes only from one's allotment (see *heleq*) and not from human striving for excessive profit (see *yitrôn*). The words "allotment" and "profit" are not used in this paragraph, but the ideas are present. Both the sovereignty of God and the portion he gives are expressed in the phrase **hand of God** (v 24).

The whole royal experiment of Qoheleth showed that striving for more wisdom, wealth, and pleasure was a futile task. What is meaningful is accepting the food, drink, and enjoyment God has given. This cannot be improved upon by human effort, and so people should be content with their lot.

■ **24** The NIV and the NRSV and other modern English translations follow the reading that suggests the idea that there are no other activities better than eating and drinking and finding satisfaction in one's work (*wĕher'â 'et-napšôṭôb*, lit., *look upon good;* see also 3:13; 5:18; 6:6). This is the portion that the sovereign God gives to humanity. The particle of comparison (*mem/min*, **than**) is missing from the Hebrew text of v 24. English translations supplement it and thus read the first part of v 24 as follows: **A man can do nothing better than to eat and drink.** The Septuagint reads it without the comparison: "Man has not the good which he shall eat and drink." Rashi took this verse as a question, "Is there no good in man that he (just) eats and drinks?" implying that people should have other goals in life (Cohen 1946, 122).

■ **25** The Hebrew text of v 25 can be translated *For who eats, and who finds enjoyment apart from me?* (**for without him, who can eat or find enjoyment?**). Qoheleth, writing as King Solomon, reiterates his choice of Solomon for the royal experiment. No one could hope to do better in wisdom, wealth, and pleasure than Solomon. Therefore the case is closed. The toilsome pursuit of excess in these areas does not bring lasting satisfaction because of the nature of wisdom, wealth, and pleasure, and not because the excess was not excessive enough. Solomon's achievements in these areas were excessive, and yet his life lacked ultimate meaning. So contentment is the only course of action (and state of mind) that leads to satisfaction, because by definition the content person is satisfied.

Some Hebrew manuscripts and the ancient versions have minor differences that yield the translation **for without him, who can eat or find enjoyment?** This reading reemphasizes the sovereignty of God in the matter of lasting satisfaction, a theme that is continued in the final verse of this unit (v 26).

■ **26** **The man who pleases** God is contrasted with **the sinner** in v 26. The literal meaning of **sinner** (*ḥôṭe'*) is *one who misses,* and it does not have the religious connotations in Wisdom literature that it does elsewhere in the OT. However, it is used in a religious sense in 8:12-13 (see also 7:26), and so 2:26 may be acknowledging the traditional retribution, which Ecclesiastes also challenges (Ginsburg 1861, 302). Or the sense here could be of someone who is clumsy or unlucky, who cannot do anything right, and thus a fool (see Herzfeld, cited by Ginsburg 1861, 302). By the incomprehensible sovereignty of God, this kind of person will end up **gathering and storing up wealth to hand it over to the one who pleases God** (see Job 27:13-17; Prov 13:22; 28:8). This may be intended as an analogy with the royal grant system of the Persian kings where the common people worked hard, only to see the results of their labor go to the emperor in the form of taxes, and also to the recipients of the royal grants who were responsible for collecting those taxes (Seow 1997, 25).

The success for the one who pleases God is not meant to be a guarantee, as Qoheleth has already rejected the oversimplification that good things happen to good people and bad things happen to bad people (1:15-18; 2:14-16). Instead, it is the sovereignty of God that determines who will have and who will not have. Striving for excess profit will not be effective. It would be easier to catch the wind. This may be incomprehensible ("vanity," *hebel*), but that is the way life is. All one can do is enjoy the portion God has given and recognize that even that enjoyment is a gift from God.

FROM THE TEXT

The portrayal of the quest for satisfaction is placed in the context of Solomon's great achievements, thus calling into question the validity of Solomon's whole orientation in life. While many people are left with the impression of Solomon's great wisdom and wealth, 1 Kgs 11 criticizes his fall into idolatry. The king in Eccl 1—2 has taken pleasure, wealth, and wisdom to extremes, so that the reader will not be fooled into seeking satisfaction in these earthly pursuits. Rather, simple contentment with food, drink, and work is the key to satisfaction in life (2:24). This is a gift from God, and not something for which to strive.

Wisdom

This unit repeatedly calls on wisdom for guidance in the king's quest for fulfillment in life, but by pronouncing the various pursuits of Solomon as meaningless, calls into question the practical value of Solomon's wisdom. The pursuit of wisdom as an end in itself is chasing after the wind, and as a means to control life it is no better, because **what is twisted cannot be straightened** (1:15). In the end, even the wisest person must live under the sovereignty of God. At the same time, wisdom is of great value, **just as light is better than darkness** (2:13).

Vanity (hebel)

The word *hebel* (**meaningless**) is used nine times in this unit. It is used with the connotation "incomprehensible" in regard to the lack of the possibility of inheritance in the postexilic periods. This fact also renders the accumulation of wealth "futile" as that wealth cannot even be kept in the family. Also futile is the pursuit of pleasure and wisdom. While life is to be enjoyed (2:24), wealth, pleasure, or wisdom should not be the orientation of one's life. Wisdom is valuable (2:13), but in the end it cannot help a person avoid death (2:14) and so should be a means to enhance enjoyment of life, but it cannot be expected to lead to control over the outcomes of life.

Enjoy Life

The pursuit of pleasure as an orientation in life is rejected in this unit, but that does not mean that life should be dreary. It is because of the hollow satisfaction of pleasure as an orientation in life that one should simply enjoy what one has as a gift from God (2:24).

Wealth

As wisdom and pleasure fail to be adequate orientations for life, so does wealth. If excess wealth leads to fulfillment in life, then Solomon should have been greatly fulfilled, but Qoheleth concludes that he was chasing the wind. Striving for excess wealth can lead to a lack of satisfaction because it prevents enjoyment of the gifts that God has given.

Greek Cynic Diogenes also challenged the common belief that wealth leads to happiness. Instead, he thought that happiness is to be found in limiting one's needs, which means that misfortune can be faced with serenity (Brunschwig 2000, 850).

Mystery of Retribution

Ecclesiastes is written against the background of the standard Wisdom literature doctrine of retribution. According to this doctrine, wisdom (and righteousness) should lead to (material) blessing and long life. There is truth in this doctrine, but it cannot be relied upon to give automatic or guaranteed results. Hence Qoheleth endeavors to nuance the doctrine by pointing to exceptions. In this case the pursuit of wisdom did not lead to the expected result of lasting satisfaction or unlimited life. The wise person will die just as surely as the fool (2:15). Even fame will not endure in the short memories of those left behind.

IV. A TIME FOR EVERYTHING (3:1-22)

BEHIND THE TEXT

The royal autobiography ends in ch 2. Chapter 3 continues with a poem that expresses the life events that are subject to God's timing. However, an autobiographical tone continues in this unit and throughout the book, with frequent use of the first person (e.g., 3:10).

No historical context is discernible for the timeless poem on time (vv 1-8) but there is specific mention of war and many (if not all) of the images present a contrast between wartime and peacetime. It seems that the writer presents war or the threat of war (a present reality for much of the postexilic periods) as one of the contingencies that make life uncertain. The poem that closes the book also appears to return to this theme (12:1-7). Death is certainly a clear theme throughout the book, and war can be a major contributor to the uncertainty of one's time of death.

The theme of God's sovereignty is continued from the previous unit as is the advice to enjoy life. Qoheleth also continues to explore the mystery of retribution and returns to the theme of the lack of profit from toil.

The subsequent unit (4:1-16) has a different format ("better than" sayings) but continues some of the same themes (such as contentment and wisdom) while introducing new themes (such as companionship).

The premise of ch 3 is that only God knows the timing of events that he has ordained. However, ancient wisdom teachers attempted to discern proper times for various activities by means of their wisdom (Crenshaw 1987, 92). In 8:5, Qoheleth declares that the wise do know when and how to act. But he returns to the idea that everything has its time and that humans do not know the future (8:6-7). This again shows the limitations of wisdom. Wisdom is useful for knowing how to act, but ultimately only God has the knowledge of when and how things will happen. The OT mentions a number of events that are subject to God's timing (von Rad 1965, 100). There is a time for giving birth (Mic 5:3), gathering animals (Gen 29:7), for kings to go to battle (2 Sam 11:1), for temple building (Hag 1:4), for trees to bear fruit (Ps 1:3), and for food (Ps 104:27). The psalmist declared, "My times are in your hands" (Ps 31:15).

The genre of ch 3 is reflection, which is a common genre in Ecclesiastes. The poem in 3:2-8 begins with the word pair **born** and **die** and ends with **war** and **peace.** These words provide a chiastic framework for the entire poem (Crenshaw 1987, 96; J. A. Loader discerns a more intricate chiasm for this poem; 1979, 11). There is also a chiastic pattern in the last verse of the poem (v 8; **love, hate, war, peace**). Each line of the poem presents a contrast between two aspects of life, one positive and one negative. There is some alternating between verses (positive actions before negative actions in vv 2, 6, 8*a*; negative actions before positive actions in vv 3, 4, 7, 8*b*). Jarick has discerned a pattern to this alternating (2000, 79-99). He considers scattering stones in v 5 to be a positive action, although it is not clear which action—sending stones or gathering stones.

Other literary devices include repetition (especially of the word **time**). The verb *to see* is repeated in this unit, reflecting Qoheleth's observation methodology (vv 10, 13, 16, 18, 22). *To see* is a key word, used forty-seven times in the book.

Chapter 3 can be outlined as follows:

In God's Time (3:1-8)

What to Do? Enjoy! (3:9-22)

(A Time for Judgment [3:16-17])

IN THE TEXT

A. In God's Time (3:1-8)

■ **1** Verse 1 introduces the main theme of vv 2-8. There is a season and a time **for every activity under heaven.**

The word **season** (*zĕmān*) does not refer to the four seasons of the year. Israel only has two seasons, wet and dry. Adding "seedtime and harvest" gives the impression of four (Gen 8:22). In Hebrew, **season** is used of set times such as the Passover festival (as in the Talmud, *Zebahim* 1:1). The word is only used in late biblical Hebrew (Neh 2:6; Esth 9:27, 31) and Aramaic (six times in Ezra and Daniel), which is consistent with a postexilic date for Ecclesiastes. In Aramaic documents outside the Bible this word is first found in the fifth century B.C. (Seow 1997, 13). The earlier biblical word with the same meaning was *môʿēd*, which also comes from a root meaning "to fix, appoint."

Qoheleth uses the word **season** for predetermined or set time. This implies that the timing of the events described in the poem is determined by God, and not by human choice. Time belongs to God, as v 11 clarifies, but for now perhaps the reader is being drawn into the illusion that human choice is the decisive factor. This illusion will soon be shattered with another affirmation of the sovereignty of God (v 10).

The Hebrew word *ʿēt* (**time**) is the most common word for time in the Bible and is used of specific times, rather than time in an abstract sense (which was not a Hebrew concept). It comes from the root *ʿānah*, which is an important word in Ecclesiastes with the meaning "be busy"; it is not clear that this meaning is connected with the noun **time** in the book (*ʿānah* also means "answer," "be afflicted," and "sing," BDB 772-77). Some of the experiences in the poem are afflictions, others are reasons to sing, and others are more neutral activities.

The word **activity** can also be translated *pleasure, delight* (*ḥēpeṣ*, 5:4; 12:1, 10). It is an activity or business in the sense that it represents the things people do because they take delight in them (3:1, 17; 5:8; 8:6). This will resonate later in this passage with the admonition to enjoy what God has given (v 22; see 2:24). The timing for every delightful activity comes from God; therefore, all one can do is to enjoy both the time and the activity while they last.

■ **2** The poem itself occupies vv 2-8 and comprises fourteen opposites. The literary device of opposites (merism) is commonly used in Hebrew to express totality (e.g., "the heavens and the earth" means "universe" in Gen 1:1; see also Eccl 11:6; Gen 49:27; 2 Sam 3:25; Pss 92:2; 139:2). However, this literary device does not seem to be in use here. Crenshaw suggests that Qoheleth is giving opposites that cancel each other out, as death cancels out birth (1987, 96). However, the opposites probably relate to wartime and peacetime.

The poem begins with the theme of life and death. Most of the lines in this unit are two groups of two words each, which establish the simple pattern of the poem. **A time to be born** is thus two words in Hebrew (*ʿēt lāledet*); the verb **to be born**, literally *a time to give birth* in Hebrew, is not passive but active (although Jer 25:34 has an intransitive use of the infinitive; Ginsburg 1861, 304). This means that the first line does not have the birth and death of a single person in view, but instead it indicates the categories of birth and death. The specific timing of giving birth is beyond human control and so this first word pair emphasizes the focus on God's timing, not human timing. **A time to die** emphasizes the opposite of birth. In the context of war and peace, war is a

81

time of dying, and a disastrous time for giving birth, both because of the chaos of the battle and also because of the uncertain outcome. Jesus reflected this reality in his warning about the difficulties for pregnant women in the coming disaster (Matt 24:19).

In the second line of v 2 the activity under God's timing is planting. Planting is not under human control because its timing is determined by the weather. Planting could not begin until the rains came, as the ground would be too hard to plow in summer (using a stick plow of wood or metal). In the ancient worldview, rain was the result of water above the firmament (*rāqîaʿ*) being released by God (or the gods) through windows (although Qoheleth speaks of rain coming from the clouds, 11:3; see Prov 25:14). It followed that the timing of the rain and, therefore, planting, were completely controlled by God.

Agricultural Calendar

In the agricultural economy of ancient Israel, a lunar calendar was used rather than a solar calendar. Harvesttimes would be connected with the phase of the moon. For example, the Passover festival fell on the 14th of Nissan. The month began with the new moon (i.e., dark moon) so the 14th of the month would be at the full moon. This allowed more time for the harvest, and also a brighter night for the harvest festival. The timing of the harvest month, however, was set by its relation to the solar equinox. So the counting of the months for the year depended on the sun.

The reader might expect that the matching activity for planting would be harvesting. This is one interpretation of the word **uproot** (*laʿăqôr*), but it is not the usual meaning. Ginsburg suggested that the uprooting relates to root vegetables, which are harvested this way, but this would only apply to a small portion of the crops (1861, 305).

For some of the couplets in this poem, the second line mirrors the first. If this is true for v 2, then planting and uprooting may also be intended as metaphors for giving birth and dying. This would relate to peace and war. But battles were generally conducted in the dry season (2 Sam 11:1), not the time of planting. The uprooting could relate to destructive activities by an invading army (Eccl 3:5; 2 Kgs 3:19, 25). Armies were known to throw stones on fields to reduce productivity of the enemy's fields. Samson destroyed the crops of his enemies with foxes and fire (Judg 15:5). In a more recent analogy, Kit Carson demoralized the Navaho by destroying their peach orchards in 1864 (Brown 1970, 27; see 2 Kgs 3:25).

The only other occurrence of the rare word **uproot** (*ʿāqar*) in this conjugation (Qal) relates to the destruction of a city in war (Ekron, in a play on words; Zeph 2:4). The word may be related to similar roots meaning "dig" (*qûr, nāqar, kûr, kārâ, ʾākar*; BDB 881, 669, 468, 500, 38). A different word for "uproot" (*nātaš*) occurs repeatedly in Jeremiah in the context of destroying nations (i.e., war; Jer 1:10; 12:14-15; 18:7; 24:6; 31:28, 40; 42:10; 45:4). Thus the word **uproot** has strong connections to wartime activities rather than being a neutral word for harvesting.

■**3** **A time to kill, and a time to heal** are opposites in war and peace settings. During the battle is the time to kill, but healing can occur when the war is over. Ginsburg thought that the pairs should be truly antithetical; since **heal** is not the opposite of **kill,** he suggested "save" instead of **heal,** based on the Syriac version (1861, 305). In the context of wartime, **heal** may refer to the healing of the disrupted relations caused by war. The Hebrew word *rāpā'* ("heal") is commonly used for healing from illness. Thus the text could also refer to a time for healing from illness. In modern thinking, any time is a **time to heal.** Extreme interpretation of the OT doctrine of retribution considered illness as a punishment from God; this would then mean that the act of healing interfered with God's justice. Sirach defended the medical profession with his argument that the physicians are engaged in continuing the work of God through their gift of healing, which they have received from God (Sirach 38:1-14).

A time to tear down is literally *break through (a wall)* (*liprôs*, but see Isa 5:5 where this verb is used for breaking down a wall). Wartime would be an appropriate context for either breaking down an enemy's wall, or breaking through to attack a besieged city (or to escape one). **A time to build** could refer to the peacetime activity of building of walls and buildings that had been destroyed during wartime.

Formation of Tells

Conquest, war, and earthquakes often meant that existing structures had to be cleared before construction on new buildings could begin. The difficulty of removing rubble meant that existing materials that could not be reused would be leveled out, thus raising the level of the building site. Over the centuries towns would become higher and higher, forming tells (artificial hills on which the latest level of occupation stood). This phenomenon has allowed archaeologists to dig down through the layers, thus reconstructing the histories of ancient cities.

■**4** The weeping and laughing of v 4 are appropriate responses to the killing and healing of v 3. Verse 3 ends with the phrase *'ēt libnôt* ("a time to build") and v 4 begins with a similar sounding phrase *'ēt libkôt* (**a time to weep**). In v 4 the opposite of mourning is dancing. This connection is also found in Ps 30:11 where mourning is exchanged for dancing. Weeping and mourning have obvious connections with wartime, while laughing and dancing would be appropriate activities in times of peace or after a victory.

■**5** Verse 5 begins with the activities of scattering and gathering stones. Scattering stones (*šālak* literally means *to throw* or *to cast*) could refer to slinging stones in war (either from the city wall or in the battlefield; *qālaʿ* is the usual word in the OT for slinging stones). *Šālak* is usually used for throwing bodies down (e.g., Isa 34:3). Scattering stones could also refer to the enemy activity of scattering stones in the fields to disrupt agricultural activities during wartime (2 Kgs 3:19, 25). In the same way the gathering (*kěnôs*) of stones could be related to the removal or gathering of field stones for ease of plowing and planting during peacetime (Isa 5:2).

The Targum and Ibn Ezra viewed the stones as building materials that would be discarded when useless or gathered when needed (Ginsburg 1861, 306; Wesley shared this view). If this is so, then gathering (and building, v 3) relate to peacetime, while scattering relates to war.

The word **embrace** is usually used literally for the hug of greeting (e.g., Gen 29:13). This would be appropriate during times of peace, but during war the activities of defense would mean a **time to refrain** (lit., *be far from*) from embracing, and one would not embrace an enemy. It is unlikely that sexual intercourse is in view here (Cohen 1946, 124, citing the Targum and Prov 5:20), but if so, this activity was inappropriate in wartime (2 Sam 11:11; Joel 2:16).

■ **6** In v 6 the activity in question is seeking and losing. The Hebrew verb *bāqaš* ("to seek," "to desire") is in the intensive form, which indicates active pursuit or search for something that is lost. The desire would be to hold on to the object when it is found. The opposite is the willingness to let go or **to lose** the object of one's seeking (**to give up**) or something that is already in one's possession. An item would be permanently lost once the seeking ceased.

The second line (**a time to keep and a time to throw away**) seems to express a parallel idea. Both lines of v 6 seem to convey the idea of war and peacetime activities. Searching and keeping are activities for times of peace. In wartime, possessions are discarded in order to escape with one's life, or they are confiscated by the invading army. The Midrash gives an example of a time to throw away. When travelers on a ship feared for their lives because the sailors planned to kill them for their treasure, they threw the treasure overboard (Cohen 1983, 80).

■ **7** **A time to tear** in v 7 must refer to garments because the counterpart of tear is **mend**. The verb **to mend** (*litpôr*) is rare, used only four times in the OT (Gen 3:7; Eccl 3:7; Ezek 13:18; Job 16:15). Garments were torn in a time of grief (and later mended, as most people could not afford to buy new garments; e.g., Gen 37:29). If the following line (**to be silent** and **to speak**) is related to the first, then this might be the silence of grief, just as Job's friends sat in silence for seven days (Job 2:12-13). Both lines in v 7 seem to relate to grief, which is common in wartime when mending and casual conversation would be inappropriate.

■ **8** Verse 8 makes explicit the war and peacetime motif of vv 2-8. Two stylistic changes occur in this last verse of the poem. The infinitives (characteristic of the entire poem) are abandoned in the final line, in favor of nouns (**war** and **peace**).

The other change is a reversal of correspondence. For the other pairs the first elements in each line are related, and the second elements in each are related (except perhaps v 5). In v 8, the first element in the first line (**love**) corresponds with the second element in the second line (**peace**), and the second element in the first line (**hate**) with the first element in the second (**war**). This amounts to a chiasm in this verse, and together with v 3, a chiasm that frames the whole poem.

The change in grammar (nouns instead of infinitives) apparently confirms **war** and **peace** as the theme of the poem. **War** and **peace** are not just more activities in an average lifespan (or the infinitives "time to fight" and "time to cease fighting" would have been used). They are external conditions under which life is lived (ultimately controlled by God, not humans) and thus make life uncertain and unpredictable. The actions (participles) of the poem are appropriate depending on whether the noun **war** or **peace** is present. A major theme of the book is that hoarding wealth and studying wisdom have unreliable results. This is made more true by the threat of war.

A time to hate seems to contradict the biblical ideal of love. But the context of this poem is an emphasis on the sovereignty of God, especially his timing. Individual aspects of the poem should not be taken as license for selfish behavior. The time for hate and war is not when humans decide to take revenge, but when God's timing thrusts the necessity of such action upon people.

The Hebrew definitions of love and hate focus more on action and less on emotion than modern conceptions. Deuteronomy 6:5-6 commands love, which indicates that an action is required (since emotions cannot be commanded). The content of the love commanded is keeping commandments, including exclusive loyalty to Yahweh, which is the essence of covenant. In the Amarna letters, kings who were in covenant together were said to love each other (NIDOTTE 1:278). This included a relationship of mutual aid in case of attack. The word **hate** characterizes a relationship without a covenant, and it could mean war. The Egyptian Pharaoh designates military enemies as *hating ones* (NIV, "enemies") in Exod 1:10. In Jesus' use of the words "love" and "hate" the focus seems to be on allegiance; for example, he tells his disciples that they should "hate" their parents (Luke 14:26).

B. What to Do? Enjoy! (3:9-22)

■9 The poem ends in v 8 and the Hebrew text has a paragraph break here (*sĕtûmâ*). One might expect in the next section a celebration of God's sovereignty because of his control of time for various human activities. But Qoheleth returns to the usual complaint about the lack of profit from toil. This would be particularly relevant in wartime. Wealth hoarded in time of peace could be quickly lost in wartime. Reflection on the poem begins with the question, **What does the worker gain from his toil?** (v 9), which echoes 1:3. The "human" of 1:3 is replaced by **the worker** in 3:9. These are used synonymously, but "worker" or "doer" (*ʿōśeh*) is chosen in the context because it is tempting for humans to think that they are in control, but it is really God, the ultimate worker/doer/maker who controls time (see v 11).

■ 10 Qoheleth continues to emphasize the verb "to see" in this chapter (six times), designating God's sovereignty as a **burden** (ʿinyān) in v 10. The verb *to see* (rāʾâ) occurs forty-seven times in Ecclesiastes and is one of the most common words in the book. Observation is the major source of revelation in Wisdom literature, rather than the direct revelation from God common in the prophetic literature. **Burden** (or "business") that God has given to humanity is another echo from ch 1 (see 1:13). The verb from which this word derives can also mean "to afflict," which shows the negative aspect of the business God has given, hence the translation **burden.** God's timing could be a blessing but, to Qoheleth, it is a **burden God has laid on men** or, literally, *given* them (nātan). The verb *to give* is also an important word in this chapter. It emphasizes the sovereignty of God in the timing of human affairs.

■ 11 The point is expanded in v 11, which affirms that God **has made everything beautiful in its time.** While humans may appear to be the workers/doers/makers (v 9), it is really God who works/does/makes everything. The word **beautiful** (yāpeh) is more than appearance in this context ("suitable" in the NRSV). God has made everything right and good, or appropriate (one of the meanings in postbiblical Hebrew; Fox 1999, 209). Everything God made has an appropriate time to show forth its purpose. In fact, time itself is his, if the pronoun attached to **time** is taken to refer to God and not **everything** ("his time" rather than **its time**). Either way, God is the subject of the verb "work/do/make," and he is the one responsible for assigning a time to everything.

This positive assessment of God's sovereignty and order is what one would have expected at the close of the poem in vv 2-8. It is possible that Qoheleth returned to the theme of human work and its futility in vv 9-10 to contrast human work with the purpose and design of God's work and his time in v 11. Human effort cannot lead to excessive gain because of God's sovereignty. Human efforts to control outcomes (even through wisdom) are futile and become a "burden" (v 9) because of their futility. It is God (not humans) who has the power to make things of beauty, just as his creation in Gen 1 was pronounced "good" (Sirach 39:16 expressed a similar idea using "good" instead of **beautiful**).

Not only is God responsible for time, but **he has also set eternity in the hearts of men** (v 11). The meaning of **eternity** (ʿōlām) is disputed by commentators. Suggested translations (including emendations) are "duration" (Murphy 1992, 34), "toil" (Fox 1999, 211), "ignorance" (Whitley 1979, 31-33), "darkness/ignorance" (Gault 2008, 57), and "world" (Septuagint, Latin). The translation **eternity** is supported by the contrast with **time.** While humanity is limited by the timing that God in his sovereignty gives, people are nevertheless aware of a reality that is not confined to the moment. Humans are aware of the past and they know about the future, but they cannot control the timing of future events, nor change the occurrence of past events. This awareness is a gift from God, and the challenge for humanity is to accept this gift and work within the parameters of God's timing.

A strange phrase unknown in other Hebrew literature underlies the translation **yet they cannot** (*mibbĕlî ʾăšer lōʾ*) in v 11. *Bĕlî* has the basic meaning "defect, failure" and is used as an adverb of negation ("not, there is not, without"). It can be combined with various prepositions, in this case, *min* ("from"). The double negative (*lōʾ*) provides intensity (the negatives do not cancel each other out; GKC §152y). *Mibbĕlî* may have been chosen in Eccl 3:11 because of the similarity in sound to the preceding word (*bĕlibbām*, **hearts of men;** Crenshaw 1987, 98).

The remainder of v 11 is literally, *which the human cannot find the deed which God has done from beginning until the end* (**they cannot fathom what God has done from beginning to end**). This fits with Qoheleth's use of *hebel* (vanity) as "incomprehensible." The sovereignty and timing of God is beyond human comprehension. A search for such answers would be like chasing the wind; the rationale for the deeds of God cannot be found.

John Ruskin on Beauty, 1885-89

The woods, which I had only looked on as wilderness, fulfilled, I then saw, in their beauty the same laws which guided the clouds, divided the light, and balanced the wave. "He hath made everything beautiful in His time," became for me thenceforward the interpretation of the bond between the human mind and all visible things. (*Praeterita*, in Christianson 2007, 177-78)

■ **12** Verse 12 is introduced with **I know,** a verb that is more relational than "I saw" (3:10, 14, 16) but can also apply to knowledge that is merely cognitive. Qoheleth's experience here is consistent with the conclusion in 2:24 (see also 8:15). Precisely because of God's sovereignty and his control of timing, humanity should be content with living in the moment and doing good.

There is nothing better is a negative form of the "better than" saying that is a feature of Wisdom literature (e.g., "Wisdom is better than rubies," Prov 8:11 KJV; Eccl 4:3, 6, 9, 13).

The translation **for men** represents an emendation (or at least an explanation) of *bām* ("for them") to *bāʾādām* ("for man," see 2:24). There are some manuscripts that have this reading, suggesting that *bām* could be a scribal error, although the plural may simply indicate a collective understanding of the singular pronoun of *in his life* later in this verse (*bĕhayyāyw*, **while they live**). Grammatical agreement is not always very precise in Hebrew, and Ecclesiastes has a large number of linguistic anomalies.

The phrase **do good** (*wĕlaʿăśôt ṭôb*) is assumed by some to be influenced by the Greek expression *eu prattein* ("to do good," i.e., to fare well; Zirkel, cited by Delitzsch 1875, 262). If so, this would be a suitable parallel for **be happy,** as this chapter is not really giving ethical advice (although it is advising a certain philosophy of life).

■ **13** While God has given humanity activity (v 10) and knowledge of eternity (v 11), he has also given the gift of enjoyment (lit., *see good*). This verse contains two *waw*-consecutives, a grammatical construction common in narrative but not in Ecclesiastes (*wĕśātâ wĕrāʾâ;* see 1:17).

The Tavern Keeper's Advice to Gilgamesh

> Let your belly be full,
>> Make merry day and night.
> Turn each day into a feast of rejoicing,
>> Dance and play day and night.
> Put on fresh garments,
>> Wash your hair and body in water.
> Play with your children,
>> Take pleasure in your wife.

(Epic of Gilgamesh, Old Babylonian version; Matthews and Benjamin 2006, 26)

■ **14** Verse 14 is again introduced by **I know** (see v 12). The emphasis is also on what God does, which is not temporary (vanity) like the deeds of humanity, but enduring. God's deeds last forever, not in the sense that there is no change or decay, but in the sense that his actions have lasting significance. His actions are designed to lead humans to fear him. This is an important theme in Wisdom literature and Qoheleth makes this explicit in 8:12 and 12:13. The fear of God is not a terror that is counterproductive to a healthy relationship but a recognition that there is a significant distinction between God and humanity. God's sovereignty over nature, human activity, and time should be recognized by humanity. The fear of God is Wisdom literature's expression of right relationship with God (see von Rad 1972, 66).

Crenshaw argues that Qoheleth's concept of the fear of God is different from the usual wisdom teaching, even approaching "terror before an unpredictable despot" in some cases (Crenshaw 1987, 100, citing E. Pfeiffer). There is no clear indication of such a view in this context, however. The fact that God's actions have lasting significance does not invoke terror, but according to Qoheleth's argument so far, should bring enjoyment of the gifts that God has given (Eaton 1983, 82). Based on the paraphrase in Sirach 18:6, Fox writes, "Fearing God means accepting one's own limitations" (1999, 213).

■ **15** Ecclesiastes 1:10 is echoed in v 15: **Whatever is has already been, and what will be has been before.** The second half of the verse has been interpreted in various ways (**and God will call the past to account**). A literal translation is *And God will seek what is pursued* (*wĕhāʾĕlōhîm yĕbaqqēš ʾet-nirdāp*). Humans pursue a legacy in life, but there is no remembrance of what they have done (1:11), and they cannot control the timing of events (3:1-11). God's seeking is, however, successful. He has what humans cannot find (3:11).

The Septuagint and Targum interpreted the object of God's seeking as "the persecuted," which is the meaning of *nirdāp* (*what is pursued*) in the Talmud. Modern interpreters who follow this reading have tended to move this verse since the idea does not seem to fit the context. Crenshaw favors the idea that God is pursuing events of the past to bring them back into the present, which is a cycle he sees represented in 1:9 (1987, 100). A more likely meaning is that God is not confused by the endless motion of nature, but that he is able to grasp the significance that human actors find elusive and incomprehensible.

(A Time for Judgment [3:16-17])

■ **16** At v 16, Qoheleth changes the subject slightly to the topic of justice, a topic he will take up again in 4:1. Using the verb "to see," he observes wickedness in the place of justice and righteousness (*mišpāt* and *ṣedeq*). Is wickedness also under the sovereignty of God? Christians, while needing to be careful about facile answers to the problem of evil, find the solution in the final judgment. Qoheleth has no such luxury as he apparently has no concept of the resurrection or the final judgment. Yet he does not let go of the idea that God will bring justice in this life, although this justice will not always be obvious since God's ways are inscrutable and incomprehensible.

The concept of order was very important in Israel and the ancient Near East. The observation of v 16 provides evidence of a lack of order. A similar observation is made in the document *A Sufferer and a Friend in Babylon*, where the sufferer says, "I have searched the world for order, / Everything is upside down. / The divine assembly is powerless to restore order" (ca. 700 B.C.; Matthews and Benjamin 2006, 242).

■ **17** Verse 17 affirms that injustice is a temporary situation, as **God will bring to judgment both the righteous and the wicked.** As God sets a time for every human activity, he also brings every human activity to judgment in his time. The standard Wisdom literature doctrine of retribution ("you reap what you sow") is operating in the view of Qoheleth, even though the results of human action may be delayed. In the standard view, the doctrine of retribution is seen to work almost automatically although Ecclesiastes is not the only OT book to challenge this (see Job; Prov 11:16; 13:23; 14:13; 21:31).

Qoheleth probably does not have an eschatological day of judgment in mind (see Eccl 3:18-21). Judgment can come in the form of consequences for righteousness and wickedness in this life. These consequences are delayed to a time of God's choosing and justice will have the final word, even though wickedness may seem to prevail.

The Targum and others have interpreted this as a reference to "the great day of judgment" (Ginsburg 1861, 315). These interpreters take Qoheleth's statements at face value, that there is no justice (*mišpāṭ*) in the world (3:16) and that God will bring justice (*yišpōṭ*, 3:17). Crenshaw sees this as an apparent contradiction, which could be a later addition by a more conservative wisdom teacher (1987, 102). It seems, however, that Qoheleth is saying that God will bring justice in his own timing and way, despite current evidence to the contrary.

■ **18** In 2:16 Qoheleth saw no distinction between the wise and fools since both would die (with no hope of a meaningful afterlife). Now in 3:18-21 the same point is made regarding humans and animals. Both will die and Qoheleth is not certain about the (apparently common) assumption of the day that the life breath of humans is distinct from that of animals (**all have the same breath,** v 19).

An unusual Hebrew phrase underlies the translation **as for men** (ʿ*al-dibrat bĕnê hāʾādām,* v 18). ʿ*Al-dibrat* means *concerning, so that* and is common in Aramaic (Dan 2:30) but occurs only four times in biblical Hebrew (Ps 110:4; Eccl 3:18; 7:14; 8:2). A number of words in v 18 are difficult to translate (*lĕb-ārām,* **tests them;** *wĕlirʾôt,* **they may see;** and *šĕhem-bĕhēmâ hēmmâ lāhem,* **they are like the animals**). The general idea is that God tests or purifies humans so that they will see that they share mortality with the animals.

■ **19** The word **breath** is the same Hebrew word that is translated **spirit** in v 21. The literal meaning of this word in Hebrew is *wind* or *breath,* and it did not have the same connotations for the Hebrew audience that "spirit" has in English. It is quite literally the breath that characterizes all living beings. If it goes up or down after death, this is not a continued existence of a personal entity. It is merely an affirmation that God is responsible for all life. Once a person loses the life breath, no human effort can bring a corpse back to life again (even modern medical techniques have only a short period of opportunity for this). This interpretation is supported by the phrase "the breath in our nostrils is smoke" in the apocryphal book the Wisdom of Solomon, which is in some sense a commentary on Ecclesiastes (Wis 2:2, see Ginsburg 1861, 28).

The Hebrew for **advantage** (*môtar*) is used only here in Ecclesiastes (also Prov 14:23; 21:5). Qoheleth's usual vocabulary is *yitrôn* or *yôtēr* (e.g., 1:3; 7:16). All three are from the same root. The Septuagint took the phrase as a rhetorical question: "What is the advantage?" The lack of distinction between humans and animals is *hebel* (**meaningless**) in the sense of being profitless and incomprehensible.

■ **20** This lack of distinction can be observed in the fact that **all come from dust, and to dust all return.** Much of the ancient understanding of the world was based on simple observation, a kind of scientific method but with less data with which to work. Since a corpse soon decays to dust, it was assumed that dust was the raw material of humanity (Gen 2:7). This is more explicit in Gen 3:19 where the sinful humans are condemned to return to dust (see Job 10:9; 34:15; Ps 104:29; Sirach 40:11). The point of Qoheleth is that since both humans and animals seem to be made of dust, there is no evidence that there is any distinction between the life breath of the two.

The fact that bodies decompose did not diminish the belief in Sheol, an insignificant afterlife, as this realm was believed to be populated by "shades" ("weak ones," *rĕpāʾîm*) not spirits or souls. The destiny of the body could easily be observed, it returned to dust (Prov 9:18; Isa 14:9).

■ **21** As for the life breath, no one can observe, therefore no one knows **if the spirit of man rises upward and if the spirit of the animal goes down into the earth.** This translation follows the ancient versions that raise doubt about the commonly held distinction between people and animals. The Hebrew text does not have **if,** which could mean that there is doubt about who knows of the distinction (*who knows [that] the spirit of man . . .*) or who knows the spirit (NIV margin, "who knows the spirit of man . . ."). This reading does not seem right because it amounts to an affirmation of the commonly held perception that something different happens to people after death than what happens to animals, a perception that Qoheleth is challenging in 3:18-20. Ginsburg thought that the denial of the immortality of the soul seemed unorthodox to the Masoretic scribes (who preserved the Hebrew text) leading them to change the interrogative *he* to the definite article (also the letter *he*) by supplying different vowels, (*hāʿōlâ* and *hayyōredet* for *haʿōla* and *hăyōredet*; Ginsburg 1861, 319; see GKC §100*m*, 150). If this is correct, then the ancient translations are right (along with the NIV reading). In any case, the interrogative *he* is not necessary for the formation of a question in Hebrew.

■ **22** Verse 22 concludes this thought and the whole chapter with **there is nothing better for a man than to enjoy his work, because that is his lot. For who can bring him to see what will happen after him?** This is consistent with the conclusions Qoheleth has given so far (2:24; 3:12). Humans cannot control the timing of events. Instead people must accept the sovereignty of God. They cannot know what happens after death, either personally or to their legacy, so they must enjoy what they have now as a gift from God. Elsewhere Qoheleth describes human activity with the negative word "toil" (*ʿāmāl*). Here he uses the word **work** (*maʿăśāyw*), a more neutral word (Crenshaw says there is no distinction; 1987, 105).

Divine Sovereignty

It is perhaps common to read Eccl 3 as an injunction to determine the appropriate action for a particular time. However, the meaning of the word **season** (3:1) and the theology of the book elsewhere suggests that it is God's timing that determines these contrasting events. The issue is not human choice but divine sovereignty. Humans can only respond with the appropriate action for the time that has been thrust upon them (von Rad 1972, 138).

Enjoy Life

Another concern of the book is striving for wealth or control through wisdom (and righteousness). Chapter 3 exposes the futility of this philosophy and advises, instead, contentment, accepting whatever food, drink, and work God has given (3:13, 22). If there is to be a change in status, it will have to wait until God's timing and cannot be forced through human effort (including wisdom or righteousness).

Mystery of Retribution

One of the main concerns of the book is injustice, and this chapter uses the poem on timing to lead up to the assertion that God will bring justice—in his time (3:17). The apparent breakdown of the doctrine of retribution is only temporary, but it does show that humans cannot control outcomes.

Compared with modern Western culture, ancient Israel was more event-oriented than time-oriented. The modern invention of clocks and watches has allowed more precision in time orientation and, along with other technological advances, has given Western culture the illusion of control. Qoheleth would disagree with this perception. Despite human efforts to control events, through technology or wisdom, it is God who is in control and he determines the timing of everything.

Beyond Physical Death

It is not difficult to acknowledge Qoheleth's view that both animals and humans die and both become dust again. But does this mean for humans that there is no hope beyond the grave? Qoheleth denies the possibility of human life beyond death. The Christian doctrine of resurrection provides a clear alternative to the pessimistic view of Qoheleth. For Christians, the resurrection of Jesus of Nazareth gives hope to all who anticipate God's work of raising the dead—from "perishable" to "imperishable," from "a natural body" to "a spiritual body" (1 Cor 15:42-44).

V. WHAT IS BETTER? (4:1-16)

BEHIND THE TEXT

Ecclesiastes 4:13-16 is one of the few paragraphs in Ecclesiastes that could betray a specific historical context. The scene involves an old foolish king, supplanted by a poor youth; this is probably a hypothetical scenario. The Targum suggested that the characters in this text are Abraham and Nimrod, or Jeroboam and Rehoboam; the Midrash and Rashi suggested Joseph, David, and Zedekiah; and others have suggested Amaziah and Joash, or the high priest Onias (245-221 B.C.) and his nephew Joseph (Ginsburg 1861, 330).

The genre of ch 4 is reflection, but it introduces a literary device called "better than" sayings (*tôb min*) (see also 7:1-12). This is a known feature of Wisdom literature and allows comparisons, often showing the superiority of wisdom, righteousness, and relationships over wealth (Prov 3:13-14; 8:11, 19; 15:16, 17; 16:8, 16; 17:1; 19:1, 22; 21:9, 19; 25:24; 27:10; 28:6). For example, Prov 16:16 says, "Better to get wisdom than gold." There may be a certain irony in Qoheleth's use of the device as he often says *there is no good* (NIV, **nothing better;** 2:24; 3:12, 22). The "better than" sayings in 9:16 and 9:18 are qualified in the same verse (Seow 1997, 67). However, many of the "better than" sayings present a serious comparison, such as **two are better than one** (4:9), while others seem more cynical or ironic, such as **better . . . is he who has not yet been** (4:3).

In ch 4, Qoheleth continues some of the themes from the previous unit. The author explores further the issues of contentment and wisdom, revisits vanity from earlier units, and introduces the theme of relationships for the first time. The frequent use of "two" is another key characteristic of this chapter (vv 3, 8, 9, 10, 11, 12, 15).

The "better than" sayings provide the structure for Eccl 4:1-12. The first two paragraphs end in "better than" sayings, while the last two begin with "better than" sayings. This leaves the climactic central paragraph without a "better than" saying. The unit can be outlined as follows:

Better Not to Be Born (4:1-3)
Better a Little with Contentment (4:4-6)
No Contentment (4:7-8)
Better Two than One (4:9-12)
Better Poor but Wise (4:13-16)

IN THE TEXT

A. Better Not to Be Born (4:1-3)

■ I Chapter 4 begins with the phrase *Again I turned* (*wĕšabtî*), which has not been used in this sense up to this point; however, this phrase continues the idea represented by two other words in previous texts (see *sābab* and *pānah*, in 2:11, 12, 20). Qoheleth turned **and saw** (*wā'erʾeh*) oppressions and the oppressed. In ch 3 there was no mention of oppression in God's timing. Qoheleth's turning is to consider a new topic, namely oppression, wealth, and power. The issue of oppression is perhaps part of the wickedness that Qoheleth saw in the place of justice and righteousness (3:16). For the phrase **under the sun** see comment on 1:3. Qoheleth also observes the tears of the oppressed (NIV supplies **I saw**). **They have no comforter,** no one to show mercy. This is a serious lack from the viewpoint of biblical culture (Ginsburg 1861, 321; Lam 1:2).

Qoheleth also saw that **power was on the side of** those who are **oppressors** (lit., *from the hand of their oppressors, power*). In the Hebrew Bible, the word "hand" is often used in the sense of power, for it is the hand that enforces. For example, in the Song of Moses and Miriam, it was Yahweh's right hand that shattered the enemy (Exod 15:6). The word **power** (*kōah*) conveys the idea of force or violence (Ginsburg 1861, 321; see 2 Chr 26:13). The hand of the oppressors stands in contrast to Qoheleth's usual mention of the hand of God as an expression of his sovereignty (2:24; 9:1).

They have no comforter is repeated at the end of v 1 and could be a case of dittography (the error of copying something twice). But the second occurrence adds dramatic effect to the lack of mercy that the oppressed receive, and so it is probably original. Qoheleth does not utilize his observation of oppression as an opportunity to give some ethical advice, but instead he alerts his readers to the problem of oppression and the lack of comforters. Some commentators see in Qoheleth's observation lack of sympathy for the oppressed who are without a comforter or an advocate to bring an end to oppression. This has led some to think that the author "belonged to the upper classes by birth and position" (Murphy 1992, xxi).

■ **2-3** In the royal autobiography of chs 1 and 2, Qoheleth in his persona as king declared that he hated life because of a lack of lasting satisfaction (2:17). Verses 2-3 also convey the idea of dissatisfaction with life. In these verses the author categorizes people into three groups in the ascending order of happiness—the living, the dead, and those who were never born. In v 2, Qoheleth regards the dead as more fortunate than the living. This does not mean that he is advocating suicide. In his thinking the severity of the oppressions makes life not worth living (see Job 3:11-19). He is less sympathetic in v 3 where it is the mere nuisance of having to observe the suffering of others that makes life unbearable.

A Sufferer and a Soul in Egypt, ca. 2000 B.C.

My soul, do you really want me to go on living?
When my life smells worse than . . .
. . . bird drop on a hot day,
. . . rotten fish in the full sun,
. . . the floor of a duck coop,
. . . the sweat of fishermen,
. . . a stagnant fish pond,
. . . the breath of a crocodile?
(Matthews and Benjamin 2006, 227)

Better than both in v 3 is an example of a "better than" saying. While the one who dies in v 2 is happier than the living, the one never born is happier still in v 3. **Who has not seen the evil that is done under the sun** could refer to those who have not experienced the evil of oppression in the world. Calvin saw in this a foil for the NT doctrine of resurrection (*Institutes* 3.9.4; 3.25.5; Brown 2007, 76).

Theognis on Not Being Born

Not to be born, never to see the sun,
No worldly blessings is a greater one!
And the next best is speedily to die,
And, lapt beneath a load of earth, to lie!
(Quoted in Ginsburg 1861, 323)

B. Better a Little with Contentment (4:4-6)

■ **4** The "better than" saying in v 3 signals the end of the first paragraph, and a new paragraph begins in v 4. The verb "to see" introduces the next item, which Qoheleth wishes to highlight in this chapter, namely the fruits of excessive toil, hoarded for oneself alone. In the postexilic empires, rights of inheritance were controlled by the king or his representative. Qoheleth has already remarked that excessive toil is fruitless as one does not know who will inherit the fruits of that toil (2:18-19). For the unique word *kišrôn*, **achievement,** see comment on 2:21.

The problem with excessive toil is that it is not motivated by the necessities of life, but by **man's envy of his neighbor.** This is truly **meaningless** (*hebel*) and futile. The Egyptian *Teachings of Ptah-Hotep* also decried covetousness: "If you inherit land, take only your own portion of the land. Do not covet the land of others" (ca. 2500 B.C.; Matthews and Benjamin 2006, 286; see also Prov 15:27).

■ **5** Verse 5 has a contrast with the envious neighbor—the fool who does not bother to work at all but instead ends up eating flesh. Idle hands are empty hands, and Qoheleth seems to envisage here individuals who are so lazy that they would eat their own flesh before lifting a hand to help themselves, a ridiculous image that emphasizes the point through exaggeration. The literal translation, *eats his flesh*, conveys the idea of destroying oneself. The book of Proverbs shows the consequence for laziness: "A little sleep, a little slumber, a little folding of the hands to rest—and poverty will come on you like a bandit" (Prov 6:10-11; 24:33-34; see also 19:24). Lohfink offers an alternate reading, namely that despite being lazy, such a person has plenty of meat to eat, another example of the breakdown of retribution (2003, 69-70).

■ **6** There must be a balance between feverishly working to "get ahead of the Joneses" and doing absolutely nothing. Qoheleth provides this balance in v 6 with another "better than" saying: **Better one handful with tranquillity than two handfuls with toil.** The first **handful** (*kap*) uses the Hebrew word for an open hand, while the **handfuls** (*hāpĕnayim*) are closed hands (Delitzsch 1875, 275-76). Work should provide a comfortable living, without becoming a tiresome effort to accumulate more than is needed. This is similar to the preference in Proverbs for a simple meal with peace, over a feast with strife (Prov 15:16; 16:8; 17:1).

Krüger translates this proverb "a handful of rest" (more literal than **handful with tranquillity** in the NIV) (2004, 97). Crenshaw thinks it comes close to stifling individual initiative (1987, 107-8). However, like all proverbs, it is open to distortion and must be applied to the appropriate situation. The situation that Ecclesiastes consistently addresses is toil and striving, not laziness and inactivity. Qoheleth's theology of contentment is not one of complacency or laziness (10:18).

C. No Contentment (4:7-8)

■**7** *And I turned* (**again**) signals a new paragraph in this chapter. This paragraph is central to the chapter and has no "better than" saying. This verse contains the central thought of the chapter, namely the value of companionship, cooperation, and contentment versus miserly lonesome hoarding, which characterizes oppression (4:1-3), competition (4:4-6), and lack of joy (4:16). Nevertheless, Qoheleth opens the paragraph with his characteristic declaration that he has observed vanity. Perhaps the meaning of *hebel* (**meaningless**) here is "incomprehensible" or "difficult to obtain." Why do we need each other? And why is it so hard to find a faithful friend and contentment? These seem to be questions that Qoheleth attempts to answer here.

■**8 There was a man all alone** (v 8) is literally, *There is one and there is no second*. The phrase in Hebrew reflects the Wisdom literature device called the "numerical saying." The numbers used in these sayings are one and two (Deut 32:30; Job 33:14; Ps 62:11; Jer 3:14), three and four (Prov 30:15, 18, 21, 29; Amos 1—2), six and seven (Job 5:19; Prov 6:16), and seven and eight (Eccl 11:2; Mic 5:5). The list of observations may then contain any number of elements. The number in the announcement is not to be taken literally, as in the English expression "three or four things" (Exod 20:5; 34:7; Job 33:29; Isa 17:6).

The individual in Qoheleth's example has no companion, and neither son nor brother. Yet he insists on working arduously and endlessly even though he has no one with whom to share the results of his labor. Neither is he satisfied with the accumulation of wealth that he sees with **his eyes,** which are also insatiable (like the "sea," "eye," and "ear" in 1:7-8). So he asks himself (or perhaps Qoheleth asks for him), **"For whom am I toiling?"** The extra toil is depriving him of **enjoyment** (lit., *good*). This endless toil deprives the miserly hoarder of enjoyment, good, and a better way. Such a needless deprivation is vanity (*hebel*) in the sense of profitless, futile, or meaningless. It is incomprehensible that someone would act this way. Business conducted alone and for oneself is an evil business (**miserable business**). Earlier Qoheleth had complained about working hard when no one worthy would inherit the wealth earned (2:18). Verse 8 carries the argument further since wealth should also be shared during one's lifetime, not merely after death.

This verse is key to the whole book, which is probably addressed to the young entrepreneurs of the new commercial systems of the Persian or Hellenistic periods. The temptation in such systems is to work unceasingly to gain excessive wealth. This is a meaningless pursuit, and Qoheleth helps his audience ask themselves the question, Why? As the rest of the chapter will argue, meaningful relationships are much more satisfying in the long run.

D. Better Two than One (4:9-12)

■ **9** A better way is the subject of the next paragraph. It is companionship that leads to success in toil. The workers receive their wages or **return** (*śākār*). This is a commercial term that stands in contrast to *yitrôn*, the excess profit that Qoheleth cannot find in life or as a result of toil (1:3). Qoheleth is not against hard work and earning wages. He is against orienting life around oneself and excess profit. The productivity of toil has been in question in the whole book up until now. Now toil is declared fruitful if it is conducted in the context of companionship and cooperation, not isolation and competition. The importance of friendship is seen in the proverbs "either friendship or death" and "a man without friends is like a left hand without the right" (Talmud, quoted by Ginsburg 1861, 327).

■ **10-12** A travel scenario seems to underlie vv 10-12. Traveling alone was dangerous in many areas of the ancient world. A companion might be needed to help in the event of a fall on rough ground (v 10). While traveling, it may not be possible to light a fire for warmth, so a companion could provide body heat (v 11). And robbers would find a lone traveler an easy target (v 12). Even when not traveling, body heat was important as windows did not have glass, and outer garments served as blankets (Exod 22:26; Ginsburg 1861, 328).

Qoheleth ends this paragraph with a proverb: **A cord of three strands is not quickly broken.** A similar thought is found in the Epic of Gilgamesh (Kovacs 1989, 37). The word for **cord** (*ḥûṭ*) is the light material that was used to contrast with new ropes in the binding of Samson (Judg 16:12). Alone, a cord could easily be snapped, but three cords twisted together are significantly stronger. The numerical saying may be in the background here as there was mention of one, then two, and now three (see Behind the Text and comment on 4:8). **Overpowered** (*tāqap*) is another rare word in the OT (Job 14:20; 15:24; Eccl 4:12; 6:10). It is found in Aramaic and postbiblical Hebrew (Dan 4:11, 20; 5:20; Talmud, *Abot* 3:8).

Henry Howard on Friendship (1546)

For as the tender frend appeasith euery gryef;
So yf he fall that liues alone, who shall be his relyef?
  The frendly feeres ly warme, in armes embraced faste;
Who sleapes aloone at euery tourne dothe feale the winter blast:
  What can he doo but yeld, that must resist aloone?
Yf ther be twaine, one may defend the tother ouer-throwne:
  The single twyned cordes may no suche stresse indure,
As cables brayded thre-fould may, together wrethed sure.
(In Johnson 1810, 356)

E. Better Poor but Wise (4:13-16)

■ **13** The final paragraph of this chapter is again introduced with a "better than" saying (v 13). The comparison this time is between an old king and his successor. This is reminiscent of the monologue of Qoheleth as king in 1:12—2:26 where the position of King Solomon was examined and his activities were found to be vanity. In that context Solomon was not described as a fool but his actions, priorities, and lifestyle were certainly called into question. Here in 4:13 the elderly king is described as **foolish** and he does not take advice. Wisdom tradition held old age in great honor (Job 12:12; 15:10), but here the portrait of an old king is negative. An old and foolish king would be replaced with a king who is young (inexperienced) but wise. Rehoboam, Solomon's successor, though young, was unwise and did not listen to the wise counsel of the older men who were counselors of Solomon (1 Kgs 12:1-15).

This is one of the few units in Ecclesiastes that hint of specific historical events, and this has led to several suggestions about which historical setting may be in mind. Scholars have suggested a range of time frames, including events in the history of Israel and events from the Persian period (see Behind the Text).

The youth who will replace the king is **poor** (*miskēn*), which is more a designation of social rank than a measure of wealth. This person is a commoner, rather than someone of royal lineage. The word for **youth** (*yeled*) is usually reserved for young children. Sometimes it has a broader meaning, though, as Rehoboam's young advisers were described with this word, and he was forty-one years old (1 Kgs 12:8; 14:21). The word may be chosen here to emphasize youth and inexperience, although in Israel's history some kings really were very young (Josiah, eight years old, 2 Kgs 22:1; Joash, seven years old, 2 Kgs 11:21).

Esteeming a poor youth above an elderly king is contrary to ancient values since age was considered to be necessary to gain wisdom, and the wisdom of the elders was respected (unlike modern technological societies where the elders often have trouble negotiating rapid change). Also, wisdom and wealth went together under the doctrine of retribution, so this scenario adds to Qoheleth's challenge of this doctrine when oversimplified.

■ **14** In v 14 the young successor to the throne may have come from prison. This was the case with Joseph, who represents one of the suggested historical settings for this scenario. The prison was not a penitentiary to reform criminals (who were dealt with through fines and corporal punishment), but rather a prison for political prisoners or debtors. This is the function of prisons in Joseph's story and in Jeremiah (Gen 39:20; Jer 37:15). The new king is not a criminal but a person of low social standing.

Some translations suggest that the young successor is the subject of both parts of v 14 (so NIV). He may have come from prison or have been born in poverty. It is possible that the old king is the focus of v 14*b*. He has lost his kingdom to find himself in poverty. Krüger suggests that *ki gam* (**or he may**) should be taken to introduce a new subject, suggesting that poverty continues under the new leadership; "poor people would still be born under his rule" (2004, 104).

■ **15** Verse 15 refers to the crowds who follow the youth, possibly **the king's successor.** The Hebrew reads literally, *the child, the second who stands under him.* This could be another youth (the second) who has already replaced the wise youth, who replaced the foolish king. Crowds now follow him, but this will not last either. This mention of a second, while somewhat unclear, links 4:13-16 with 4:9-12 where the word "second" or "two" is found five times.

■ **16** In v 16 the crowd is soon displeased again and is ready to support a new king. It is better to have an inexperienced king who is wise than an old king who is foolish. But this is vanity (*hebel*, futile, profitless, incomprehensible), and it would be better still to have a wise king who is also experienced and has the continued support of the crowd. But Qoheleth does not say so, because the world does not work so. Instead, life is incomprehensible. The lack of clarity in vv 13-16 makes it difficult to see the connection with **chasing after the wind,** which usually signifies the futile or unattainable nature of something.

FROM THE TEXT

Vanity (hebel)

This unit highlights the futility of envy as a motivation for labor (v 4) and also of hoarding wealth without sharing it (vv 7-8). A lack of satisfaction is the root of both these problems. Also, there is something incomprehensible about the people's lack of satisfaction with the king's successor in vv 13-16.

Enjoy Life

The whole discussion in ch 4 about what is better is tempered by the notice in 3:22 (see also 5:18) that there is "nothing better." This is typical of Qoheleth's style, which often sees him accused of contradictions. Some of the "better than" sayings do seem sarcastic, some serious, but this reflects contradictions and enigmas in life. Injustice and oppression in the world can lead to despair, but they should lead to contentment with one's own lot, although not complacency about the suffering of others. While there is nothing better than to enjoy whatever God has given (3:22; 5:18), there are also some things in life that are better than others, such as companionship, which should be grasped when available (4:9-12).

In the 1851 novel *Moby-Dick*, Herman Melville portrays the main character Ahab as losing the enjoyment of simple things in life. In a symbolic act he throws his pipe overboard, which gives no more protest than a fizzle, and like the rivers in Eccl 1:7 makes no difference to the ocean whatsoever. The brief passage (ch 30) uses vocabulary reminiscent of Ecclesiastes like "vapour," "puffs," "smoking," "toiling, not pleasuring," "smoking to windward," "windward," "whiffs," "dying," "trouble," "business," "vapours," "smoke," and "bubble," at which point Ahab proceeds to pace the planks (getting nowhere). The reason for his loss of pleasure is his obsession with catching the white whale Moby Dick, an elusive goal that amounts to chasing the wind. In the front of the book, Melville lists the etymology of several words, including "whale," which is said to originate with the Danish word *hval*, a word that has a remarkable similarity to the Hebrew word for "vanity" (*hebel*).

Relationship and Wisdom

The movement of ch 4 is oppression, envy, companionship, and wisdom. Much oppression comes from the oppressor's desire to accumulate more, which may be motivated by envy of others. It is companionship that can alleviate the pain of oppression, as one's **friend can help him up** (4:10). Wisdom will help to recognize this and may even lead to someone who is impoverished in debtors' prison rising to kingship.

4:1-16

VI. LET YOUR WORDS BE FEW (5:1-9)

BEHIND THE TEXT

Ecclesiastes 5:1-9 focuses on the fear of God and the mystery of retribution, two topics that are not shared by the preceding and following units. The imperative mood also sets this unit apart from its context. Most of what precedes has been philosophical reflections on life, not instructions. There have been some hints at advice, especially with the "better than" sayings. But here and in 9:7-10 and 11:9—12:8 the advice is more direct and resembles the instructions in the book of Proverbs. Verses 8-9 continue the imperative mood (*'al* plus imperfect) but introduce the new topic of oppression (which was also dealt with in 4:1).

Verses 4-5 give advice on vows that were regulated but not required in OT law. Nazirite vows were a special kind of vow that required abstaining from wine. These could be temporary or life-long (as in the case of Samson and Samuel, whose parents dedicated them in this way; Num 6:1-21). Other vows were taken as a kind of bargain with God when circumstances required his intervention. Upon deliverance the vowed action would be taken, usually payment, but sometimes another type of gift (e.g., Hannah promised to give her son, 1 Sam 1:11; Elwell and Comfort 2001, 1287).

The genre of this unit is instruction and includes a rhetorical question and hypothetical quotation (v 6). This unit gives the first advice in the book. Verses 1-9 can be outlined as follows:

Conduct Before God (5:1-7)

Oppression and Justice (5:8-9)

IN THE TEXT

A. Conduct Before God (5:1-7)

■ I Verse 1 begins with advice for conduct in the temple. **Guard your steps** could be translated *watch your steps* or more literally *watch your feet* (*raglēkā*). The steps are to be watched as the worshipper goes to the house of God, the temple. In Wisdom literature, right living is often characterized as a way of walking, hence obedience is in mind here (e.g., Ps 1:6; Prov 1:15).

The reader is encouraged to **go near** (to God) **to listen rather than to offer the sacrifice of fools.** *To go near* (infinitive) can be translated as imperative (**go near**) on the basis of the first word in the verse (**guard**), and the singular verb can be taken as collective with **fools** as the subject ("gift [that] the fools sacrifice"). What seems to be missing is "better than," which is supplied in the ancient Syriac translation and gives a better reading, "To go near to listen is better than to give (what) fools sacrifice" (see GKC §133*e*). Still, it is unusual to sacrifice a gift. Usually a gift (e.g., grain) is given and a sacrifice (usually an animal) is sacrificed (lit., *slaughtered for sacrifice*).

The foolish behavior contrasts with listening and is explained in the next part of the verse. Fools are so slow to listen that they do not even know that they do wrong. When Saul disobeyed God after the battle with the Amalekites, Samuel emphasized the priority of obedience and listening over sacrifice (1 Sam 15:22). Saul claimed that he took plunder in order to sacrifice, even though Samuel had delivered the command to destroy all the plunder. Amos and Micah also preached the priority of obedience over sacrifice (Amos 5:21-22; Mic 6:7-8; see also Prov 15:8; 21:3; 21:27; Jer 6:20).

The Hebrew of the final phrase in v 1 is difficult; it reads literally, *for they do not know to do evil* (*ki-ᵉênām yôdᶜîm laᶜăśôt rāᶜ*). This looks like fools do not do evil because they do not know how, which does not make sense given the usual connection between folly and wickedness. BHS suggests adding "than," which gives the reading "fools do not know how to do anything other than evil" (*milaᶜăśôt*; the same translation results from adding *ki ᵓim* as found in 3:12; 8:15). This seems a bit extreme, and modern translations settle for adding "that" (**that they do wrong**). Ginsburg translated it "as they who obey know not to do evil" (1861, 336).

■ **2** Verse 2 continues with instructions to be careful with speech, implying that fools are not so. Bumper sticker wisdom puts it like this: "Engage brain before putting mouth into gear." The word *bāhal* (**be quick**) can mean "be disturbed" or "hurry." It is one of many rare words in Ecclesiastes, and the usage here is found in late texts (Esth 2:9). The Egyptian wisdom teacher Ani had similar advice: "Do not raise your voice in the house of god, he abhors shouting" (Lichtheim 2006, 137).

The rationale for this instruction is the distance between God, who is in heaven, and people, who are on the earth. This idea is part of the concept of "the fear of God," which is included in the closing instruction of this unit (v 7). The distance between God and humanity is an expression of divine sovereignty, which is an important theme in the book. For example, ch 3 argued God's control over the timing of events in life. Appropriate reflection on God's sovereignty will result in less being said to God (see Matt 6:7). Job was very open with God about his frustrations, but when God responded with a statement of his sovereignty, he soundly put Job in his place, which caused Job to reflect, "Surely I spoke of things I did not understand, things too wonderful for me to know" (Job 42:3). Psalm 115:3 also emphasizes God's sovereignty (rather than just distance), where God's abode in heaven is connected with his ability to do "whatever pleases him."

■ **3** A fool utters **many words** is the alternative to keeping one's words few (v 3). The phrase **As the dream comes when there are many cares** seems to be a different way of saying that much business amounts to nothing. A dream amounts to nothing, and so is similar to the key word "vanity" (*hebel*). Dreams and vanity are connected in v 7. **Many cares** is literally *much business* (*běrōb ʿinyān*), using a key word that is used in 1:13 and eight times in Ecclesiastes. In the same way, **many words** amount to the **speech of a fool.** This verse is a proverb, which could be a quote from an older tradition.

■ **4** Verse 4 continues the focus on speech, this time in regard to vows made to God. The reader is encouraged to pay a vow quickly. Only fools would delay. **He has no pleasure in fools** is literally *there is no pleasure in fools;* this phrase indirectly implies God as the subject of the action (circumlocution). This is typical of Wisdom literature, which avoids direct speech about God's action in the world. Ginsburg thought that **fools** was the subject; that is, fools have no pleasure (hence he translated it, "fools have no fixed will") (1861, 338-39). Deuteronomy 23:21-23 also warns against delaying the payment of a vow, with some differences in language (see also Prov 20:25; Sirach 18:22). The Deuteronomy version is more specific about the action of God whereas Ecclesiastes is more general. Deuteronomy 23:21 warns against the sin of delay in paying a vow. However, v 22 makes clear that refraining from making vows is not a sinful act while v 23 emphasizes the importance of keeping promises to God once they are made.

■ **5** Verse 5 discourages making vows if they will not be fulfilled. The implication is that those who make vows have an obligation to fulfill them. Once a vow is made it cannot be rescinded. The caution here is again on excessive or meaningless words. Jephthah apparently fulfilled his vow to kill his daughter (Judg 11:39), but the community would not let Saul fulfill his vow to kill Jonathan (1 Sam 14:45). Numbers 30 begins with a prohibition against breaking the vow taken by a man but then focuses on the law regarding the ratification of vows taken by women. The law provided a father or a husband with the right to nullify such a vow under certain circumstances.

■ **6** Making a vow and failing to fulfill it is sin, according to Qoheleth (**do not let your mouth lead you into sin**). If the word **messenger** (*mal'āk*) in the Hebrew text is correct, it implies that someone from the **temple** (a word supplied by the NIV) would come and check (demand?) on fulfillment of the vow, which must have been registered in the temple. There is no other evidence for this practice, and ancient versions (Greek and Aramaic) have the excuses made to God. Ginsburg translated **messenger** as "angel," citing the preposition "before" (*lipnê*), which he viewed as appropriate in the presence of God or angels, whereas one would speak "to" (*'el*) a fellow human (see Deut 26:3, 5) (1861, 340, 343). Qoheleth also warns against making the claim that the vow made was a **mistake** (*šĕgāgâ*); this word is used elsewhere to designate unintentional sin (see Num 15:22). In any case, a mistake required the sacrifice of a young bull in Num 15:22-31 and Lev 4:2-35.

■ **7** **Much dreaming and many words are meaningless** in v 7 is a difficult construction in Hebrew (lit., *For in many dreams and vanities and words increase*). Delitzsch suggested that the text has been copied incorrectly and should be rearranged to read "for in many dreams and many words there are also vanities" (1875, 291). This verse may contain a literary device called hendiadys, in which two words are linked together by the conjunction "and" to convey a complex idea. Thus the phrase *many dreams and vanities* conveys the idea of "vacuous dreams" (Seow 1997, 200), or "meaningless words" (Longman 1997, 156). The meaning of *hebel* here is probably "futile, profitless."

The next advice of the unit is the standard foundation of Wisdom literature: fear God (**stand in awe of God,** mentioned seventeen times in Proverbs; see From the Text and 3:14; 7:18).

B. Oppression and Justice (5:8-9)

■ **8** Verses 8 and 9 are something of a diversion from the topic of the present paragraph (advice on approaching the sanctuary, and making vows) and also from the following paragraph (a chiasm focused on contentment). The topic is now oppression **in a district,** which does bear some relation to the present paragraph because of the hierarchy involved in encountering both God and king. There may also be a relation to the following paragraph in the sense that oppression is the result of greed, and hence a lack of contentment.

Qoheleth begins with the advice that one should not be **surprised** to see oppression and the denial of justice and rights **in a district** (v 8). The second part of v 8 indicates that the hierarchical system is corrupt on every level, making any attempt to improve the lot of the poor hopeless (which may explain why Qoheleth did not encourage action on behalf of the oppressed in ch 4). At every level of administration, there are those who watch over those who are below them. The verb *watched* (NIV, **eyed,** *šōmēr*) can have a variety of connotations, including the watchmen who patrol the city at night (Song 3:3; 5:7), God who watches over Israel, and those who watch a victim with hostile intent (Ps 56:6). Palestine in the postexilic periods was tightly controlled by foreign powers, unlike the loose preexilic monarchies that to some extent tolerated the prophetic voice and even allowed some prophets to address the king himself (see Jer 26:16-19). Ginsburg took the whole sense of this verse differently (1861, 345). He translated **do not be surprised** (*titmah*) as do not be "alarmed" (see Ps 48:5; Jer 4:9; Job 26:11) and thought Qoheleth expressed the view that oppression is no cause for alarm or fear because the injustice is limited by the ultimate oversight of God. It is difficult to choose between these two interpretations because of the ambiguity of the vocabulary and because Qoheleth elsewhere presents both views: the whole idea of retribution is oversimplified, yet God will ultimately bring evildoers to justice.

■ **9** The sense of v 9 is difficult to grasp. There may have been a scribal error in the transmission of the text. The first part of the verse continues the theme of profit (**increase,** *yitrôn*), which is important in the book (5:11, 16; 6:11). What is not clear is to what the profit of the land refers (**increase from the land**). There is an unexpected feminine pronoun, which the Masoretic scribes have marked as a masculine. The verse is literally, *And profit [of] land in all he/she/it [is], a king for a cultivated field.*

The word *ne ʿĕbād* (**profits**) could modify **king** or **fields.** The most natural connection is **fields** since this verb is used to mean "cultivated" in several contexts (Deut 21:4; Ezek 36:9, 34). Thus the king belongs to (or is committed to, *lĕ*) cultivated fields. *Ne ʿĕbād* can also mean "served," which would give the sense of the **king** being served by the **fields** (**the king himself profits from the fields**). Either the king is involved in the hierarchy of corruption, and is making a profit from the productive fields, or the land as a whole depends on productive fields and will therefore prosper if the king recognizes this and encourages production (see Buhlmann 2000, 108). The former option seems to fit better with the oppression observed in 5:8, but requires an unusual interpretation of the preposition *le* ("from" or "by," where usually it is "to, for, belonging to").

Fear of God

The major theme of the sovereignty of God is developed further in 5:1-9 with the application of showing respect to God in the sanctuary. The concluding statement, "fear God" (5:7 NRSV), is the standard Wisdom literature expression of right relationship with God.

Empty Words

Qoheleth's warning against excessive words and the practice of meaningless religion calls us to reflect on our contemporary ways of worship where speaking to God rather than listening to him has taken a dominant role.

Let My Words Be Few

You are God in heaven
And here am I on earth,
So I'll let my words be few—
Jesus, I am so in love with You.
(Matt Redman and Beth Redman, 2000)

Mystery of Retribution

If the doctrine of retribution were working as expected, there would be no oppression because the oppressors would be punished by God. The observation of oppression shows that the doctrine needs to be nuanced and that ordinary humans have little control over outcomes. Elsewhere this control was attributed to God (e.g., Eccl 3) but here it seems to be connected with human hierarchy, culminating with the king.

VII. LIMITATIONS OF WEALTH (5:10—6:9)

BEHIND THE TEXT

Ecclesiastes 5:10—6:9 follows the advice of the previous unit to guard one's steps before God. Themes from prior units are revisited (contentment, wealth, joy, vanity). The next unit (6:10—7:14) focuses on wisdom rather than wealth; these two units thus complement the themes of the royal autobiography (especially 2:1-16).

The introduction of coins to the economy of the Persian and Hellenistic periods helped turn money into a commodity that could be hoarded and invested. Ecclesiastes does not specifically mention coins, but the extensive commercial interests in the book suggest the period of coinage. The improvement of shipping and trade at the same time meant that wealth could be increased rapidly and lost just as quickly. Qoheleth warns against the dangers of orienting one's life around these new values.

The genre of 5:10—6:9 is reflection. This unit forms a chiasm that has its climax in 5:18-20. The featured thought is the enjoyment of, and contentment with, the toil and wealth that one has, since these are a gift from God. They are, in fact, God's method of bringing joy to one's heart. This unit ends the first half of the book, or 111 verses out of the total 222 verses. A. G. Wright has observed that the key word *hebel* (**meaningless,** 6:9) has the numerical value of thirty-seven (1980, 44). This word occurs in the book thirty-seven times, equal to its numerical value (assuming that the second occurrence of *hebel* in 9:9 is an error).

Ecclesiastes 5:10—6:9 can be outlined as follows:

A. No Satisfaction (5:10-12)

    B. Grievous Evil (5:13-17)

        C. Contentment (5:18-20)

    B'. Evil (6:1-6)

A'. No Satisfaction (6:7-9)

This analysis differs from that of Seow, who sees the boundaries of the chiasm as 5:8—6:9 and the climax as 5:20 (1997, 217). Seow also makes the focus of this unit contentment ("Enjoy the Moment"), but excludes two important verses on this topic from the climax (18-19). Contentment with the portion that God has given is the focus of 5:18-20, and also the focus of this passage, and the book as a whole. Thus, 5:18-20 should be seen as the climax of this chiasm.

IN THE TEXT

A. No Satisfaction (5:10-12)

■ **10** Verse 10 deals with the lack of satisfaction that money and wealth give. A unique use of the preposition *bĕ* (*ʾōhĕb behāmôn*, lit., *whoever loves in wealth*) is probably a scribal error where the last letter of the previous word is repeated by mistake (dittography, so BHS). Another difficulty is the lack of a verb in the phrase *lōʾ tĕbûʾâ* (lit., *no gain* or *no produce* or *no increase*). One option is to assume that the verb "satisfied" from the beginning of the verse (*Whoever loves money will not be satisfied with money;* NIV, **Whoever loves money never has money enough**) applies to this clause also (**whoever loves wealth is never satisfied**). Crenshaw suggests an ironic ellipsis and supplies "gets" in his translation, "whoever loves wealth gets no gain" (1987, 119-21). This gives the same sense as the Targum, which supplied the vowels for "it will not come [to him]." These interpretations suggest a lack of wealth, rather than a lack of satisfaction in wealth. The latter is really the focus of this verse.

Verse 10 states the theme of the passage in the negative: money and wealth do not bring lasting satisfaction (the positive is stated in the climax to the chiasm in vv 18-20). This is *hebel* (**meaningless**) in the sense that it is incomprehensible. It is a mystery, one of the paradoxes of life; money is believed to be the solution to the problems of life, but it is not. More money, even a *multitude* (**income,** *hāmôn*) of it, does not bring satisfaction, but instead brings the desire for more. This theme has already been covered in 1:8 (eyes not satisfied with seeing) and 4:8 (eyes not satisfied with seeing riches, *ʿōšer*). The vocabulary in the verse covers wealth in the form of cash (*kesep*), possessions (*hāmôn*), and produce (*těbûʾâ*). All three will be summarized by the word **goods** (*tôbâ*) in the next verse.

Juvenal on Satisfaction

Besides, while thus the streams of affluence roll,
They nurse the eternal dropsy of the soul,
For thirst of wealth still grows with wealth increased,
And they desire it less, who have it least.
(*Satires* 14:138-40, in Ginsburg 1861, 348)

■ **11** Like the continuous flow of river water in 1:7, excess production never really brings a surplus, because **as goods increase, so do those who consume them.** Qoheleth may be talking about the population increase that tends to accompany prosperity or increase in the demand for goods by consumers or the increase in the number of employees to maintain one's wealth. When a wealthy man cannot personally consume all his wealth or possessions, his only benefit is to see them with **his eyes** before they are consumed by others. But this will not lead to contentment either, as the eye is never satisfied (1:8; 4:8).

Teachings of Ptah-Hotep, ca. 2500 B.C.

Follow your heart as long as you live,
Do no more than is required,
Do not shorten the time of "follow-the-heart,"
Trimming its moment offends the *ka*.
Don't waste time on daily cares
Beyond providing for your household;
When wealth has come, follow your heart,
Wealth does no good if one is glum!
(In Lichtheim 1975, 66)

■ **12** In v 12 Qoheleth returns to a theme already stated in 2:23, namely restlessness at night experienced by those who are involved in troublesome toil. The focus here is on the sleeplessness of those who are never satisfied with their wealth. **The abundance of a rich man permits him no sleep, but the sleep of a laborer is sweet.** Laborers sleep well because they do not have wealth that they are concerned about hoarding and protecting from others. In their tired state they sleep well whether their stomachs are empty or full. The rich, on the other hand, worry that a thief may break in or some other misfortune will cause the loss of their stored wealth; this anxiety leads them to have sleepless nights (see Prov 25:16; Sirach 31:1-4). Overeating and indigestion also contribute to the sleeplessness of the rich.

Henry Howard on Sleep (1546)

The sweet and quiet slepes that weryd limmes oppresse,
  Begile the night in dyet thynne, and feasts of great excesse:
But wakenlye the riche, whose lyuely heat with rest
  Their charged boolks with change of meats cannot so sone dygest.
(In Johnson 1810, 356)

B. Grievous Evil (5:13-17)

■ **13** Qoheleth explores the issue of wealth further in vv 13-17 (these verses echo 2:18-23). Hoarding wealth is not only a mystery (*hebel*, v 10) but also a **grievous evil** in that wealth does not have lasting effects. Wealth does not offer protection to its owner, but only harm. Ahiqar wrote, "Amassing wealth corrupts the heart" (Matthews and Benjamin 2006, 308).

■ **14** To make matters worse, wealth could be **lost through some misfortune** (v 14). The Hebrew for **misfortune** is literally *bad business* (*'inyan rā'*). The word "business" is a key word in Ecclesiastes (see comment on 1:13).

The loss of wealth through misfortune leads to more evil because the owner of wealth will have **nothing left** to pass on to a **son** (v 14). Elsewhere Qoheleth is pessimistic about the value or possibility of bequeathing wealth to the next generation (2:18, 21). In the old agricultural economy, a son would be a blessing because there would be someone to work the fields and to increase the family's wealth. But in the Persian period where land was granted by the king, there was no guarantee of establishing a hereditary estate.

■ **15-16** Verses 15-16 lament the inability to keep anything after death. The inability to retain material possessions after death is no longer specific to inheritance, but to the fact that wealth is not permanent. As Job observed, everyone was literally naked at birth and is metaphorically naked at death (Job 1:21; see also Ps 139:15; Sirach 40:1). The work of the "laborer" (*'ōbĕd*) in v 12 was positive because it led to satisfying sleep. But Qoheleth returns in v 15 to the negative nature of work as "toil" (**labor,** *'āmāl*) because it results in no lasting accumulation.

Qoheleth again laments wealth's lack of permanence as a **grievous evil** (v 16). The "grievous evil" in v 13 was the unexpected disadvantage of wealth; in v 16 it is the situation that possessions cannot be retained after death. There is no **gain** for this toil, as in the English expression, "You can't take it with you." Toil and gain are key concepts in Ecclesiastes and should be related; however, Qoheleth does not link them together because the gain that human beings expect is lasting material satisfaction and toil is oriented around this unattainable goal. Qoheleth's usual pronouncement on such a pursuit is "chasing after the wind" (e.g., 2:11), but here he varies the phrase to **he toils for the wind** (see Prov 11:29; Isa 26:18; Job 16:3).

■ **17** **All his days** the owner of wealth **eats in darkness.** The literal reading of the second line is *and he is greatly frustrated, and his sickness and anger* (**with great frustration, affliction and anger,** *wĕkāʿas harbēh wĕhālĕyô wāqāṣep*). The NIV reading is based on changing the vowel of *frustrated* (*kāʿas*) in Hebrew to form a noun. An orientation around toiling for material accumulation is toiling for the wind and leads *not* to satisfaction and contentment but to **great frustration, affliction and anger.** Such a person **eats in darkness** because he or she has used up all the daylight hours striving for satisfaction from accumulated wealth, which does not bring lasting satisfaction. This is a foretaste of the destiny of all: the land of darkness (Sheol) where the worker is no longer "under the sun." It is "the fool" who "walks in the darkness" (2:14; see also 6:4).

C. Contentment (5:18-20)

■ **18** Verse 18 states an important theme of the book: **it is good and proper** to find satisfaction with what one has. The word **proper** (*yāpeh*) is the same word as "beautiful" in 3:11 where it is said that God "made everything beautiful in its time." In 5:18 it is Qoheleth who observes what is **proper** in life, but later in the verse it is God who has given that life, and in the following verse God has also given **wealth and possessions** and the ability to enjoy them. The sovereignty of God in the timing of ch 3 is also evident in his gift in ch 5.

The climax of the chiasm in vv 18-20, then, argues that lasting satisfaction is not to be found in striving for more, but in contentment with what one has. Qoheleth uses the emphatic pronoun to contrast his view from those around him (although he often adds the pronoun for no apparent reason). Others may strive for profit, but **I realized that it is good** to be content with the **lot** that God has given. The lot or portion that one has is a gift from God in contrast to the gain or profit that one strives for in a commercial economy (see comment on 2:10). Whether little or much (v 12), what one has is a gift from God, and even life itself, though short, is God's gift.

■ **19** Verse 19 emphasizes **possessions** as a gift from God. The word **possessions** (*nĕkāsîm*) is an Aramaic word known from the fifth century B.C. Egyptian Aramaic texts and reflects the commercial interest of Ecclesiastes as well as suggesting a postexilic date (this word is not known before the fifth century; Seow 1997, 13; also used in 6:2; Josh 22:8; 2 Chr 1:11, 12).

It is truly **a gift of God** to be able to enjoy life and to be happy in one's work (v 19). The secret to this happiness is contentment with what God has given (portion), accepting it as a gift from God, and not trying to accumulate excess (profit). This correlates with Qoheleth's view of the sovereignty of God. Humans try to control their destiny through toil and investment, but lasting joy is under divine, not human, control.

Crenshaw thinks that some people are stingy by nature and therefore they would not enjoy wealth (1987, 125). Qoheleth does seem to recommend generosity in 11:1-2. But in the context of the striving, which Qoheleth condemns, the main reason for failing to enjoy wealth is greed. It is those who are always striving for a greater profit who cannot enjoy the portion that God has given.

■ **20** The lack of remembrance was negative and another evidence of the futility of human toil in 1:11. In 5:20 it is the one who toils who will not greatly remember the **days of his life.** The reason given for this is the preoccupation that God gives **with gladness of heart.** Thus lack of memory or reflection is positive in this setting. For the cynical youth who is disillusioned with the emptiness of the commercial system and its values, Qoheleth has given a message of hope.

Toil was described earlier as an evil business with which man busies himself (4:8). Now the same root is used for the occupation that God gives (*maʿᵃneh*). Business is evil when it is motivated by greed, but it brings **gladness of heart** when it is accepted as a gift from God. This seems to be an analogy from the royal grant of Persian kings (see 2:10) and indeed much of the vocabulary from 5:18-20 echoes the language of the royal grant (Seow 1997, 24).

B'. Evil (6:1-6)

■ **1** In 6:1-6 the structure of the chiasm moves away from the main point to reiterate the evil that Qoheleth has seen under the sun. The phrase *there is an evil* (*yēš rāʿâ*) links 6:1 with 5:13. In 5:13-17 the grievous evil was the harm from, and loss of, wealth. In 6:1-6 the evil is the possession of wealth without the power to enjoy it. Qoheleth views it as a heavy burden on human beings.

■ **2** Qoheleth begins with the assertion that God is the One who gives **wealth, possessions and honor;** however, he considers it an evil that **God does not enable** the recipients of his gifts **to enjoy them** (v 2; see also 2 Chr 1:11 where Solomon is described as having these as gifts from God). The power to enjoy these things is a gift from God. Thus the sovereignty of God is emphasized yet again. The word for **enjoy** is literally *eat* (*ʾākal*), which is also used earlier in this unit in the context of a satisfied laborer who sleeps well whether he or she has eaten much or little (5:12). Again, this evil becomes only worse, a **grievous evil**, and **meaningless** in the last line, because **a stranger** ends up enjoying God's gifts. What good are God's gifts of wealth, possessions, and honor if the recipient of these gifts does not enjoy them or dies with the knowledge that a stranger will enjoy them instead of his own children?

The identity of the **stranger** is not specified, but the word is literally *foreigner, alien* (*nākěrî*), although nationality may not be in mind here. Under foreign rule, either Persian or Greek, the one who inherited one's property could very well be a foreigner. This could be an allusion to the royal grant of the Persian kings, which did not pass automatically to the recipient's heir, but could be given to someone outside the family (Seow 1997, 25).

■ **3** Verses 3-6 contrast the man who lives a long time with a stillborn infant. Qoheleth begins with the emptiness of the man with a large family and prosperity and long life. The element of fathering is present in 6:3 (**a man may have a hundred children**) and in the counterpart to this section of the chiasm (5:14). In ch 5, the evil is the loss of an inheritance to pass on to a son. In ch 6, the evil is the lack of ability to enjoy one's prosperity despite the blessing of many children and long life (see Gen 25:8; Job 42:17). In a moment of exaggeration, Qoheleth declares **that a stillborn child is better off than** this person who does not get to enjoy his prosperity and **does not receive proper burial.** Yet he never recommends suicide, even in 4:2 when he declares that the dead "are happier than the living" (contrast the Egyptian document *A Sufferer and a Soul in Egypt* and the Mesopotamian *A Pessimistic Dialogue Between a Master and Servant*, Pritchard 1969, 405-7, 437-38).

The hypothetical man in question has insult added to injury after his death as he receives no **proper burial,** which is a reversal of the honor he received in life (2 Kgs 9:34; Eccl 8:10; Isa 14:19; Jer 22:19). Murphy thinks that this lack of burial applies to the **stillborn child,** which would receive no burial (1992, 48, 54). This fits the context better, but it does not fit the syntax well. Ginsburg's argument fits the context, syntax, and vocabulary better, namely that *qěbûrâ* (**burial**) should be rendered by its usual meaning "grave." The text could thus be translated *even if the grave did not wait for him*, which extends the thought of this person living many years (from the beginning of the verse) (Ginsburg 1861, 361). Even if he were never to die, there would be no point in wealth without satisfaction and contentment (see 6:6).

■ **4** The element of coming and going in v 4 (**It comes without meaning, it departs in darkness**) is also common to the counterpart of this section of the chiasm (5:15). In both verses coming and going is a metaphor for life and death. The sense of *hebel* (**without meaning**) here is apparently *fleeting* (Ginsburg suggested "nothingness"; 1861, 361). **Darkness** is also an element common to the counterpart in the chiasm. In 5:17 the greedy owner eats in darkness because he cannot stand to waste any of the sunlight. In 6:4 it is the stillborn baby that lives and dies in darkness (see Job 3:16). Babies that survived were named on the eighth day (and males circumcised, Gen 17:12; Luke 1:59), unlike the stillborn child whose **name** departs **in darkness** and is also **shrouded** in darkness. **Name** also means renown or memorial (Deut 9:14; 1 Sam 24:21; 2 Sam 14:7; Ps 72:17; BDB 1028). The child will not be able to carry on the father's name, as Jacob had wished for Ephraim and Manasseh (Gen 48:16).

■ **5** Verse 5 deals with the experience of the stillborn child. The stillborn finds rest, while the prosperous person who lives many years does not. The verb *to know* in this verse does not seem to have a subject, thus the interpretation that the stillborn child never **knew anything.** It could be that the verb is still modifying the object of **saw;** the phrase could thus be translated as *it never saw or knew the sun.* The ancient translation of Symmachus took **rest** as the object ("it never knew rest"; Crenshaw 1987, 127).

The sun was a blessing in the ancient world, where the light of the sun was essential for daily life (see 7:11; 11:7). *Seeing the sun* or *light* is used elsewhere for life (7:11; Job 3:16; Pss 49:19; 58:8). The stillborn child never experiences this blessing, and yet **it has more rest** than the man who lives his life in discontent.

■ **6** In v 6 Qoheleth declares a long life to be worthless if a person does not have the opportunity to enjoy prosperity. This verse has a number of rare linguistic features (Ecclesiastes is known for its unique language). *'Illû* (**if**) is an unusual form influenced by Aramaic and also found in Esth 7:4. It is a combination of *'im* and *lû*, which is the form found in the Dead Sea Scrolls fragment of this verse. The expression **years twice over** is also rare (*šānîm paʿămayim*).

Verse 6 expands on v 3. Dissatisfaction with life not only ruins enjoyment for one who lives many years, but even if someone could live **a thousand years twice over**, there would be no satisfaction if he or she could not *see good* in life (**enjoy his prosperity**). This point is made positively in the climax of this chiasm in 5:18 where Qoheleth states that it is the human lot to eat, drink, and *see good* or find satisfaction. If there is no enjoyment in this life, then there is no meaning, as **all go to the same place,** that is, Sheol, the place of the dead. Since the OT has no concept of a meaningful afterlife, life must be enjoyed now, "under the sun," for there is no second chance for joy. The NT will move beyond this viewpoint (1 Cor 15:32).

A'. No Satisfaction (6:7-9)

■ **7** Verse 7 begins the final paragraph of this chiasm (6:7-9) and corresponds to 5:10-12. In contrast to the climax of the chiasm that focused on the positive side of contentment (5:18-20), this paragraph, like the rest of the chiasm, focuses on the negative side, namely dissatisfaction. In 5:10 the lover of money is not satisfied; in 6:7 a person's **appetite is never satisfied.** This is a positive thing in Prov 16:26, where a man's appetite urges him to work hard. Here it is negative because there is no end to the work, and satisfaction is never reached, like the sea and ear in 1:7-8, which are never full. The word **appetite** shows the literal meaning of the word *nepeš*, which is usually translated "soul"; *nepeš* has various meanings, including throat, gullet, life, self, soul in the sense of a living being, and so forth. Here it is used in parallel with **mouth.** Hebrew thought had no concept of a soul that could exist independent of its body.

■ **8** The portion or lot given by God is the basis for contentment in the climax of the chiasm (5:18-20) and is contrasted in v 8 and elsewhere in Ecclesiastes with the profit that people strive for, but without lasting satisfaction. The profit in this case is the **advantage** (*yôtēr*) that a wise man should have, but does not have, over a fool. This theme (the limitation of wisdom) is also explored elsewhere in Ecclesiastes (2:14) and will be the climax of the chiasm in the following unit (7:7). In the counterpart to this section of the chiasm, the profit was the advantage (*kišrôn*) that a wealthy owner should have, but does not have, from accumulated wealth (5:11). This thought counters the traditional wisdom teaching of the absolute superiority of wisdom over folly (a view that Qoheleth still holds in a relative sense [e.g., 4:13]).

The second half of v 8 is obscure. It is literally *what [gain] for the poor, knowing [how] to walk before the living* (*mah-lleʿānî yôdēaʿ lahălōk neged haḥayyîm*). "To walk before the living" is an idiom for successful conduct (Crenshaw 1987, 129). But appropriate conduct does not always lead to success, which calls into question the advantage of the wise person over the fool. Thus the word **advantage** must carry over from the first half of the verse. The wise person has no advantage over the fool, just as a poor person has no advantage from knowing how **to conduct himself before others.**

■ **9** The element of **eyes** in v 9 has a counterpart in the first section of the chiasm. In 5:11 the rich owner has no use for accumulated wealth except to look at it, since no one could eat so much. In 6:9, **what the eye sees** is contrasted positively with **the roving of the appetite.** An insatiable appetite will not bring satisfaction, which can only come through contentment (as a gift from God). To *see good* is the idiom used for satisfaction and enjoyment in 5:18 and 6:6. Joy in life comes when a person sees the good in the gifts that God has given instead of allowing the mind to wander after other things (looking "over the fence" to the "greener grass").

Verse 9 qualifies *hebel* (**meaningless**) as **a chasing after the wind,** which suggests something futile or elusive. Lasting satisfaction is elusive in part because appetites do tend to wander. It is difficult to be content with the gifts that God has given, and it is futile to desire more. The Masoretic scribes marked the midpoint of the book between vv 9 and 10.

Wealth

The lack of lasting satisfaction that wealth gives correlates to the sea, the ears, and the eyes in ch 1, which are never satisfied by water from rivers, hearing, or seeing (1:7-8). Hoarded wealth can even cause harm, it can be easily lost, and it cannot be taken from this life (5:13-15). Song of Songs emphasizes the value of wealth relative to love in the declaration, "If one were to give all the wealth of his house for love, it would be utterly scorned" (8:7). Jesus' parable of the rich man's barns shows both the lack of lasting satisfaction from wealth, and the impossibility of keeping wealth after death (Luke 12:15-21). This man is condemned for his plan to "eat, drink and be merry," which is remarkably similar to Qoheleth's advice to enjoy food and drink (5:18). The important difference is that Qoheleth is advising contentment with the food and drink that God has given him, whereas the rich man in Jesus' parable has hoarded an excess so that he can make pleasure the orientation of his life. Hoarding wealth will never lead to lasting satisfaction because it is open-ended. One's current possessions, however, are finite and if enjoyed with contentment, will offer immediate satisfaction.

Enjoy Life

Contentment is the main thrust of this passage and is a theme that has already been presented with force in Ecclesiastes. As for the king in chs 1—2, wealth that is hoarded and accumulated does not bring lasting satisfaction but leads to desire for more (5:10), additional consumers (5:11), lack of sleep (5:12), harm (5:13), loss (5:14), frustration, affliction, and anger (5:17), lack of ability to enjoy (6:2), and lack of satisfaction (6:7). In the NT, Paul provides Christians with the key to contentment: "Rejoice in the Lord always. I will say it again: Rejoice!" (Phil 4:4; see also Phil 4:11-12; Luke 3:14; 1 Tim 6:6-8; Heb 13:5; James 4:1-2; 5:1-5). Joy that is found in the Lord and not in wealth leads to lasting satisfaction, and the hope of the resurrection in the NT means that this contentment continues on into eternal life (1 Cor 15:32).

Vanity (hebel)

The use of *hebel* (**meaningless**) in this unit is very negative and is coupled with the designation **evil**. The accumulation of wealth does not bring the expected profit (5:10; 6:1-2, 9). The lack of enjoyment from wealth, and even loss of wealth, is evil (5:13, 16; 6:1-2). Fortunately this negative outlook is balanced by the call to enjoy life and be satisfied with what one has (5:18-20).

VIII. LIMITATIONS OF WISDOM (6:10—7:14)

BEHIND THE TEXT

Ecclesiastes 6:10—7:14 is the start of the second half of the book according to the Masoretic scribes, and it follows the chiasm of 5:10—6:9 with a chiasm of its own. The previous chiasm focused on the limitations of wealth, and this one focuses on the limitations of wisdom. These are major themes in the book and this unit also revisits the themes of divine sovereignty and fame.

The chiasm is broken up by pleas for the value of wisdom in 7:5-6 and 7:11-12. This sets the stage for the climax of the chiasm, which suggests the limitations of wisdom; even a wise person can be turned foolish by a bribe (7:7). The whole unit is flanked by assertions of the sovereignty of God, which is the very thing that limits human wisdom (6:10-12; 7:13-14).

119

The unit is a reflection and includes "better than" sayings. Other literary devices are the alliteration of 7:1 and the wordplay of 7:5-6. A key word in Ecclesiastes is **good** (fifty-two times), which is very frequent in ch 7 (fifteen times) because of the many "better than" sayings. Ecclesiastes 6:10—7:14 can be outlined as follows:

A. Sovereignty of God: Humans Do Not Have Foreknowledge (6:10-12)

    B. Don't Depreciate the Past/Present in Favor of the Future (7:1-4) (Wisdom Is Still Valuable, 7:5-6)

        C. Wisdom Is Limited (7:7)

    B'. Don't Depreciate the Future/Present in Favor of the Past (7:8-10) (Wisdom Is Still Valuable, 7:11-12)

A'. Sovereignty of God: Enjoy Life (7:13-14)

IN THE TEXT

A. Sovereignty of God: Humans Do Not Have Foreknowledge (6:10-12)

■ **10** Ecclesiastes 6:10-12 forms the theological structure for this unit, along with 7:13-14. The Masoretic scribes designate the center of the book between vv 9 and 10, and here Qoheleth seems to begin his argument again. The unpredictability of life as expressed here seems to be an admission of the sovereignty of God. Not even wisdom can give a person control over life. One must be content to accept what God has given and to recognize human limitations, for **Whatever exists has already been named** (lit., *its name is called*). This idiom is an expression of designation and is used in biblical and Babylonian texts (Isa 40:26; *Enuma Elish;* see Matthews and Benjamin 2006, 12). The passive mood expresses God's involvement behind the scenes. It is God who has already designated what happens. His foreknowledge is expressed in the next phrase: **and what man is has been known.**

This translation fits the context (and follows the Septuagint) but represents an unusual interpretation of the relative pronoun (*'ăšer*). Fox suggests transposing the words **man** and **and,** giving the translation "and what it is, is known" (1999, 247). Seow's emendation is preferable as it requires less adjustment of the consonants. He assumes that an extra letter (*alef*) has been added by scribal error (dittography, *'ăšer-hû' 'ādām* instead of *'ăšūrēhû 'ādām*); his emendation results in the translation of this clause as follows: "the course [step, going] of human beings is known" (1997, 230-32). The sovereignty of God is further emphasized with the statement **no man can contend with one who is stronger than he.** The **one who is stronger** is presumably God (see Job 9:19).

Ahiqar on Rulers

Make a ruler's order to be your heart's desire.
Can kindling conquer the flame?
Can flesh conquer the knife?
Can farmers conquer rulers?
(Matthews and Benjamin 2006, 305)

■ 11 Contending with God would require many words, and Qoheleth regards this as *hebel* (that is, inconsequential) in v 11. Arguing with God would not be to anyone's advantage (Job 42:3). The use of more words only means more meaningless speech. To reinforce this point Qoheleth uses alliteration, giving the effect of babble (*dĕbārîm harbēh marbîm hābel*). *Hebel* (**the less the meaning**) is used in the sense of profitless in this context. The last line, **how does that profit anyone?** conveys the same idea.

■ 12 Verse 12 exposes the lack of human knowledge in this brief life. People pass through **meaningless** (*hebel*) **days** of living like a **shadow. A shadow** can provide welcome shade and protection but, like breath or vapor (other meanings of *hebel*), it is not lasting and cannot compare with the everlasting sovereignty of God (see 1 Chr 29:15; Ps 144:4; Job 8:9; 14:2; Eccl 8:13).

He passes through is literally "and he does them [the days]" (*wĕyaʿăśēm*), which has led to the theory of Greek influence, since the Greek verb "to do" is also used to express "spending time" (see Ruth 2:19 and postbiblical Hebrew; Fox 1999, 248). Theories about Greek influence on the thought of Ecclesiastes have been popular in the past, but there are no Greek loanwords in the Hebrew text, and many of the ideas can be found in Semitic sources as well as Greek. Also, similar life settings may have given rise to similar ideas that are not necessarily dependent on each other.

Divine foreknowledge is contrasted with the limitations of human knowledge in v 12. **Who knows?** is a rhetorical question with the assumed answer: "No one." Not even the wisdom teachers know what is good, even though they have many proverbs about what is good. Chapter 7 will list some of these and show their weaknesses; they are not absolute truth, although Qoheleth will still admit some advantage to wisdom. He is a wisdom teacher himself, after all.

B. Don't Depreciate the Past/Present in Favor of the Future (7:1-4)

■ 1 Ecclesiastes 7:1-4 is the second paragraph of the chiasm in 6:10—7:14. Qoheleth seems to quote a proverb in 7:1: **A good name is better than fine perfume,** which has striking chiastic alliteration (*ṭôb šēm miššemen ṭôb*) (see the proverb, "A good name is more desirable than great riches" [Prov 22:1]). To some extent 7:1-14 is a list of proverbs, some quoted, perhaps some composed by Qoheleth himself. They are carefully arranged to make his point that wisdom, while valuable, is limited.

A great name was one of the blessings of Abraham in Gen 12:1-3 but, for the builders of the tower of Babel, desire for their own renown resulted in divine judgment (Gen 11:4; see also Job 30:8). Even God is concerned about his reputation. This was part of his motivation for the exodus (Deut 28:58-59; see Amos 2:7). A good name is connected with perfume in Song 1:3 and bad smell with poor character in Gen 34:30; Exod 5:21. Luther translated this phrase "a good odour (i.e. reputation) is better than good ointment" (Delitzsch 1875, 313).

A good name is better than fine perfume, but efforts will be counterproductive if fame (**a good name**) becomes one's orientation in life. Qoheleth goes on to develop the limitations of fame by pointing out the absurdity of taking this proverb to its logical conclusion (vv 1-4). If all that really matters is the legacy one leaves behind, then to die is more valuable than to be born, **the day of death better than the day of birth.** This is absurd as life is to be enjoyed in each moment as Qoheleth emphasizes repeatedly elsewhere (e.g., 2:24; see introduction).

■ **2** Verse 2 continues this argument. If the day of death is more valuable than life, then **It is better to go to a house of mourning than to go to a house of feasting.** That is, a funeral is better than a wedding or birth (see Esth 7:8; Jer 16:8). The Dead Sea Scrolls and one Hebrew manuscript have "joy, pleasure" (*simhâ*) instead of **feasting** (*mišteh*), which does not really change the meaning (Krüger 2004, 37, 134). The house of mourning also accommodated eating and drinking (Jer 16:5-9). Whybray takes v 2 seriously and sees the point as the necessity to face death and mortality, without retreating to the "empty, raucous laughter of fools" (see 7:6) (1989, 11). Likewise Towner sees this verse as a reminder that one should approach all human experiences with a "keen sense of mortality" (1997, 326). However, Qoheleth is probably using sarcasm to show that an unhealthy desire for fame is to wish for one's own death so that fame can increase (see Spangenberg 1996, 65).

■ **3** The sarcasm continues in v 3 with another proverb, **Sorrow is better than laughter,** although there may be some truth in this proverb too. **Sorrow** or vexation (*kaʿas*) is not seen in a positive light elsewhere in the book. Along with suffering it is the experience of the workaholic in 2:23 and the result of wisdom in 1:18. But it is the nature of proverbs to be situational and to contain some truth but not absolute truth or universal applicability. Suffering can bring a depth of character that is missing in those who have only known frivolity (see 2:2; Prov 14:13). Luther states, "The heart is made better by sorrow" (Delitzsch 1875, 315).

Verse 3 continues this thought, declaring that **a sad face is good for the heart. A sad face** is literally *in evil of face* (*bĕrōa' pānîm*, Gen 40:7; Neh 2:2). **Good for the heart** is literally *the heart is good/glad* (*yîṭab lēb*, Ruth 3:7; Judg 19:6, 9). This is similar to the idiom *ṭôb lēb* meaning "glad in heart" (2 Chr 7:10; Judg 16:25; Esth 1:10; 5:9).

Along the Road

> I walked a mile with Pleasure,
>> She chattered all the way;
> But left me none the wiser,
>> For all she had to say.
> I walked a mile with Sorrow,
>> And ne'er a word said she;
> But oh, the things I learned from her
>> When Sorrow walked with me!
> (Robert Browning Hamilton, in Felleman 1936, 537)

■ **4** Verse 4 closes this look at the logical conclusion of the proverb in v 1 with another proverb, **the heart of the wise is in the house of mourning, but the heart of fools is in the house of pleasure. The house of mourning** was already mentioned in 7:2 in contrast to the **house of feasting.** Here the contrast is to the **house of pleasure** (or "joy," *śimḥâ*). The connection between **feasting** and **pleasure** was also made in Esth 9:17.

Is Qoheleth still showing the absurdity of making fame one's goal in life, or is he now serious about the connection of wisdom and folly with mourning and pleasure? Earlier he argued that more wisdom leads to more grief because of all the oppressions that a wise person must witness. But he has also argued that one should enjoy life in the moment. There is some ambiguity here and a double meaning may be intended. The wise recognize the limitations of life, but the fools do not. This does not mean that Qoheleth rejects his own previous advice. This unit, too, will conclude with advice to enjoy good times, but also to accept bad times as these also come under the sovereignty of God (7:14).

(Wisdom Is Still Valuable [7:5-6])

■ **5** Having quoted a proverb in v 1, only to reject any universal application of the principle, Qoheleth seems to switch to some serious advice in v 5: **It is better to heed a wise man's rebuke than to listen to the song of fools** (see Prov 12:1; 13:1, 18; 15:5, 12, 31-32). The words of the wise can be vanity when stretched beyond logical limits (so 7:1-4), but they are still superior to the **song of fools.** Instead of feasting and laughter (vv 2-3), the focus is now a **song** that is in some sense related to the first two (see Amos 6:5). **Song** (*šîr*) is

123

sometimes used in the sense of "praise" (Isa 42:10; Ps 149:1; Jer 20:13, which may also be relevant here. The praise of fools is contrasted with **a wise man's rebuke.** This is one of two statements on the value of wisdom (also 7:11-12). These come before and after the climax to the chiasm, which exposes once again the limitations of wisdom (7:7).

■ **6** In a remarkable wordplay the **song** (*šîr*) of fools in v 5 now turns to the **crackling** (*sîr*) **of thorns** on fire **under the pot** (*sîr*). This is an image of brevity amid much commotion as dry thorns do not take long to burn up but make a great deal of noise doing so. Dry twigs from a thorn bush would provide a hot but brief fire with little heating energy (see Ps 118:12; Joel 2:5). Barton catches the wordplay in his translation "as the crackling of nettles under kettles" (although nettles do not burn with the same crackle as thorns) (1908, 138). The nuance of *hebel* (**meaningless**) here is fleeting or profitless.

John Hookham Frere on the Mirth of Fools (1801)

> The mirth of fools, somewhere the preacher says,
> Is like the cracking thorns when in a blaze;
> So unsubstantial are their liveliest joys,
> Made up of thoughtless levity and noise:
> Tho' at the first the mantling flame looks bright,
> 'Tis but a momentary glare of light,
> With nothing solid to sustain the fire,
> It quickly sinks, and all their joys expire.
> (In Christianson 2007, 191)

C. Wisdom Is Limited (7:7)

■ **7** Verses 5-6 are now balanced with another look at the limitations of wisdom (see 7:1-4). Even wisdom can be corrupted by oppression and bribery, **Extortion turns a wise man into a fool, and a bribe corrupts the heart** (7:7).

In Hebrew, the sentence begins with *kî* ("for," "because"), which usually follows an antecedent, but there is none here. Also the Dead Sea Scrolls have "perverts" (*wîʿawweh*) instead of **corrupts** (*wîʾabbĕd*), which does not really change the meaning (Krüger 2004, 37, 134). The Dead Sea Scrolls fragment also has a blank space large enough for about fifteen letters between vv 6 and 7 (Longman 1997, 186).

The word **bribe** is literally *gift* (*mattānâ*, see also Prov 15:27). This shows the fine line between gift and bribe. The Bible is generally negative about bribes (Exod 23:8), but the realism of Prov 21:14 can be shocking to modern audiences: "A gift given in secret soothes anger, and a bribe concealed in the cloak pacifies great wrath."

B'. Don't Depreciate the Future/Present in Favor of the Past (7:8-10)

■8-10 The importance of contentment, in the form of patience, is addressed in vv 8-10. It is unwise to dwell on the good **old days** (v 10), or to become impatient to the point of **anger** (v 9), for **patience is better than** anger, and better days are coming (v 8). The vocabulary of **patience** and **pride** provides a helpful visualization. **Patience** is literally *long of spirit* (ʾerek-rûaḥ), while **pride** is *high of spirit* (gĕbah-rûaḥ; see Prov 16:5).

These three verses correspond to 7:1-4 in the chiasm. Those verses focused on depreciating the past/present in favor of the future, while 7:8-10 focus on depreciating the future/present in favor of the past. This apparent contradiction provides a balance and prevents distortion of either perspective. Dissatisfaction with Persian or Hellenistic domination easily could have made this yearning for old days commonplace (Delitzsch 1875, 320).

Phoebe Hesketh on the End of a Party (1989)

And the end of a party is better than the beginning.
Quietness gathers the voices and laughter
into one cup—
we drink peace.

Crumpled cushions are smoothed as our souls
and silence comes into the room
like a stranger bearing gifts
we had not imagined,
could not have known
without such comings
and such departures.
(In Christianson 2007, 192)

■9 Verse 9 warns against **anger**. The word **anger** (kaʿas) appears in Eccl 1:18; 2:23; 5:17; and 7:3 with the meaning *sorrow, grief*, or *frustration*. Anger **in the lap of fools** is the opposite of the proverb, "Wisdom reposes in the heart of the discerning" (Prov 14:33). The image of anger *resting* (yānûaḥ, *residing*) in the **lap of fools** is a contrary image, as anger does not rest (Crenshaw 1987, 137). Fox suggests that the image portrays anger being nurtured and fed, like a baby resting in his or her mother's arms (1999, 254).

■10 Qoheleth advises against dwelling on the past in v 10. The classic example of Israelites dwelling on the good old days is when they were traveling in the wilderness and wished to be back in slavery in Egypt (Exod 16:3; Num 11:5-6; 14:1-4). Qoheleth considers elevating the past as a sign of a lack of wisdom.

(Wisdom Is Still Valuable [7:11-12])

■ **11** In the chiasm, 7:11-12 corresponds to 7:5-6, which also balances the value of wisdom against the limitations expressed elsewhere in this unit (6:10—7:14). Verse 11 interrupts the strict chiastic structure to reinforce the value of **wisdom**. The translation **wisdom, like an inheritance** assumes an unusual meaning for the preposition ʿim. The usual meaning is "with," which would yield the translation: "wisdom with an inheritance is a good thing." The first line thus suggests that while wisdom may be as good as wealth, wisdom *with* wealth is better. **Those who see the sun** refers to those who are alive and is equivalent to Qoheleth's usual phrase **under the sun** (see also Job 3:16; Pss 49:19; 58:8).

Although the limitations of wisdom are addressed in this unit, Qoheleth is positive about wisdom. It **is a good thing and benefits those who see the sun.** Like money, it provides protection. One might have expected Qoheleth to say that wisdom is *better than* money, especially since there are several "better than" sayings in this unit (see Prov 8:11). But the protection of wisdom, like that of money, also has limitations.

■ **12** Verse 12 also expresses the value of wisdom but, as in v 11, it is not clear whether wisdom is superior to wealth, or if both together provide **a shelter.** Eaton points to a possible wordplay as **shelter** can also mean "glitter" in Ugaritic; he thus sees here a reference to the glitter of money (1983, 113). The literal translation of the first phrase is *for in the shade of the wisdom, in the shade of the money* or *for in a shade is the wisdom, in a shade is the money* (*kî běṣēl haḥokmâ běṣēl hakkāsep*). In the light of Qoheleth's other statements about the limitations of wealth it would seem that the superiority of wisdom over wealth is assumed in 7:11-12. However, this unit climaxes with the limitations of wisdom. Yet overall, Qoheleth is concerned to show that wisdom is limited because it cannot guarantee wealth or other positive outcomes. Qoheleth also taught that there is no lasting contentment in accumulated wealth. Despite its limitations, wisdom is superior to accumulated wealth.

The second half of 7:12 is open to several interpretations regarding the relationship of **knowledge** and **wisdom**. The Septuagint and Targum understood them as genitives of **advantage** ("the advantage of knowledge and wisdom") while the Vulgate took them as subjects ("knowledge and wisdom are an advantage"). The Hebrew text links **knowledge** (but not **wisdom**) to **advantage** ("the advantage of knowledge [is]"). But the form of the noun **knowledge** is the same as the infinitive, so the Hebrew text could be translated "the advantage of knowing wisdom [is]" (see Crenshaw 1987, 138). All these alternatives confirm the value of wisdom.

A'. Sovereignty of God: Enjoy Life (7:13-14)

■ 13 The final two verses of this unit provide the closing theological framework of the chiasm (13-14), as 6:10-12 provided the opening. The limitations of wisdom are set in the context of the sovereignty of God. Ecclesiastes 6:10-12 did not mention the involvement of God but implied his presence with the use of the passive voice and mention of "one who is stronger than he" (6:10). Now Qoheleth is explicit in his mention of God, who is sovereign even to the point of making things **crooked** (even though the sages had a goal to set people on a straight path). God was implied but not mentioned in the statement "What is twisted cannot be straightened" (1:15). Wisdom is limited in that it cannot supersede the sovereignty of God. His foreknowledge and control are absolute, despite the best efforts of wisdom. This affirmation of God's sovereignty is very general and does not give enough information to support Crenshaw's interpretation that some things were twisted in creation (1987, 139). The issue at hand is the limitation of human wisdom, not the nature of creation.

■ 14 Verse 14 places Qoheleth's theme of contentment in the context of the sovereignty of God. A wordplay is present in the first line, **When times are good, be happy; but when times are bad . . .** (bĕyôm ṭôbâ hĕyēh bĕṭôb ûbĕyôm rāʿâ rĕʾēh). The word **good** is used twice (**good, happy**), and the words **bad** and **consider** have similar sound (rāʿâ, rĕʾēh). The word **therefore** translates ʿal-debrat še, which occurs only in this verse in the OT and is modeled after the Aramaic phrase ʿal-debrat dî.

Qoheleth advises joy in good times and a philosophical attitude in bad times, given that divine foreknowledge is absolute and human foreknowledge is limited. This amounts to a variation of his usual advice to enjoy life (see e.g., 3:12-13, 22). Wisdom is valuable, but it has its limitations, and in the end, one must be content with the portion that God in his sovereignty has given (see Job 1:21). To make this point, Qoheleth has apparently quoted common proverbs in this unit and shown their limitations by taking them to their logical conclusion.

Horace on Living in the Present

But God, in goodness ever wise,
    Hath hid, in clouds of depthless night,
All that in future prospect lies
    Beyond the ken of mortal sight,
And laughs to see vain man opprest
With idle fears, and more than man distrest.

Then wisely form the present hour,
    Enjoy the bliss that it bestows;
The rest is all beyond our power,

And like the changeful Tiber flows,
Who, now, beneath his banks subsides,
And peaceful to its native ocean glides.
(Odes 3:29; 29-36; in Ginsburg 1861, 378)

FROM THE TEXT

Divine Sovereignty

Qoheleth expresses the sovereignty of God in terms of his knowledge and strength (6:10, contrasted to human lack of knowledge in 6:12). Sovereignty is also expressed in a proverb stating that what God has made crooked cannot be straightened (not even by wisdom). The implication of God's sovereignty is that humans cannot control outcomes and must therefore accept (with joy) the lot that God has given (7:14). There are some things we might wish to change, "but we cannot alter what God has made" (Towner 1997, 327).

Fame

In the thought of OT times there was no developed doctrine of resurrection or belief in a meaningful afterlife. Instead, people found immortality in the success of their children and future generations, as well as in their reputation. Qoheleth mocks this idea with the conclusion that the funeral house is better than the feasting house (7:2). Instead of dwelling on the past, Qoheleth advises enjoyment of God's good gifts, and acceptance of his sovereignty in bad times (7:14).

Wisdom

The previous unit (5:10—6:9) emphasized the limitations of wealth. Apparently some people had been orienting their lives around attaining wealth, and they were attempting to use wisdom to gain it. This passage (6:10—7:14) emphasizes the limitations of wisdom. Even if wealth were a worthy goal, wisdom is not a reliable path to that goal. This is because of a limitation of knowledge (6:12; 7:14); and wisdom is limited by corruption (7:7) and by God's sovereignty (7:13). Yet there is value to wisdom despite its limitations (7:5, 11).

IX. JUDGMENT, RIGHTEOUSNESS, AND WISDOM ARE ELUSIVE (7:15-29)

BEHIND THE TEXT

Ecclesiastes 7:15-29 follows two chiasms that focused on the limitations of wealth and wisdom. It continues to challenge a simplistic view of retribution and advocates the fear of God (v 18) despite the elusiveness of righteousness and wisdom. The following unit continues these themes and also revisits the sovereignty of God.

Reflection is the main genre of this unit; it includes instruction (v 21), and rhetorical questions (vv 16-17). The word **find,** used eight times in this unit, conveys a key theme in the book. Qoheleth seeks answers in life (1:13; 7:25, 28, 29) but does not find satisfaction in the expected pursuits. He wishes to escape (*mālaṭ*) the woman folly (v 26), but he finds that satisfaction and even wisdom escape him (v 24). In the end satisfaction comes not from trying to find something elusive but from accepting the gifts that God has already given (8:15). Verses 15-29 can be outlined as follows:

Judgment Is Elusive (7:15-18)

Righteousness Is Elusive (7:19-22)

Wisdom Is Elusive (7:23-24)

There Is Judgment; Righteousness and Wisdom Are Superior (7:25-29)

A. Judgment Is Elusive (7:15-18)

■ **15** This unit continues a common theme of Ecclesiastes, the value and limitations of wisdom. The autobiographical, conversational tone is reminiscent of the reflections of the king in chs 1—2. Qoheleth does not, however, present himself as Solomon or as a king in this unit. He is at times critical of kings (4:13; 5:8; 10:16) and even gives advice regarding kings (8:2-4; 10:4, 20). The exaggeration of chs 1—2 ("I have seen all the things," 1:14) is continued in the phrase **I have seen both of these.**

The context of this observation is Qoheleth's **meaningless life.** The meaning of *hebel* in this context could be "fleeting," although the context does not allow a very precise definition in this case. The immediate context is the breakdown of the standard wisdom concept of retribution. Thus *hebel* could have the sense "incomprehensible" here. What Qoheleth has observed is unexpected and puzzling.

In the doctrine of retribution, which was the standard view of the wisdom teachers, those who are righteous are believed to be rewarded by God with material blessings such as prosperity and a long life. At the same time, the wicked will suffer punishment through material disaster and even death. Qoheleth's observations do not support this doctrine as a universal principle. Instead, he has seen a **righteous man perishing in his righteousness, and a wicked man living long in his wickedness.** Qoheleth adds no further commentary, as his audience immediately sees that the world is not operating as it should. The more cynical among his audience would be drawn into his argument because they would have already made this observation and challenged the doctrine of retribution themselves. They would be among those who challenge the claim of the psalmist: "I was young and now I am old, yet I have never seen the righteous forsaken or their children begging bread" (Ps 37:25; see Prov 10:24-27).

■ **16** Qoheleth then gives some surprising advice to cope with this glaring anomaly. He seems to advocate moderation in righteousness and wisdom. This is contrary to all the teaching of the wisdom teachers, the Law, and the Prophets, which all recognize a general lack in these areas, not an overabundance. Qoheleth, too, had advocated wisdom, while recognizing its limitations (1:18; 2:13; 2:16; 6:8; 7:7). Thus it is highly unlikely that Qoheleth is advocating second-class righteousness and wisdom, although this is the understanding of Crenshaw (1987, 140). Some have suggested that Qoheleth is writing of self-righteousness or hypocrisy (Whybray 1989, 120) or of bragging about one's own righteousness and wisdom (Seow 1997, 253, 267). Proverbs speaks of being wise in one's own eyes (3:7; 26:12, 16; 28:11). Ginsburg related this to being overly rigid and scrupulous in religious and moral conduct (1861, 379), and Delitzsch characterized the advice as "be not a narrow rigorist" (1875, 325).

Qoheleth states that self-destruction is the result for an **overrighteous** and **overwise** individual (v 16). It is possible that Qoheleth is speaking of a pursuit of righteousness and wisdom that leads to self-destruction (see Prov 16:18). The word *harbeh* (**over-**) probably modifies **be** rather than **-righteous** (Seow 1997, 252-53, citing Whybray) so that it is not an extreme righteousness that is in view but an extreme pursuit. Such an extreme pursuit of wisdom and righteousness could result from someone who is using this behavior *for the sake of* long life or material benefits. Retribution is not very reliable, and such a pursuit will be counterproductive, leading to frustration and destruction. This may be supported by the syntax of **neither be,** which is literally, *and do not make yourself wise profit* (*yôtēr*). The final noun is usually taken in an adverbial sense, modifying "wise" (e.g., **overwise**). But it could be an indirect object so that a preposition would have to be supplied (e.g., "for the sake of profit"). This is consistent with Qoheleth's general view that righteousness and wisdom should not be pursued for the sake of profit but under the motivation of the fear of God.

Robert Burns on Rigid Righteousness and Wisdom (1786)

My Son, these maxims make a rule,
 An' lump them aye thegither;
The Rigid Righteous is a fool,
 the Rigid Wise anither:
The cleanest corn that ere was dight [before was winnowed]
 May hae some pyles o' caff in;
So ne'er a fellow-creature slight
 For random fits o' daffin [frolicking].
(In Christianson 2007, 194)

7:16-17

■ **17** Verse 17 stands in contrast to v 16 as Qoheleth gives the advice **do not be overwicked, and do not be a fool.** If a cynical youth were ready to plunge into folly on the basis of v 16, this advice brings the expected balance. Qoheleth could have said "do not be wicked" (instead of **overwicked**). Perhaps he wishes to be more realistic, as he has been about the human ability to be righteous (7:20, 29), but this should not be read as a license to be a little wicked. There is no qualification of folly in v 17; Qoheleth advises against all folly. Qoheleth is a wisdom teacher after all and despite all the incongruities of life, he could never advocate wickedness and folly. The result of being overly wicked is dying **before your time,** which parallels the result of an extreme pursuit of righteousness (v 16). God's sovereignty over the timing of events is implied in the phrase **why die before your time** (see 3:1-8). The idea of a time for death is also found in Job 22:16, *Ahiqar* 7:102, and the Phoenician Eshmunazar inscription (Crenshaw 1987, 142).

Verse 17 shows that while Qoheleth is willing to challenge the universality of the doctrine of retribution, he is not willing to abandon it. He fully expects an overly wicked person to meet an untimely death.

■ **18** Verse 18 gives the advice to **grasp the one and not let go of the other;** it is not clear what is intended by the pronoun *this* (*zeh*), which occurs twice and is translated **the one** and **the other.** Probably there are not two things in mind, but only one, namely the warnings given in vv 16-17. The reader should hold on to the advice given in these warnings and not let them go. **The man who fears God will avoid all extremes** is literally, *the one who fears God sends all things out* (*yāṣāʾ*). Another use of *yāṣāʾ* is "escape" (Gen 39:12, 15), which could suggest the idea of escaping the extremes of Eccl 7:16-17 (**avoid all extremes**). Although he is willing to challenge accepted wisdom teaching, Qoheleth still believes in the fear of God as the foundation for life. The fear of God is not an unhealthy dread but a healthy respect of God that means a relationship of obedience and trust (see 3:14; 5:7; 8:12-13). Perhaps the sense of this phrase in v 18 is "fear of God will make everything come out fine" or "everything will come out fine for the one who fears God." Even though righteousness and wisdom cannot guarantee a long and happy life, they are still the best principles to live by and will lead to the best result, subject to the sovereignty of God.

B. Righteousness Is Elusive (7:19-22)

■ **19** The positive value of wisdom is reemphasized in v 19 as it will make one man **more powerful than ten** or literally, *wisdom is stronger for the wise than ten*. The variant reading of the Septuagint is "helps" (*boēthēsei*) in place of **powerful,** giving the sense "wisdom helps the wise person." This reading is supported by the Dead Sea Scrolls fragment (ʿzr, meaning "to help").

There is no apparent reason why Qoheleth specifically chose the number ten, except that it is a round number. Davis suggests that this is a quotation of a popular proverb (2000, 204). Seow suggests that scribal errors involving word division and letter confusion (*shin* as a *sin*) corrupted the original meaning, "the wealth of the proprietors" (*mēʿōser haššallîṭîm* for MT *mēʿăśārâ šallîṭîm*, **ten rulers**) (1997, 5, 14). This emendation supports Seow's argument that the word **ruler** (*šallîṭîm*) really means "proprietor" in the Persian period (where he dates Ecclesiastes). However, the Hebrew text is ambiguous as to whether the ten are **rulers** or "proprietors" because there is not enough information in the context. Krüger suggests that **rulers** is probably correct (2004, 36).

■ 20 The argument now oscillates back to the limitations of righteousness. According to v 20 there is no one who is overly righteous, so the effort described in v 16 leads to destruction partly because the goal of absolute perfection is unattainable, even though righteousness and wisdom are valuable (see Rom 3:10, 23; Pss 14:1-3; 53:1-3).

The word *sin* is usually used in a nonreligious sense in Wisdom literature. Rather than wickedness and rebellion against God, it has its more literal connotation of missing the mark or failing to reach a goal. In this setting the nonreligious meaning (a mistake) is probably in mind because in Ecclesiastes **righteous** is connected more with wisdom than with religious institutions and because the immediate comparison is with doing good. Even with the religious meaning of "sin" (which is broader than just intentional disobedience), the OT recognizes no sinless perfection (1 Kgs 8:46; Ps 143:2; Prov 20:9; also Sirach 19:16).

There is no obvious connection between the universality of sins (or mistakes) in 7:20 and the value of wisdom in 7:19. The connecting word *ki* ("for," "because") usually indicates such a connection, but it can also be emphatic with no causal connection to the preceding. Alternatively, it is possible that 7:19 is an interruption and that v 20 refers back to 7:16-18. If this is correct, then v 20 may be seen as an instruction against an extreme pursuit of righteousness because there is no one who does not sin. Ginsburg did see a connection between vv 19 and 20, arguing that *ki* never begins a new subject (1861, 382-83).

■ 21-22 The reality of the universality of sin leads to some advice in vv 21-22 against listening to malicious gossip. The literal meaning of **do not pay attention** is *do not give your heart*, sometimes translated as "do not take to heart" (ESV). While everyone knows how painful it is to overhear something bad said about oneself, almost everyone is willing to spread such criticism about others. Qoheleth's advice, then, is that it is better not to **pay attention to every word people say,** and also to make allowances for the indiscreet speech of others, knowing that everyone has also been indiscreet, as v 20 asserts.

Qoheleth refers to the past indiscretions of his readers as an argument for tolerating the indiscretions of others, but in so doing does not condone further indiscretions (while being realistic that no one is perfect, 7:20). **Cursed** (*qillaltā*) is the intensive form (Piel) of the verb meaning "be lightly esteemed" (BDB 886). An example of cursing is found in Shimei's insults when David fled Absalom (2 Sam 16:7-8).

C. Wisdom Is Elusive (7:23-24)

■ 23-24 Qoheleth returns to the topic of the limitations of traditional wisdom teaching with his focus on the elusiveness of wisdom. Qoheleth, who tested the lasting satisfaction of pleasure (see 2:1), now says that he tested the attainability of wisdom. He fails the test and comes to the same conclusion as Job 28:12-22 and Prov 30:1-4. Like the strong woman of Prov 31, absolute wisdom cannot be found (Prov 31:10). In the end, "who can find it?" (**who can discover it?** Eccl 7:24; see also Sirach 24:28-29; Baruch 3:14-23). The phrase **All this** seems to refer to the observations in 7:15-22, but it could also refer to the content of the following verses.

The elusiveness of wisdom is reiterated in v 24 with the phrase **most profound,** which is literally *deep, deep* (*ʿāmōq ʿāmōq*), using repetition to indicate the superlative. **Far off** and "deep" represent horizontal and vertical dimensions, which accords with the horizontal (*wĕlātûr*, "explore") and vertical (*lidrôš*, "study") of the examination of all things in 1:13.

D. There Is Judgment; Righteousness and Wisdom Are Superior (7:25-29)

■ **25** Qoheleth has **turned** (*sābab*; see also 2:20) to consider other topics more deeply and now he turns **to search** (see 2:12) for wisdom and even to examine **the stupidity of wickedness,** as he had investigated pleasure and wealth in chs 1—2.

One of the things he is searching for is **the scheme of things** (*ḥešbôn*). This is an important word in Ecclesiastes but is used in a variety of ways. Like so much of Qoheleth's vocabulary, it is a commercial word and means "reckoning, account" (Sirach 42:3 and the Talmud; Murphy 1992, 74). It is used in the sense of "considered assessment of life, that is, what is arrived at by a deliberate process of reckoning" (see Eccl 7:27, 29; 9:10; Machinist 1995, 170). It is one of the words Seow identified as occurring in fifth century B.C. Egyptian Aramaic texts (but not occurring before the fifth century, thus suggesting a postexilic date for Ecclesiastes) (1997, 13). Perhaps the best understanding of *ḥešbôn* in this context would be "answer." There are many legitimate questions in life, and Qoheleth is attempting to engage the young audience that has begun to question the standard answers. Like them, Qoheleth has been looking for the answer.

To make this search complete, it must involve knowledge of folly and madness, and so perhaps will prevent others from falling into these traps. Qoheleth already hints at the outcome by providing negative adjectives: **the stupidity of wickedness and the madness of folly.** The words **stupidity** and **folly** have the same root letters, in different combinations (*ksl; skl*).

■ **26** Although absolute wisdom cannot be found (7:23-24), a bitterness worse than death can be found when one experiences wickedness and folly. The meaning of **more bitter than death** could also be "stronger than death," as *mar* has this meaning in Ezek 3:14. It is love that is as strong as death in

Song 8:6 (using different vocabulary). The bitterness is the result of the **snare, trap,** and **chains** that come from association with a certain **woman.** The **snare** (*māṣôd*) is a siege work in 9:14; in Proverbs (7:22-23; 22:14) the adulterous woman leads those without sense to a snare. **Chains** (*ʾāsûr*) are associated with Delilah's entrapment of Samson with new ropes (Judg 16:11-12) but are positive in Song 7:5 where the king is held captive in the woman's hair.

Fox thinks this is a statement against women in general (1999, 269). This would be plausible coming from the patriarchal society of the biblical world where Adam blamed Eve for his sin and Zech 5:8 personified evil as a woman in a basket (see also Sirach 25:24; 42:13, 14; 1 Tim 2:14; Testament of the Twelve Patriarchs). This is not necessarily the point of Qoheleth here, though. Elsewhere he is positive about women (**wife, whom you love,** 9:9). Ecclesiastes 7:26 uses the definite article (**the** woman) and seems to be using the term as a personification of folly, just as wisdom is often personified as a woman (Prov 1:20-33; 8:1—9:6; 9:13-18; and probably 31:10-31; see also Sirach 6:24-31; Krüger 2004, 147; Bartholomew 2009, 266).

The one who escapes the snare of folly is the one who **pleases God.** The one who fears God (see v 18) is perhaps meant here as the one who pleases God. Krüger suggests that the opposites **man who pleases God** and **the sinner** are not moral categories but refer to lucky and unlucky individuals (2004, 146). **Sinner** (*ḥôṭēʾ*) is not usually religious in Wisdom literature but has the literal meaning of missing the mark.

7:26-28

■ **27** Verse 27 seems to provide the answer for the search expressed in v 25. The answer to the limitation of retribution, righteousness, and wisdom is to pursue these things in the fear of God (v 18) because the alternative of wickedness and folly leads to great bitterness. It takes some investigation; one must add **one thing to another** (lit., *one to one*) **to find the answer** (the scheme of **things**). This equates to the English idiom "put two and two together." The doctrine of retribution may not be absolute, but wickedness nevertheless leads to bitterness (v 26) or even death (v 17).

■ **28** The theme of seeking without finding is continued in v 28, although the subject of the seeking is different. In this case, an **upright man** is found among a thousand, but an **upright woman** is not found (the word **upright** is not in the Hebrew text in both cases). This seems to suggest that while righteousness is elusive for everyone, it is more elusive for women than for men. It may also mean that, in Qoheleth's judgment, men are only slightly better than women. It would not be surprising that someone of Qoheleth's time and culture would make a negative statement about women (and even someone from more recent times, e.g., Delitzsch 1875, 335).

This is not the tone of the book as a whole, however, although like other Wisdom literature Ecclesiastes seems to be addressed mainly to men. Neither is it the tone of Scripture as a whole, which although it reflects the patriarchal culture from which it came, nevertheless tends to raise the place of women above that of the cultures that it addressed.

Some plausible suggestions have been made to explain the presence of this statement. It is possible that the whole saying is a quotation of a popular (nonbiblical) proverb. This kind of argument was used by Jerome (Ginsburg 1861, 103). Ecclesiastes does contain other sayings that seem to be quotations, and they are often included so that Qoheleth can reject them. If 7:28 contains a quoted proverb, then the rejection of it could be signaled by the introductory remark about not finding what he sought repeatedly to find in his life. Thus Qoheleth searched for the truth of the proverb but found it to be false (Lohfink 2003, 103). Upright men are not easier to find than upright women. However, this is a departure from the topic of the chapter (Seow 1997, 265).

The word ʾādām is usually a generic word for human beings (there are other words for "male"; ʾîš, zākār). Qoheleth uses ʾādām only in the generic sense elsewhere (against Whybray 1989, 127), which supports the theory that he is not the author of a proverb that degrades women. In any case, the proverb does not exalt men very highly above women, since only **one upright man among a thousand** is found, that is, virtually none.

Another plausible suggestion is that a scribe has added a proverb here thinking it was appropriate to the context, when it is not (see Whybray 1989, 126). The reference to the woman in v 26 could have been misunderstood as a reference to all women, instead of a personification of folly (or a reference to the adulterous woman). Thus a misogynous proverb was inserted, possibly first in the margin that, for later copies, led to the confusion that it belonged in the text. There are no actual copies of Ecclesiastes that support this theory, but this kind of mistake is well known from other cases.

A very probable possibility is that **woman** is a metaphor in v 28, as it apparently was in v 26. There she was personified folly, and here she seems to personify wisdom (Prov 9:13-18; 1:20-33; 8:1—9:6; Bartholomew 2009, 267). This Lady Wisdom is difficult to find (see Prov 31:1) and may only be found in one person (ʾādām) **among a thousand,** but among the other nine hundred and ninety-nine (**them all,** běkol ʾēlleh) wisdom (**one upright woman**) is not found. This interpretation would be strengthened by an emendation of the first word in v 28, from ʾăšer ("which") to ʾiššâ ("woman") (Fox 1999, 270). This would give the sense, *I myself have been searching for Lady Wisdom, but I have not found her. One person among a thousand I have found (to have wisdom), but I have not found Lady Wisdom among all others.* This is consistent with Qoheleth's views on the elusiveness of wisdom in vv 23-24 and elsewhere.

Louise Erdrich on Qoheleth and Women (1995)

There is misery in Koheleth's enjoyment of everything, but an inability to love or at least respect the opposite gender is an embarrassment to any complex intelligence. Somebody told this guy what, or he was jilted, let down royally. He used that as an excuse to write three self-righteous, arrogant, and mean little verses of diatribe. Men are made by God, he concludes, but there's not one good woman in a thousand. (In Christianson 2007, 201)

■ **29** In v 29 the theme of searching and the search that resulted in finding bitterness (v 26) has also resulted in a more positive discovery, namely, **God made mankind upright.** If the question is whether righteousness has value, then part of the answer is that God has made people upright. Although the vocabulary is different, there is a close connection between being righteous (*sedeq*) and **upright** (*yāšār*). Righteousness, though elusive, should be pursued (but not to the point of self-destruction, 7:16) because that is the lifestyle that God has ordained.

Even though God has made people to serve him in righteousness and wisdom, people continue to search for alternative answers (**schemes,** *ḥiššĕbōnôt*), which lead only to bitterness, folly, and madness. Fulfillment is a gift from God, and fearing him is an end in itself. The answer (*ḥešbôn*, **scheme of things,** 7:27) can be found simply enough. Endless searching for the rewards of righteousness will lead to self-destruction (v 16).

7:28-29

FROM THE TEXT

Mystery of Retribution

In the simplified world of instruction for children, as found in the book of Proverbs, the reality and merits of judgment, righteousness, and wisdom are presented in a way that is no longer believable for the growing adolescent who begins to see anomalies and can develop tendencies to become cynical. To this audience Qoheleth is honest about the limitations of the values that were taught to children, but he does not advocate a cynicism that goes too far in the opposite direction. Instead, he continues to uphold the value of wisdom and righteousness in a complex world and to alert his audience to the trap that waits for the wicked and the fool, even though that trap may for the moment be hidden. God's way is still better than the schemes that people are continually inventing to bypass the sovereignty of God.

The NT addresses the elusiveness of judgment by promising a final eschatological judgment for everyone (Heb 9:27). The elusiveness of righteousness is addressed by a call to a sincerity of heart. This amounts to a righteousness that exceeds the self-righteousness of the Pharisees (Matt 5:20; see Matt

5:6). The answer to the elusiveness of wisdom is so simple, "Ask God . . . and it will be given" (James 1:5).

Fear of God

The benefits of the doctrine of retribution are for those who are righteous and wise, but Qoheleth challenges the possibility of righteousness in an absolute sense, and also the quest for such righteousness, which leads to either despair or hypocrisy. Instead he advocates living under the fear of God and recognizes that human **schemes** have distorted God-given righteousness (v 29). Paul quoted Eccl 7:20 (**There is not a righteous man on earth**) in Rom 3:10, and then went on to connect the lack of righteousness to the lack of fear of God (Rom 3:18; see Eccl 7:18).

The emphasis on the fear of God is part of traditional wisdom teaching. It is mentioned in Ecclesiastes five times and according to Crenshaw has several meanings (1987, 156, citing Pfeiffer). The "awe in the presence of dreadful power, the numinous" is found in 3:14; 5:7; and 7:18, while religious devotion is more important in 8:13 and 12:13. However, the context does not always give enough data to make a distinction. The connection with God's gift and with keeping the commandments would seem to put 3:14 and 12:13 into the category of religious devotion. However, disobeying God's commandments could be dangerous, and there is also judgment in the context of 12:13. Fear of God's dreadful power would also seem relevant for 5:7 (God may become angry), 7:18 (deals with being overwicked), and 8:13 (God will cut the life of the wicked short).

Wisdom

In response to the overconfident pursuit of wisdom, Qoheleth warns **it is far off and most profound** (v 24). Wisdom is a valuable guide in life (v 25), but it is not something that can be easily grasped and relied upon to control outcomes in life. Wisdom is not a means to a material end but an expression of right relationship with God.

X. THE DAYS OF THE WICKED WILL NOT LENGTHEN (8:1-17)

BEHIND THE TEXT

Chapter 8 continues important themes from ch 7: the value of wisdom, although it is elusive; the elusive nature of justice, although ch 8 expresses confidence that justice is coming. Chapter 8 also introduces instructions for conduct before the king (who is sovereign) and commends joy. Many of these themes will also be explored in ch 9, which once again expresses less confidence about the certainty of justice.

The postexilic period saw the rise of emperors whose power was absolute (see Introduction). Ecclesiastes 8:2-4 advises obedience to these dictators. Qoheleth's advice on how to approach kings suggests that the book is not specifically addressed to kings or nobility, but it is not addressed to the poor either. His audience has access to the king and they have opportunities; they can cast bread (11:1); they can hoard wealth (5:13).

The genre of ch 8 is a loose collection of sayings (vv 1, 6-8), instruction (vv 2-5), and reflection (vv 9-17). The chapter begins with rhetorical questions. The threefold repetition of **find** in v 17 shows that the unsuccessful search emphasized in ch 7 is still in view. The lack of human success in this search is contrasted with God's timing (v 6) and sovereignty (v 17). Verses 1-17 can be outlined as follows:

Sovereignty of the King (8:1-9)

Mystery of Retribution (8:10-15)

Sovereignty of God and Limitation of Wisdom (8:16-17)

IN THE TEXT

A. Sovereignty of the King (8:1-9)

■ I Chapter 8 begins with the rhetorical question, **Who is like the wise man?** which has the implied answer, "No one." It is such a wisdom teacher who **knows the explanation of things** (*pēšer dābār*). The word for **explanation** (*pēš er*) is Aramaic and so is consistent with a postexilic or northern origin of the book (Ginsburg 1861, 390). *Pēšer* is common in the Aramaic text of Daniel but is found only here in biblical Hebrew. The unusual presence of the letter *he* in **like the wise man** (*kĕhehākām*) suggests that a scribal error may have led to incorrect word division (*kĕhehākām* instead of *kōh hākām*, meaning "so wise," Murphy 1992, 80). The former would be positive about wisdom, the latter would expose the limitations of wisdom. Both these viewpoints can be found elsewhere in Ecclesiastes, even in this chapter, so choosing between the two is difficult.

It is possible that the rhetorical question **Who knows the explanation of things?** also has the implied answer "No one." While wisdom teachers are unique, there are certain things they cannot interpret, or perhaps even they do not know the meaning of life in general. This would fit Qoheleth's criticism of traditional wisdom (e.g., 6:8). It is also possible that he is referring to something specific, which the wisdom teachers cannot interpret, namely the proverb that follows, **Wisdom brightens a man's face and changes its hard appearance** (Hertzberg, cited by Whybray 1989, 129). There is more than one way to interpret the proverb, so it may give a wisdom teacher difficulty.

Wisdom can bring a change of countenance from despair or worry (**hard appearance**) to brightness or joy. **Hard appearance** is literally *strength of his face* (*'ōz pānāyw*), which BDB (739a) translates as "boldness, impudence." This interpretation suggests that wisdom has enlightened (*tā'ir*, **brightens**) one who was arrogant (see Num 6:25; Exod 34:29-35).

It may be that some of the ambiguity of v 1 is resolved in v 2, which is about conduct before the monarch. A look of consternation or impudence before the king would be dangerous, so (by wisdom) a person would change such a countenance (Fox 1999, 275).

■ **2** In vv 2-5 Qoheleth begins some advice about dealing with kings. He seems to be speaking of the sovereignty of kings partly to make an analogy with the sovereignty of God. The sovereignty of a king implies certain behavior that is also relevant in the presence of God (see Barolín 2001, 18).

Qoheleth begins with the advice, **Obey the king's command** (v 2). In the Hebrew text this is an awkward command (the text reads literally, *I mouth of king keep*). "Mouth of king" stands for the command of the king (which comes from his mouth), but "I" (*ʾănî*) in the text is out of place. This could be a scribal error (writing *ʾănî* instead of the direct object marker *ʾet*, which has no English translation). Other suggestions include adding "I said" (as in 2:1; 3:17, 18; so NIV, **I say**), changing "I" (*ʾănî*) to "my son" (*běnî*), which is a common address in Wisdom literature (but only used once in Ecclesiastes [12:12]), and changing "I" to "in the presence of" (*ʾnpy*), which is based on a passage in *Ahiqar* (Whitley 1979, 71). Perhaps the best solution is to take *ʾănî* as an emphatic pronoun with ellipsis of the verb **say** as the NIV does in this verse.

The second part of v 2 is difficult to translate and reads literally, *even because of the oath of God* (*wěʿal dibrat šěbûʿat ʾělōhîm*). This has been translated in various ways including **because you took an oath before God** and "because of God's oath to him" (ESV). It is not clear that either God or the reader has made an oath to the king. It may be that obedience to the king's command is to be taken as seriously as an oath that one may have made to God. Thus Seow translates, "Keep the king's command, yea, according to the manner of a sacred oath" (1997, 276). Delitzsch (1875) thought that v 2*b* is not original.

■ **3** Qoheleth's advice, **Do not be in a hurry to leave the king's presence,** is opposite of the advice given in 10:4 to hurry out of the king's presence in order to obey his command. It is possible that **do not be in a hurry** belongs with the previous verse, as in the Septuagint (followed by RSV; Whybray 1989, 130). Verse 3 could then be translated *Go from his presence, do not stay for a bad cause* (this is more consistent). An alternative translation that follows the Hebrew text more closely is *do not be dismayed before him* (Gen 45:3; Job 23:15; *tibbāhēl*, Niphal, is usually "be dismayed," while BHS suggests an emendation to Piel, *těbahēl*, which is usually "hurry"). The **bad cause** could be a conspiracy (Ogden 1987, 129).

The sovereignty of the king is given as the reason for not supporting an evil cause before the king: **for he will do whatever he pleases.** This expression of sovereignty is only used elsewhere in the OT for God (e.g., Jonah 1:14). Thus Qoheleth seems to be comparing the sovereignty of the king with that of God, with the implication that God should also be obeyed. Like the king, his "word is supreme" and no one would dare to challenge his actions (Eccl 8:4).

■ 4 The sailors challenged Jonah's actions (Jonah 1:10), but it is futile to challenge the actions of God (Job 9:12; Isa 45:9; Dan 4:35). No one can say to him **"What are you doing?"**

Henry Lok on God's Sovereignty (1597)

Who dare unto account his soveraigne call,
Who to no power in earth inferiour is?
Who will not at his feet all prostrate fall,
Who hath the power to punish his amis?
As deputies to God, on earth they raigne,
And by his sword of Justice state maintaine.
(In Christianson 2007, 201-2)

■ 5 The benefit of obedience is expressed in v 5 where Qoheleth says that **no harm** (*dābār rāʿ*) will come to the one who obeys the king's command. The king's command seems to be in mind because of the context of the prior verses, which are about behavior before the king, and also because of the similar vocabulary (**obey; bad cause/harm,** *dābār rāʿ*). However, use of the word **command** immediately draws to mind the divine commands and continues the double meaning of these verses: sovereignty belongs to the king and to God.

The guarantee that no harm will come to the one who obeys is remarkably similar to the doctrine of retribution, which promises blessing for the righteous and which has been challenged by Qoheleth (even in this chapter). Yet Qoheleth still retains a degree of respect for the doctrine, even though he sees the complexities of life that make it unreliable.

The benefits of obedience to the king are known to the **wise heart** that also knows **the proper time and procedure,** literally *time and justice*. This follows on from ch 3 where the times for various events were set by God. Chapter 8 now adds that the wise person can discern the proper time for an event. The word "and" (**time and procedure**) is not found in the Septuagint; thus the proper understanding could be *time of justice* (or judgment), that is, when the results of obedience to the king (and God) will be revealed. Ginsburg identified this as a hendiadys, two nouns linked by a conjunction to express a single idea (1861, 395). Does the wise heart really know when God will bring judgment? This may be an instance of Qoheleth introducing traditional wisdom for the purpose of refuting it (see 8:7).

■ 6 Qoheleth turns to challenge the knowledge of the timing of justice (v 6) and even the certainty of justice (v 7) from the king or God in the next verses. *For there is a time of justice for every matter but the evil of humanity is great upon them.* The evil of humanity, or **man's misery,** is this: he does not know the time of justice, or even if there is going to be justice (v 7). The doctrine of retribution, though widely accepted, cannot be relied upon to operate in every case or in a timely fashion (v 11).

■ **7** While 8:5 was optimistic about a wise heart knowing the time of judgment, v 7 is less so and accords more with the notion of God controlling the times and seasons in ch 3.

■ **8** The primary operation of divine retribution in OT thinking was death. Since there was no significant view of an afterlife in ancient Israel, blessing was experienced through a long and peaceful life, while punishment came through an untimely (and presumably violent) death. But Qoheleth observes that **no one has power over the day of his death** (v 8), even the wise or righteous person. This inevitable and final event lies only within the sovereignty of God. This was already stated in 3:2, along with God's sovereignty over the time of birth.

People can no more control their death than contain the **wind.** The Hebrew word for **wind** (*rûaḥ*) is the same as "breath" or "spirit." This leads to a double meaning. People cannot control the timing of death, because they cannot guarantee that they will continue to breathe. At first the meaning **wind** seems primary and recalls the discussion about the movements of the wind (1:6) and the refrain regarding chasing the wind (e.g., 1:14, 17; 2:11, 17, 26). But as the reader progresses, the meaning "breath" becomes primary as the day of death looms closer (see 3:19, 21; 12:7).

No one will be released from the final battle of death, as **no one is discharged in time of war.** In the Persian period, there was release from military service for those who could afford to pay a substitute (Seow 1997, 28-29). Deuteronomy also provided for release from military duty (20:5-8; 24:5). But there can be no such release from death. Rashbam read this as the impossibility of sending a delegation to delay the angel of death (Medieval rabbi Shmuel son of Meir; Japhet and Salters 1985, 170). If this is true for the righteous and the wise, it is certainly true for the wicked. For **wickedness will not release those who practice it.**

The introduction of war is usually taken as a hypothetical comparison, but it could be that it is meant literally as a major cause of death and a real possibility in the postexilic periods. There is no release from war, not only for soldiers, but also for civilians who are caught in the battle zone. The timing of death, and thus the operation of retribution, is unknown in wartime (see Davis 2000, 208).

■ **9** These are the reflections that Qoheleth had in his observation of **everything done under the sun.** The inhumanity that he witnessed seemed to go unpunished. The word for **lords it over** (*šālaṭ*) is an important word in Seow's argument for a Persian period date for Ecclesiastes (1997, 14). But Krüger objects that Seow's definition of "right of disposal" is probably incorrect in 8:9

(2004, 36). The usage here is the usual definition of "rule over," but it is possible that Seow's translation is correct ("people exercise proprietorship over one another") (1997, 276). There is not enough evidence to determine the exact meaning here (as in 7:19). The last phrase **to his own hurt** could also be interpreted as bringing evil on the one oppressed, rather than the oppressor.

B. Mystery of Retribution (8:10-15)

■ **10** The opening word **then** (*ûběkēn*) shows the continuity between vv 9 and 10, although some commentators take v 10 as the beginning of a new unit (Krüger 2004, 158). Qoheleth states that he **saw the wicked buried** as an example of the breakdown of retribution (v 10). This is not a reference to a deserved, untimely death but to a decent burial that they do not deserve. Burial was a sign of honor, and this courtesy should not have been afforded to the wicked (see 6:3). This is somewhat a change of topic from 8:1-9, but it is an example of the breakdown of retribution and an extension of the royal sovereignty to divine sovereignty.

These people who received the burial were not only wicked but also hypocrites as they **used to come and go from the holy place and receive praise.** The translation **receive praise** (*wěyištabběhû*) follows a minority of manuscripts but makes better sense than "were forgotten" (*wěyištakkěhû*) as in the Masoretic Hebrew text (unless there is a quick change of subject from the wicked to the righteous). Apparently there was scribal confusion of the consonants *bet* and *kaf*, which look similar in Hebrew.

Verse 10 closes with the declaration, **This too is meaningless** (*hebel*), in the sense of "mysterious, incomprehensible." It does not make sense that the wicked are rewarded like this.

■ **11** The whole problem is made worse by the fact that the divine **sentence for a crime is not quickly carried out,** which leads the wicked to fill their hearts **with schemes to do wrong.** Since the action of retribution is not obvious and immediate in many cases, the wicked continue with their oppressions because they seem to be getting away with it. The word **sentence** (*pitgām*) is one of the two examples of Persian words used in Ecclesiastes (also used in Esth 1:20; Ezra; Daniel). The literal meaning is *word* (Ezra 5:7; BDB 834, 1109), which, when it comes from the king is by definition a decree or sentence. This has been a major indicator of the postexilic date of the book. The lack of timely divine retribution may be an allusion to injustices in the contemporary legal system. In an Aramaic text from Elephantine (Egypt), a commoner complained that field work was not remunerated and that the "judges of the province" did not bring justice (Seow 1997, 34).

■ **12** The long life of the **wicked man** is an anomaly. While **wicked man** or "sinner" (*hōte᾿*) is usually used in a nonreligious sense in Wisdom literature, it seems to be used here in a religious sense (see 2:26; 7:26; 9:2, 18). This is not just a bungling fool but a sinner who deserves to die (Fox 1999, 286).

The first part of v 12 presents some ambiguity. The phrase *sinner does evil a hundred* (**a wicked man commits a hundred crimes**) may be short for "a hundred times" (ESV) or it may mean "a great (hundredfold) evil" (see Gordis 1968, 297). Ginsburg's suggestion, "a hundred years," is attractive because it accords with the lack of retribution, that is, a long life for the wicked (1861, 403). *He prolongs* (*ûmaʾărîk lô*, **lives a long time**) probably means that the wicked presumably prolong their lives, even though, according to the doctrine of retribution, they should die young (e.g., Prov 10:21).

Yet in the face of all this evidence to the contrary, Qoheleth cannot give up on the doctrine of retribution (as he has shown elsewhere). While there is no simple correlation between wickedness and early death, Qoheleth is still convinced **that it will go better with God-fearing men, who are reverent before God.** Despite the limitations of righteousness and wisdom, and the mystery of retribution, the benefits of fearing God still outweigh those of wickedness and oppression.

■ **13** Verse 13 is a direct contradiction of v 12, though it uses the vocabulary of v 12. The sinner's life is prolonged (**lives a long time,** *maʾărîk*, v 12) and the wicked person's life will not be prolonged (**not lengthen,** *lōʾ-yaʾărîk*, v 13). It is possible for one writer to contradict himself or herself, even in the next breath. Sometimes this is done for effect and sometimes because the writer is conflicted about which position to take. An alternative explanation is that an editor has added v 13 with the intention of balancing v 12 with a more orthodox perspective. Ecclesiastes 8:12*b*-13 fits with the theology of the epilogue (12:14), which was probably added by an editor. This led Barton to the conclusion that 8:12*b*-13 may also be an addition (1908, 154). But the theology of the epilogue is found elsewhere in the book, except for the call to obey commandments (12:13).

Another possible explanation for contradictions is that traditional wisdom is quoted for the purpose of refuting it. Since Hebrew has no quotation marks, it is difficult to know when a quote is offered (if the writer wishes to clarify this, then certain vocabulary is available, but not all quotes are so marked). A similar explanation is the "yes . . . but" reasoning in which Qoheleth is saying, "Yes, this is true, but this is also true." This is the solution of Hertzberg and Zimmerli (cited by Krüger 2004, 160).

All of these possibilities can be defended by the available evidence. The last has the advantage of making sense of the text as we have it (which is preferred unless there are clear indications of an addition [e.g., the use of the third person in 1:1]). The book as a whole makes sense if Qoheleth is seen as a wisdom teacher who wishes to nuance traditional wisdom teaching, but not to abandon it altogether. While he sees major anomalies with the doctrine of retribution, he cannot abandon it completely. He cannot (at least does not) say how the wicked will be repaid, but he nevertheless holds on to this belief and would never dare to take the risk of abandoning righteousness and wisdom (Crenshaw concedes this point even if it is the view of the community responsible for the final editing, rather than Qoheleth himself; 1987, 156).

■ **14** This mystery is declared **meaningless** twice in v 14 (in the sense of "incomprehensible"). Retribution is not working, although it should (and surely will) work. There is a variation on the realm of this mystery. Instead of the usual "under the sun" (twenty-nine times [e.g., 1:3]) it is **on earth** (ʿal-hāʾāreṣ).

■ **15** In the light of this anomaly, indeed contradiction, in life, Qoheleth makes a recommendation: enjoy life. The days of one's life cannot be controlled by righteousness or wisdom. The length of one's life is a gift from God. Therefore, righteousness and wisdom should not be pursued for the sake of reward, but because it is the right thing to do to fear God and to enjoy whatever lot he has given in life. Long life or wealth are not better than this. There is nothing better **under the sun.** God's sovereignty does not allow human control of destiny through retribution or any other means. Yet he often does punish sin, and a wise person will obey God, just as one would obey the king (8:2).

This enjoyment is different from the pleasure (śimḥâ, the same vocabulary) that was pursued in ch 2, which was a life of wine satisfying the flesh (bayyayin ʾet-běśārî) and of wealth and possessions. Here in 8:15 the joy (śimḥa) is eating and drinking what God has provided (not to excess) and enjoying work (rather than leisure).

C. Sovereignty of God and Limitation of Wisdom (8:16-17)

■ **16-17** The last two verses of this chapter reiterate the point that wisdom and toil are limited. They cannot lead to control or comprehension, because these belong to God alone. **Even if a wise man claims he knows, he cannot really comprehend it** (v 17). All the searching is fruitless, and in the end one must accept the sovereignty of God and enjoy the portion in life he has given.

The phrase **eyes not seeing sleep** (v 16) is unusual. The more common expression in the OT is "give sleep to my eyes" (Prov 6:4; Ps 132:4; Gen 31:40). Not seeing sleep has parallels in the Latin texts of Terence and Cicero (Barton 1908, 157).

Verses 16 and 17 belong together as the **when** of v 16 (protasis) is resolved in the **then** of v 17 (apodosis). Verse 17 reiterates the limitation of wisdom in the light of the lack of human comprehension. Another Aramaism occurs in this verse (běšel ʾăšer, **despite;** see Jonah 1:7, 12; Whitley 1979, 77). The word for **wise man** (ḥākām) seems to have the technical sense of a wisdom teacher here, although it is usually used in the OT in a more general sense (e.g., Gen 41:33; Eccl 2:14-16; Crenshaw 1987, 34).

FROM THE TEXT

Wisdom: Value and Limitations

Chapter 8 begins with a very positive statement about wisdom: it brightens the face. While positive statements have already been made about wisdom (e.g., 2:13-14), such a positive statement is still surprising given the great efforts of Qoheleth to nuance the value of wisdom, and hence the doctrine of retribution. This chapter also carries warnings about the limitations of wisdom (v 17).

Sovereignty of Kings and God

The sovereignty of God is an important theme in Ecclesiastes, and it is often illustrated with reference to an earthly king. The inability of humans to control outcomes is evident in the breakdown of the doctrine of retribution and in the inability to ask the question **What are you doing?** to king or God (v 4). This is a warning to those who would try to use the doctrine of retribution to manipulate God into providing material blessings. Righteousness should be an expression of the fear of God, not a spiritual means to a material end.

Two areas of life in particular that cannot be controlled are the timing of death (v 8) and knowledge of the future (v 7).

Mystery of Retribution

In the perfect world of the wisdom teachers, as presented to youth in their formative period, righteousness leads to a long life of blessing, while wickedness leads to destruction in an untimely death. However, in the real world, one can often observe the righteous getting **what the wicked deserve** (v 14). Nevertheless, the king should be obeyed and God feared, as **wickedness will not release those who practice it** (v 8). There is justice (**procedure,** v 6) for everything, and while the timing and method of this justice may be beyond comprehension (v 17), the days of the wicked **will not lengthen like a shadow** (v 13).

Enjoy Life

Wisdom and justice are elusive, and the sovereignty of God and king is inscrutable. The only course of action left for the ordinary person is to enjoy life (within the bounds of obedience and fear of God) for there is nothing better (v 15).

XI. THE SAME DESTINY OVERTAKES ALL (9:1-18)

BEHIND THE TEXT

Chapter 9 continues Qoheleth's argument with more reflection on the injustice of life. The themes of ch 9 are almost the same as those of ch 8. Chapter 9 presents the elusiveness of justice without the optimism of ch 8. Chapter 9 also continues the theme of the sovereignty of God. Qoheleth values wisdom but considers it ineffective because there are those who despise it (ch 8 emphasized the elusiveness of wisdom).

The story of a besieged city in 9:13-16 could have been based on a historical situation. However, there are very few clues to specific history in Ecclesiastes, and most scholars now agree that this account is a fictional example story. Suggestions for the historical context in the past included the siege of Dor by Antiochus III (218 B.C.) or Antiochus VII; the siege of Abel Beth Maacah (2 Sam 20:16) or of Beth-sura by Antiochus V, or that of Syracuse by the Romans (212 B.C.). Others suggested the city in question could be Athens or Themistocles (Kinlaw 1968, 628).

Sheol

Ecclesiastes only uses the Hebrew word for the underworld once (šĕʾôl; 9:10), which is remarkable considering Qoheleth's preoccupation with death. However, the OT mentions death and dying over one thousand times, but names Sheol less than one hundred times, and Ecclesiastes often mentions death without using this vocabulary (e.g., "All go to the same place," 3:20). Ancient Israelites did not have a developed view of the afterlife, preferring to focus instead on the present life. This began to change after the exile, and by the time of the NT events, there was a developed view of the resurrection among Jewish teachers (Pharisees), although some groups resisted this new development (Sadducees). Sheol in the OT is not heaven, for only God was believed to live in the sky (in conscious rejection of polytheism). Neither is Sheol hell, as it is not a place of torment or punishment. Its location is variously described as under the earth (Num 16:30) or in the lower part of the cosmic ocean (Job 26:7). It is a place for all the dead regardless of their relationship with God (Job 30:23), and a place where everyone is free from misery (Job 3:17). It is not a place of bliss or praising God (Ps 6:5) but a place of silence (Ps 94:17). It is a city with gates (Job 38:17) and there is no return street from this city (Job 16:22). No one wished to be trapped in Sheol and so to miss out on life (except Job in times of despair; Job 14:13; see Ps 49:15). It is a dark and gloomy place (Job 17:13). It was not the soul (nepeš) or spirit (ruah) that was believed to be in Sheol, but the shade ("weak ones," rĕpāʾîm; Ps 88:10), as those in Sheol are not alive and do not breathe (spirit/breath).

The genre of ch 9 is reflection, including sayings (e.g., v 4, "a live dog is better off than a dead lion"), instruction (vv 7-10), and example story (vv 13-16). The phrase **no man knows** is repeated with variation in vv 1 and 12, and the words **destiny** and **happen** in vv 2 and 11 come from the same root (qārah). This chapter can be outlined as follows:

The Same Destiny for Righteous and Wicked (9:1-6)
Enjoy Life (9:7-10)
Success Is Unpredictable (9:11-12)
The Results of Wisdom Are Unpredictable (9:13-18)

IN THE TEXT

A. The Same Destiny for Righteous and Wicked (9:1-6)

■ 1 In v 1, Qoheleth concludes that human destiny is subject to the will of God. The word for **concluded** (lābûr) is unique in the OT. BDB (101) lists the meaning as probably "make clear, clear up, explain" and notes the similarity with another verb "to purify, select" (bārar). Grätz observed the similarity with *lātûr* (**explore**), which is a common word in Ecclesiastes (1:13; 2:3; 7:25) (cited in BDB 101). Many of the ancient translations, however, render the word as "see."

Once again Qoheleth gives his heart (**reflected on**) to the fate of the righteous and the wise, and he concludes that their fate is in **God's hands.** Wisdom and righteousness do not guarantee escape from the destiny of death. Moreover, no one knows whether God will respond with actions of **love or hate.** Qoheleth observes in his world the failure of the doctrine of retribution, which leads him to claim that no one can predict who will experience God's love or hate. "The same destiny overtakes all" (v 2), namely death.

■ **2** In v 2 Qoheleth sums up his argument that **a common destiny** awaits all, whether **righteous** or **wicked, good** or **bad,** ritually **clean** or **unclean,** and religious or not. Here he juxtaposes the characteristics of those who are good and those who are evil. In previous chapters he already dealt with the wise and **the righteous.** The **good and the bad** are not dealt with elsewhere, and **the bad** is not in the Hebrew text (but is in the Septuagint, Syriac, and Latin). The closest parallel to this pair is **the good man** and **the sinner** in this verse. The opposites of **clean** and **unclean, those who offer sacrifices and those who do not, those who take oaths** and those who do not, are a new element, as Ecclesiastes does not often refer to religious ritual (and also avoids mention of the history of Israel).

■ **3** Qoheleth calls the lack of retribution an **evil** in that both good and bad have **the same destiny,** namely death. He has no answer to this problem. The NT will later follow further developments in Judaism that see the answer in the resurrection and subsequent judgment for all. Qoheleth is stuck with the standard OT understanding that knows of no resurrection, but sees everyone going to Sheol, the place of **the dead,** which is neither punishment nor bliss. In Sheol there is no distinction between the righteous and the wicked.

■ **4** Verse 4 argues that **anyone who is among the living has hope.** The word **among** (*yĕhubbar*, literally, *joined with*) follows the reading that is supported by many Hebrew manuscripts and ancient translations (the written text here in the MT is *yibbāḥēr*, which means "chosen") (Krüger 2004, 167). This reading is positive about life, whereas elsewhere Qoheleth has been negative about life. Nevertheless, the next verse will show the sarcasm in Qoheleth's presentation of the proverb. **Hope** is a rare word based on a more common root meaning "trust, confidence." The word is used elsewhere only in Isa 36:15 (see 2 Kgs 18:30), where it means confidence for victory in battle.

The grievous evil of the lack of justice caused Qoheleth to say in 6:3 that a stillborn child is better off than someone who lacks contentment, but here he puts life ahead of death so that it would be better to be a **living dog** than **a dead lion.** Lions were obvious symbols of strength in ancient Israel, while dogs

9:1-4

were despised as scavengers and were certainly not "man's best friend" (ABD 6:1143; 1 Kgs 14:11; 16:4; 21:19; Prov 30:30). Dogs were used as a metaphor for enemies and for derision (1 Sam 17:43; Ps 22:16, 20). To be called a "dead dog" was an even stronger insult (2 Sam 9:8; 16:9). The comparison of a living dog and a dead lion is a popular proverb that has made its way into a number of different languages and cultures (Ginsburg 1861, 412). Even in Western culture where dogs and cats are adored as pets, the lowly place of the dog is preserved in many sayings.

Rabbi Hiya on the Righteous as Living

My son, you know Scripture but not *Midrash*. FOR THE LIVING KNOW refers to the righteous who are called LIVING even in their death; BUT THE DEAD KNOW NOT refers to the wicked who, even in their lifetime, are called DEAD. (In Cohen 1983, 229)

■ **5** Verse 5 portrays a negative view of death and Sheol. The living at least have hope of seeing justice done in their lives or lifetime (v 4), but the dead are trapped in Sheol (they were not believed to have the power to roam around the earth as spirits) and **know nothing. They have no further reward** because Sheol is not a place of reward or punishment; it is not eternal life, but only eternal death. **Even the memory of them is forgotten.** There is a wordplay with the similar sounds of **reward** (*śākār*), **forgotten** (*niškaḥ*), and **memory** (*zikrām*). In a culture that has no view of a meaningful afterlife, one lives on after death through children and memory. For Qoheleth this is a shallow kind of immortality.

Qoheleth has decried the lack of memory elsewhere. There is no remembrance of former things (1:11) or wise people (2:16) or of a poor wise man who saved a city (9:15). However, lack of memory is positive for those gifted by God, for they will not remember the (difficult) days of their life (5:20). Later in the book, Qoheleth will recommend remembering the many days of darkness (11:8) and remembering one's Creator while young (12:1).

There is irony in this comparison of the living and the dead, as Qoheleth has quoted a proverb in 9:4 about the value of life, only to define that value in v 5 as the knowledge of death. This is a hollow advantage indeed (Delitzsch 1875, 360).

■ **6** In v 1, Qoheleth used love and hate as actions that would come from God as reward or punishment. In the expected justice of retribution, God's love would correlate with actions of love by the person in question, and so also for hate. In v 6, the lack of this expected justice is such that the actions of love and hate are forgotten after death and no longer make a difference. Both lovers and haters are trapped in Sheol with no further prospect for justice.

In many places, Qoheleth has proclaimed that there is no profit to be gained from toil, wisdom, and righteousness. Instead people should enjoy the portion that God has given them, as they cannot control the outcome of their future. Here in 9:6, Qoheleth argues that the dead have no portion (**part, heleq**) to enjoy. They will never again have the opportunity to enjoy what is done **under the sun,** as they do not see the sun in Sheol.

B. Enjoy Life (9:7-10)

■ **7** Verse 7 is advice to enjoy life. Qoheleth does not usually use the imperative mood when he gives his advice to enjoy life (2:24; 3:12-13, 22; 5:18; 7:14; 8:15; 11:8-9). The imperative mood here conveys strong advice. Other imperatives have involved behavior before God (5:1-8) and king (8:2-3). So once again Qoheleth advises enjoyment of food and drink (9:7). That is what God wants (**favors,** *rāṣâ*). This could be in opposition to what God does not want, namely striving for profit or attempting to control outcomes through wisdom and righteousness, since God is sovereign and outcomes are in his hand.

■ **8** This enjoyment is to be conducted with "gladness" (*śimḥâ*) and "a joyful heart" (*leb-ṭôb*) (v 7). Thus the appropriate clothing is **white,** that is, not the clothing of mourning, or clothing dirtied by the dust and ashes of grief. White clothing was worn by Mordecai on a festive occasion (Esth 8:15) and white clothing is worn by the righteous in Rev 3:4, 5; 7:9. Along with white clothing, Qoheleth advises that one's head should be anointed with olive oil, the ancient equivalent of shampoo or lotion (see Pss 23:5; 45:7; 104:15; Prov 27:9; Matthews 1991, 24, 26, 326).

■ **9** In v 9 Qoheleth adds enjoyment in marriage to his prescription to enjoy eating and drinking. Life is short (**meaningless,** *hebel*) and is a gift from God. Therefore whatever portion (**lot,** *ḥelqĕkā*) he has given should be enjoyed. There is no guarantee that righteousness or wisdom can extend life or prosperity, so this should not be the motivation for toil.

In Hebrew the word for **wife** is the same as "woman" (*ʾiššâ*). In this case the definite article is expected as in *"the* woman that you love." Since there is no article in the Hebrew text, the meaning is technically *"a* woman that you love" (*ʾiššâ ʾăšer-ʾāhabtā*). However, Qoheleth is not suggesting promiscuity here. Ginsburg argued that because of the lack of article, the meaning is not **wife** but sensual gratification with no reference to the context of marriage (1861, 417). However, this is probably just another example of the erratic use of the article in Ecclesiastes, and the qualifiers **whom you love** ("love" in Hebrew emphasizes acts of commitment) and **all the days** suggest that a life-long marital partner is in view (and not just any woman). Even though love is temporary (v 6), Qoheleth still commends it. The advice of this verse could equally apply to women but is specifically addressed to men; Qoheleth has a male audience in mind (which is usual for the wisdom teachers). The advice is similar to that given by Siduri, the tavern keeper in the ancient Akkadian document Epic of Gilgamesh (Qoheleth probably knew of the story; Seow 1997, 64).

The last half of v 9 is missing from some manuscripts, which suggests it may have been added in error. If this is so, then the occurrences of *hebel* in the book would be thirty-seven, which equals the numerical value of that word (Wright 1980, 44).

■ **10** Verse 10 advises working hard because **where you are going, there is** no **working . . . planning . . . knowledge** or **wisdom.** The word **going** in connection with Sheol (**grave**) is consistent with Qoheleth's earlier use of this word to indicate death (1:4; 6:6). The advice to work hard is linked to the enjoyment of life. Since there is no meaningful afterlife in his thinking, this life is the only opportunity to appropriate God's gift of food, drink, marriage, and life itself.

John Ruskin on Eccl 9:10 (1868)

Ask the labourer in the field, at the forge, or in the mine; ask the patient, delicate-fingered artisan, or the strong-armed, fiery-hearted worker in bronze . . . and none of these, who are true workmen, will ever tell you, that they have found the law of heaven an unkind one—that in the sweat of their face they should eat bread, till they return to the ground; nor that they ever found it an unrewarded obedience, if, indeed, it was rendered faithfully to the command—"Whatsoever thy hand findeth to do—do it with thy might." (In Christianson 2007, 213)

C. Success Is Unpredictable (9:11-12)

■ **11** The theme of 9:1-6 is repeated in 9:11-12. In the former, a common destiny awaits the righteous, unrighteous, clean, unclean, oath takers, and those who avoid oaths. Death awaits all. In the latter, **time and chance** await both **the swift** and the slow, **the strong** and the weak, **the brilliant** and **the learned.** Even those who are expected to succeed in the world are eventually overcome by death, and they do not know when that event will occur.

The sport of running footraces was part of Greek culture but not Hebrew culture. Greek contests were probably introduced into Palestine during the time of Antiochus Epiphanes IV (174-164 B.C.), who approved the building of a gymnasium (Coogan 2001, 326). In Hebrew culture the race was often important in war because a fleeing soldier would be expected to have an advantage if he were a faster runner (2 Sam 2:18-23; Amos 2:15) and speed was also important for couriers (2 Sam 18:19-32). The next statement specifies that a battle is in mind as **the battle** is not **to the strong.** The stronger soldier is expected to win the battle, but this is not always the case. The point of the story of David and Goliath in 1 Sam 17 is to show the superiority of Yahweh over Goliath and the pagan gods. Qoheleth has no such agenda. The unexpected outcome is simply chance and another indication of the unreliability of life. Elsewhere in Ecclesiastes the threat of war is possibly a major cause of the unreliability of retribution theology (see 3:1-8; 12:1-8). The specific mention of war in 9:11 suggests that the outcome of war is unpredictable, just as war makes the outcome of retribution unpredictable.

From the battle scene, Qoheleth turns to everyday life and argues that intelligence and learning do not always provide **wealth** and **favor** as expected. Instead, the mysteries of **time and chance** reduce the reliability of speed, strength, intelligence, and education. There is no explicit mention of the sovereignty of God here, unlike 9:1, where the righteous and wise are in God's hands.

■ **12** Because advantages do not always yield victory, no one **knows when his hour will come.** The time of death comes unexpectedly, like a trap that snaps on an unsuspecting bird, or *an evil net* (**cruel net,** *bimṣôdâ rāʿâ*) catching a fish. Likewise *an evil time* (**evil times,** *ʿēt rāʿâ*) will catch each person in death. The times and seasons are under God's control (3:1-8); the tone of resignation in 3:1-8 changes to resentment in 9:12 as the time of death is unexpected and unwelcome, something to be feared, as a bird takes flight at any hint of a trap. Yet the bird/fish/human is trapped anyway. This could be a return to the theme of war. If war comes upon a land, the whole population experiences **evil times** (see 11:2).

D. The Results of Wisdom Are Unpredictable (9:13-18)

■ **13** Despite the unexpected timing of death, 9:13-18 now relates a story that shows the superiority of wisdom that, if followed, could lead to some delay of the day of death. This example of wisdom **greatly impressed** Qoheleth and stands in contrast with the impotence of speed and strength in v 11. However, the power of wisdom is also limited, either because the townsfolk did not take the wise advice, or they soon forgot the wise man once the danger had passed, so that wisdom gave no lasting advantage to the man who possessed it. Perhaps the lack of lasting value of wisdom **impressed** Qoheleth as much as the superiority of wisdom.

■ **14** The story is drawn from the scenario of war, which may be one of the main contingencies that Qoheleth sees as diminishing the application of the retribution theology. The story relates a **small city** with few inhabitants being attacked by a great king who **surrounded** the city and built great siege works against it. The word for siege works in the Hebrew text has the same spelling as "net" (*maṣôd*) used in v 12. Some Hebrew manuscripts and the Septuagint favor the reading *maṣôr* (**siegeworks**) instead of the MT *maṣôd* (scribal error due to confusion between *dalet* and *resh*). The verb **built** favors the reading **siegeworks** (*maṣôr*) in this verse.

155

15 In this situation the greater power of the attacking king would be expected to prevail, but instead a **poor but wise** man was found who was able to save **the city by his wisdom.** Apparently he did save the city, thus proving the superiority of wisdom over military power, but then **nobody remembered that poor man.** The word *remember* has the sense "give thought to" in 12:1 ("Remember your Creator"). A similar event occurred in 2 Sam 20:16 where a wise woman saved her town, Abel Beth Maacah, by throwing the head of Sheba over the wall to Joab and the attacking Israelite army.

A **wise** man who is **poor** is a contradiction of the retribution theology because wisdom should lead to a level of prosperity. The word for **poor** (*miskēn*) is used only in 4:13; 9:15-16 in biblical Hebrew, but is common in Aramaic. This is typical of the affinity of the language of Qoheleth with Aramaic.

16 Nevertheless, **wisdom is better than strength** because wisdom was able to save the city when strength was lacking, and wisdom was able to overcome the greater strength of the attacking king. However, the strength of wisdom did not last long because the people **despised** his wisdom and his words were **no longer heeded.** Wisdom did not have lasting value or strength. Though **wisdom is better than strength,** it is limited in what it can achieve.

17 The attacking king may have been shouting demands for surrender as he surrounded the city, but **the quiet words of the wise are more to be heeded than the shouts of a ruler of fools** (v 17). The Babylonian attackers shouted their demands to those on the wall of Jerusalem in the time of King Hezekiah. The officials of Jerusalem asked them to speak in Aramaic rather than Hebrew so that the populace would not be demoralized by their words (2 Kgs 18:26). The general statement of 9:17, however, may have in mind the shouting of the ruler within the besieged city, who would not listen to the advice of the wise poor man.

18 "Wisdom is better than strength" (v 16) but is nevertheless vulnerable to sabotage by **one sinner** or someone who misses the point (v 18). The word **sinner** (*hôteʾ*) is not usually used in a religious sense in Wisdom literature and seems to have the more literal sense here of someone who misses an opportunity through incompetence.

The particular word for **war** in v 18 is unusual (*qĕrāb* instead of *milḥāmâ*, 3:8; 8:8). It comes from the word "approach" and is used in the sense of a hostile approach (BDB 898a; see Zech 14:3; Pss 55:18; 68:30; 78:9; 144:1; Job 38:23; Dan 7:21). The superiority of wisdom over **weapons of war** is similar to the English proverb "the pen is mightier than the sword" (see Prov 20:18).

Despite Qoheleth's awareness of the limitations of wisdom, he has yet again proclaimed the superiority of wisdom over other possibilities such as folly, or in this case, military power.

Mystery of Retribution

Qoheleth challenges the operation of retribution in ch 9 with the argument that all are alike in death, which is such a sad state that one would rather be a (live) dog. Six verses are devoted to this anomaly, which is answered by the NT doctrine of resurrection, a doctrine alien to the OT.

Enjoy Life

Given the rejection of a meaningful afterlife, Qoheleth advises joy in the present life, **for this is your lot** (v 9). This advice is connected directly with the lack of afterlife, for it is in this life that one must be motivated to work and enjoy life (v 10). While Qoheleth is serious about this advice to enjoy life, and has a positive view of life as a gift from God, he also feels the loss of justice and speaks about the lack of afterlife with a certain bitterness in his tone (9:1-3). He is not advocating "eat, drink and be merry for tomorrow we die" (rejected by Paul in 1 Cor 15:32), nor would he agree with Paul that "we are to be pitied more than all men" without a resurrection (1 Cor 15:19). Yet there is something missing.

In this sense Qoheleth serves as a setup for the NT doctrine of resurrection. In the resurrection the inequities of this life will be rectified and the enjoyment of life will not be fleeting (*hebel*, see Delitzsch 1875, 361). Bonhoeffer saw a profound connection between enjoyment of this life and hope in the resurrection (1997, 157). Davis calls the book "a kind of preface to the New Testament" (2000, 169).

Wisdom: Value and Limitations

The value of wisdom is expressed through a story of a wise poor man who saved his besieged city by wisdom. Wisdom has enduring strength only if the community remembers and pays attention to the words of the wise (even the words of the poor person with wisdom). Wisdom's words are quiet but powerful and good for those who give heed to them. However, whatever good wisdom accumulates can be destroyed by **one sinner** (v 18), a fool who refuses to pay attention to words of wisdom.

XII. FLIES IN THE OINTMENT (10:1-20)

BEHIND THE TEXT

Chapter 10 continues significant themes from ch 9, including the value and limitations of wisdom, the sovereignty of kings, and the mystery of retribution. There is a reference to laughter but not the same emphasis on enjoying life that chs 8 and 9 have. Chapters 11 and 12 emphasize joy again as Qoheleth gives concluding advice to his young audience, including advising generosity and remembering God.

A number of everyday activities are mentioned in 10:7-18. Horses were used for transport only by kings or the wealthy, certainly not by slaves (v 7); pits were dug and concealed to trap animals (v 8); stone walls were havens for snakes (v 8); stone was a prime building material for foundations and had to be quarried (v 9); timber was cut with axes (v 10); snakes were charmed to remove them from dwellings (v 11); and roofs supported by wooden beams had to be maintained every year before the rainy season (v 18).

The genre of ch 10 is a collection of sayings, including instruction (v 4) and reflection (v 10). The chapter can be outlined as follows:

Folly Can Outweigh Wisdom (10:1-7)
Results Can Be Unpredictable (10:8-15)
Benefits of a Wise King (10:16-20)

IN THE TEXT

A. Folly Can Outweigh Wisdom (10:1-7)

■ I Qoheleth continues the theme of the previous verse (9:18) in ch 10, namely that a little folly can outweigh much wisdom. In this case, a colorful and famous image is used to convey the truth, **dead flies give perfume a bad smell.** This comparison gives rise to the common English saying "a fly in the ointment," meaning that a great deal of good can be spoiled by a small amount that is bad (also in another English proverb, "One bad apple spoils the whole bunch").

The Hebrew for **dead flies** is literally *flies of death* (*zĕbûbê māwet*), but it is not really deadly flies or flies buzzing around a carcass that are in question here. It is apparently a dead fly that has begun to rot that causes a bad smell to come from the perfume. Thus BHS suggests reading "a dead fly" (*zĕbûb mēt*). This requires deleting two letters from the Hebrew text, and there is no textual evidence for this emendation, although most modern translations follow a similar emendation. In addition to **give . . . a bad smell** there is another verb (*yabbia*ʿ, meaning "makes it bubble" or "ferment") in the first line, which is lacking in some of the ancient translations. Modern translations also leave it out (so NIV). The Septuagint reading suggests the Hebrew word *gābiaʿ*, meaning "cup, bowl" (Fox 1999, 301).

The application for Qoheleth is wisdom and folly. It is part of the breakdown of retribution that folly carries more weight than wisdom in many cases. **A little folly** from a wise person can have great consequences for life and reputation, just as a small fly can spoil a whole jar of perfume (Ibn Ezra, in Ginsburg 1861, 424), and as "yeast works through the whole batch of dough" (1 Cor 5:6). This is consistent with Qoheleth's observation of the limitations of wisdom, but so is Ginsburg's interpretation, that it is the folly of others that subverts the effectiveness of the wise (1861, 424).

Often Quoted by John B. Bennett

A moment of foolishness can undo a lifetime of preparation. (Origin unknown)

■**2** The heart of the wise inclines to the right but that **of the fool to the left** conveys Qoheleth's preference for wisdom over folly. In Hebrew culture the right hand side was to be preferred as reflected in names such as Benjamin ("son of my right hand") and sayings such as "Your right hand, O LORD, glorious in power" (Exod 15:6 NRSV). Left-handedness was considered abnormal and viewed with suspicion. This characteristic is mentioned as a disadvantage of the judge Ehud, although it became an advantage in his assassination of Eglon as the weapon was concealed on the opposite side from what Eglon expected (Judg 3:21; see also Matt 25:33). The preference for the right is also reflected in English. The right hand is "right" (i.e., "correct," "proper"), while the left hand is "left" (i.e., "left over"). The English word "sinister" comes from the Latin for "left."

■**3** So the wise are on the right path, while fools are on the wrong path. The analogy of walking down a path is important in Wisdom literature, and elsewhere it is God's Word that lights the path (Ps 119:105), and God who will make one's paths straight (i.e., "easy"; Prov 3:6).

The very conduct of the fool **shows everyone how stupid he is** (see Prov 12:23; 13:16). Ancient versions convey the idea here that fools consider everyone else to be stupid. Arrogance and folly tend to go together, and Qoheleth may have intended the ambiguity (which would be consistent with his style).

■**4** As a little folly can outweigh great wisdom, the opposite is sometimes the case. In v 4 Qoheleth gives more advice on conduct before a king (see 8:2; 10:20). While he had earlier advised rushing away from the king's presence to carry out his orders, he now advises staying in place, even if **a ruler's anger rises against you.** This is because **calmness can lay great errors to rest.** This was the experience of young David, whose music would calm King Saul when "the evil spirit from God was upon Saul" (1 Sam 16:23 ESV). The vocabulary in v 4 also uses "spirit" (**anger,** *rûaḥ*). The **calmness** that is needed is literally *healing* (*marpēʾ*). There is also a dual use of the word *rest* (*nûaḥ*) in this verse. This word can also mean "leave" in the causative stem (**do not leave;** the name Noah comes from this root).

■**5** In v 5 Qoheleth moves again to his observation of the breakdown of retribution, which is **an evil I have seen under the sun.** This time it is **the sort of error that arises from a ruler,** as rulers are apparently the cause of the anomaly about to be disclosed or at least they fail to use their power to correct the wrong. It is possible to translate **the sort of** as *indeed* so that the error actually comes from the king and does not merely resemble a royal error (Whybray 1989, 170). Ultimately it is God who is the ruler responsible for the breakdown of retribution because he should be enforcing blessings for the righteous and curses for the wicked. It is a mystery of life that he, in his sovereignty, does not.

■ 6 The evil in this case is that **fools are put in many high positions, while the rich occupy the low ones** (v 6). The **rich** are associated with the competent and the blessed. The word **fools** is actually *folly* (*sekel*) in Hebrew, although ancient translations render it "the fool."

■ 7 Verse 7 continues with another example of the anomaly. Qoheleth has **seen slaves on horseback, while princes go on foot like slaves** (see Jer 17:25). The word **slave** (*'ebed*) comes from the verb "to work, serve" and has a broad range of meaning, including high-ranking officers of the king (2 Sam 19:17). In this verse, however, a contrast is drawn between the low rank of a **slave** and the high rank of a **prince** or ruler, which is why the reversal of roles is shocking (see Prov 19:10; 30:22).

B. Results Can Be Unpredictable (10:8-15)

■ 8-9 The examples change in vv 8 and 9. In a similar vein to the doctrine of retribution, workers expect to receive the rewards for their labor but so often an accident prevents the expected outcome. The one who **digs a pit** falls into it, and the one who **breaks through a wall** is **bitten by a snake** (v 8). The word **pit** (*gûmmās*) is found only here in the OT but is found elsewhere in Aramaic. The connection between the wall and the snake is apparently to be found in the habit of snakes building their nests in stone walls. These have many gaps where animals can enter (see Amos 5:19; Ginsburg 1861, 429). Verse 9 conveys a similar thought. Someone quarries stones for a specific purpose but instead is **injured by them,** and logs are split for construction but the logger is **endangered by them** (v 9). The word *yissāken* (**endangered**) is also unique in the OT but occurs in postbiblical Hebrew (Whybray 1989, 153). This preponderance of unique words (*hapax legomena*) that are also found in Aramaic or postbiblical Hebrew is often explained in terms of a postexilic date for Ecclesiastes. Even if these words existed in colloquial Hebrew from preexilic times, they are not found in the literature until later so they still suggest a postexilic date for Ecclesiastes.

Calvin on the Dangers of Life

Embark upon a ship, you are one step away from death. Mount a horse, if one foot slips, your life is imperiled. Go through the city streets, you are subject to as many dangers as there are tiles on the roofs. (*Institutes* 1.17.10; quoted in Brown 2007, 77)

■ 10-11 Verses 10 and 11 give examples of retribution in action. Wisdom makes the difference in these settings, especially the kind of practical wisdom used by an artisan such as that which was helpful to Bezalel (Exod 35:30-31). A skillful (wise) wood cutter will use a sharp ax and save strength, but **if the ax is dull . . . , more strength is needed** (v 10). The word for **ax** is literally *iron* (*barzel*, also in 2 Kgs 6:5). **Unsharpened** is an extended meaning of the verb *qilqal* ("to polish"; BDB 886b). This unusual vocabulary gives way to difficult syntax in the second half of the verse. **Skill will bring success** is literally *profit causes success wisdom*. The profit that brings success is wisdom, or wisdom (**skill**) brings success and profit (for **success** see 2:21; 4:4; 5:11; 11:6).

Likewise, an experienced snake charmer must use his skill (wisdom) to avoid a snake bite (v 11). The snake **charmer** is literally *lord of the tongue* (*lĕbaʿal hallāšôn*). This possibly relates to a profession that removed unwanted snakes, attracting them by striking the wall with a stick, whistles, clucking noises, spitting, and curses or magic formulas, as nineteenth-century travelers to Egypt observed (Ginsburg 1861, 435). Verse 11 contrasts the lack of **profit** for the unsuccessful snake charmer with the profit (*yitrôn*, **success**) of the skillful worker in v 10. Verses 10-11 convey commonsense cause and effect in action (retribution). Qoheleth is aware of the benefits of wisdom as well as the limitations. Perhaps this connection is meant to imply that wisdom would make the difference in the scenarios of vv 8-9 also (Delitzsch 1875, 379).

■ **12-15** Qoheleth is more specific about the superiority of the wise over fools in 10:12-15. The wise are careful with their helpful **words** (v 12) while fools multiply words that begin in **folly** and end in the worst kind of **madness** (vv 13-14). The translation **words of the wise . . . are gracious** (v 12) assumes that favor comes from the wise, but it could also be that favor comes to the wise. Fools do not realize the limitations of their own knowledge or even of knowledge in general (v 14). The pronouncement in v 14 about the unknown future is a quote from earlier in the book (6:12; 7:14; and 8:7) and interrupts the flow of the discussion of fools. It takes a truly wise person to know the limitations of wisdom and knowledge and to realize that retribution has serious inconsistencies. Fools have not come to this point, but they are full of their own importance and continue to make pronouncements about the future based on the standard understanding of cause and effect. They are deluded, however, as **no one knows what is coming—who can tell him what will happen after him?** Qoheleth concludes by saying that fools weary themselves as their lack of skill leads to inefficiency and they cannot even find their **way to town,** let alone to success (v 15). There may be no guarantee that wisdom will lead to success, but what is clear to Qoheleth is the fact that foolishness will only lead to disaster.

C. Benefits of a Wise King (10:16-20)

■ **16** Verse 16 has a warning for those whose ruler was a **servant** and whose princes live a life of indulgence and revelry. An unusual word is used for **woe** (*ʾî*), which occurs only twice in the Bible (4:10; 10:16) and is also used in rabbinical literature (BDB 33a). The usual Hebrew words are *hôy* and *ʾôy*, which are used when someone has died (e.g., Amos 5:16-18, where it is used in the context of punishment for breaking covenant) or is about to die (Isa 24:16). The word *naʿar* (**servant**) is usually used for someone of teenage years (a boy or a young person), even someone of fighting age (Abraham's warriors in Gen 14:24), while the word *yeled* (child) is typically for younger children. It is not certain, however, that age is in view here. As "boy" sometimes has a derogatory sense in English, so *naʿar* can refer to a servant who is an adult (e.g., Num 22:22).

The **princes** (*śar*) who **feast in the morning** are not necessarily the sons of the king in the narrow sense that "prince" usually has in English. The Hebrew *śar* is the general word for a ruler who is subordinate to the king. These rulers begin their revelry (and drunkenness?) early in the day, that is, earlier than they should, when other matters should be taken care of first. They are indulging themselves (see Acts 2:15; Isa 5:11).

■ **17** Verse 17 provides a contrast with v 16. Rather than the curse implied in the "woe" for the land whose rulers are incompetent, there is a blessing for the land whose rulers are nobility. **Blessed** is the common result for those who are wise (see Ps 1) and comes from a verb with the basic meaning "go straight" (BDB 80b). A straight path is an easier path. This blessing is for the land whose king is a son of the nobility and whose **princes** feast at the appropriate **time**. **Noble birth** is literally *son of free men* (*ben-ḥôrîm*). The assumption is that a king of noble birth has received the proper education and training to bring blessing on the land as king (see 9:15; 10:6).

The princes or rulers of this blessed land feast *in time,* that is, at the appropriate time (not in the morning as in v 16). Their reason for feasting is to gain **strength** (*gĕbûrâ*), not because they are drunkards (see Prov 31:5-7).

■ **18** Qoheleth states the consequences of laziness in v 18. The noun "laziness" (**lazy**) is in the dual number, signifying an intense laziness (Delitzsch 1875, 388). The lazy person's roof will **sag** (*yimmak*) and, as **his hands are idle** (*šiplût* means "sink"), **the house leaks.** The words **rafters** (*mĕqāreh*) and **idle** (*šiplût*) here are unique in the OT. The usual word for **rafters** is *qôrâ* (Gen 19:8; Song 1:17). **Sag** (*yimmak*) is also a rare word, occurring only in 10:18; Ps 106:43; and Job 24:24. Laziness is a common theme in Proverbs (e.g., Prov 6:10). In the context of the previous two verses, this could easily be applied to kingdoms that are ruled by lazy leaders (Ginsburg 1861, 442) as a kingdom or dynasty is often called a "house" (2 Sam 7:16).

■ **19** In v 19 Qoheleth quotes a proverb that is in line with his advice to enjoy life (e.g., 9:9), including eating, drinking, and wealth. These things should not be the orientation of life (especially for rulers, see 10:16-17), but neither should the worries of life (and death) that prevent one from enjoying the moment at hand. Wealth answers **everything** in the sense that life can have problems without it. It can be a temporary answer as with the prodigal son (Luke

15:13), or it can be used to build relationships (as with the shrewd manager who was fired; Luke 16:9).

The verb **answer** (ʿanah) can also be translated *afflict*, which is seen in the Syriac version, "money oppresses and leads them astray" (Ginsburg 1861, 443). While excess money can cause problems in life, this does not seem to be one of Qoheleth's arguments. It is likely that there is some sarcasm in Qoheleth's statement "money answers everything" (ESV) as it is possible that members of his audience had oriented their lives around money and thought more of this new commodity than they should have. Using another nuance of ʿanah, a key word in Ecclesiastes (e.g., 4:8, "business"; 5:20, "occupied"), Seow translates this line as "money preoccupies everyone" (1997, 328).

■ **20** Verse 20 has a warning not to **curse** the king or rulers, even in private. One's actions have a way of becoming known and the king may find out, with disastrous consequences (see Luke 12:3). The form of the word **in your thoughts** (běmaddāʿăkā) has been influenced by Aramaic and is found elsewhere in the OT only in 2 Chr 1:10-12 and Dan 1:4, 17 (Barton 1908, 179).

The Persian government employed spies (known in Greek sources as Eyes and Ears of the king) who would apprise the king of the dealings of ordinary people (Briant 2002, 344). Ecclesiastes 10:20 seems to have this situation in mind when it warns against speaking against the king, **because a bird of the air may carry your words.** This reference is paralleled in the Aramaic *Proverbs of Ahiqar*, which warn "a [b]ird is a word," also in the context of warning against cursing (Krüger 2004, 189; Matthews and Benjamin 2006, 304). In the Midrash of Hag 2:11, the wall is said to have ears (Ginsburg 1861, 445).

Proverbs of Ahiqar

[My] son, do not [curse] the day until you see [its end].

May [this] come to your attention, that in every place their [i.e., the gods'] [eyes] and their ears are near to your mouth. Take care that it does not destroy [your] advantages.

Before all others mind your mouth,

and [against] those who [ask], harden <your> heart;

for a [b]ird is a word,

and whoever releases it is a man without understanding. (Krüger 2004, 189)

FROM THE TEXT

Wisdom: Value and Limitations

Qoheleth continues to dialogue with standard wisdom teaching by arguing that skill (wisdom) makes up for a dull ax but that many times wisdom

165

is outweighed by even just a little folly, just as a small fly spoils perfume (see also 1 Cor 5:6). Even the results of everyday things like digging a pit can be unpredictable and humans cannot control the future (v 14).

Sovereignty of Kings

Once again care is advised when in the presence of the king who, like God, can exercise his sovereignty in unexpected ways. The ruler could make foolish decisions with disastrous results, but the right kind of king results in blessing for the land.

Retribution and Human Accountability

Humans are accountable for the outcome of their actions. The roof of the lazy man is expected to leak (v 18). This may be an illustration to show that divine retribution sometimes works as expected. But Qoheleth is more cautious about other human life experiences that are unplanned and unintended. He seems to think that some human actions have an inherent risk or danger such as digging a pit, breaking a wall, quarrying stones, or splitting logs (vv 8-9). This inherent risk demonstrates the unpredictable nature of outcomes. Human activity does not always lead to the expected results because, unlike God, humans are unable to control outcomes.

10:1-20

XIII. CAST YOUR BREAD UPON THE WATERS (CONCLUSION) (11:1—12:7)

BEHIND THE TEXT

Ecclesiastes 11:1—12:7 continues the theme of the mystery of retribution from ch 10 but also introduces generosity, enjoyment of life, and remembering one's Creator while still young. This brings the words of Qoheleth to a close, and the remainder of the book reaffirms the editor's theme (12:8) and gives a positive assessment of Qoheleth's writing (12:9-14).

167

Like the previous unit, this one has a number of activities drawn from everyday life in the ancient world. Agricultural societies are concerned about bread, clouds and rain, falling trees, wind, birth, sowing seed, and the sun (11:1-7). The imagery of ch 12 draws on a number of household activities: guarding the house, grinding grain, closing doors, rising from bed, avoiding danger in the streets, observing almond blossoms, and drawing water from springs and wells (12:3-6). Many of these activities cease in ch 12 where the imagery seems to be drawn from war or the desolation caused by war. War and the threat of war was an ongoing reality in the postexilic periods.

The genre of this unit is instruction and reflection. Literary devices include the numerical saying (11:2) and elements of a city lament, which many have seen as an allegory or extended metaphor (12:1-7). Allegory is not a common literary device in the OT (see Judg 9:7-15; Ezek 17:1-8) despite a long history of widespread allegorizing by subsequent interpreters. This makes metaphor a more likely device here, but the imagery is more likely a city lament in anticipation of the possibility of war (neither metaphor nor allegory, but literal). The verb *know* is repeated five times (11:2, 5 twice, 6, 9) reiterating the lack of human knowledge that was emphasized in previous chapters. This realization of human limitation and divine sovereignty must come **before** (*'ad 'ăšer lō'*, 12:1, 2, 6) death or the desolation caused by war. Ecclesiastes 11:1—12:7 can be outlined as follows:

11:1—
12:7

> Generosity (11:1-2)
>
> Knowledge Is Limited (11:3-6)
>
> Happiness in Youth (11:7-10)
>
> Remember Your Creator (12:1-7)

Interpretation of this unit has baffled readers of Ecclesiastes for centuries, and Jerome's assessment is still largely true, "almost as many opinions as there are people" (quoted by Murphy 1992, 115). Of course the book as a whole is enigmatic and perhaps this unit is another example of Qoheleth using enigmatic writing to express the enigma of life ("an unsettled style that imitates life itself"; Davis 2000, 164).

Qoheleth makes reference to disaster that **may come upon the land** (11:2), **days of darkness** (11:8), and **days of trouble** (12:1). It is difficult to determine what Qoheleth has in mind in these texts. This difficulty has led Jewish (Targum, Talmud, Midrash) and some Christian interpreters (e.g., Delitzsch, 1875) to an allegorical interpretation of this unit. Some others have resorted to a hybrid reading of this unit that seeks to find a literal meaning but resorts to allegorical or metaphorical meaning when the literal meaning is elusive (e.g., Crenshaw 1987; Eaton 1983). Others see in this unit descriptions of old age and death, the coming of nightfall or winter, some cosmic eschatological disaster, a community in mourning or the coming of a storm. It is quite likely that Qoheleth is speaking literally about events that are associated with a war. The postexilic empires experienced periods of peace and prosperity, but they were also ravaged by war. Qoheleth may have been suggesting that the imminent possibility of war should not mean that everyday activities should be suspended (such as planting crops, 11:4).

IN THE TEXT

A. Generosity (11:1-2)

■ **1** Chapter 11 begins this literary unit with the famous proverb, **Cast your bread upon the waters, for after many days you will find it again** (the word find, *māṣaʾ*, sounds like another word for [unleavened] bread, *maṣṣâ*). The flat, round bread of biblical times was perhaps likely to stay afloat longer than modern Western bread. Some have interpreted this proverb as advice to make an investment, perhaps by sending trading ships across the seas (Delitzsch 1875, 391; Bartholomew 2009, 337; see Isa 18:2). This would be unique in the book of Ecclesiastes, because elsewhere Qoheleth does not advise an orientation around wealth (5:10). In 5:14 he observes that the outcome of an investment cannot be guaranteed, as all could be lost in a venture (see 9:11; Davis 2000, 219).

Qoheleth's attitude toward the poor is more positive than his attitude to wealth. He is sympathetic to the oppressed (4:1; 5:8) although up to this point he does not recommend any action on their behalf. Here in 11:1 he seems to be advising generosity, which will bring its own rewards. This is consistent with the Middle Eastern practice of hospitality; ancient and medieval Jewish commentators follow this line of interpretation. It is also reflected in an Arab proverb, "Do good, cast thy bread upon the waters, and one day thou shalt be rewarded" (Ginsburg 1861, 447). An Egyptian document has similar sayings: "Do a good deed and throw it in the water; when it dries you will find it," and "Give one loaf to your laborer, Receive two loaves from the work of his shoulders" (Ankhsheshonq 19:10; 22:19; in Fox 1999, 312; Matthews and Benjamin 2006, 316).

Isaac of Nineveh on Generosity (ca. A.D. 700)

When you give, give generously, with a joyous countenance, and give more than you are asked for, since it is said, "Send forth your morsel of bread toward the face of the poor man, and soon you will find your recompense." Do not separate the rich from the poor or try to discriminate the worthy from the unworthy, but let all persons be equal in your eyes for a good deed. (In Christianson 2007, 220)

■ **2** Qoheleth continues the theme of generosity in the next verse (11:2) and advises giving a portion to **seven** or **eight. Portions** (*ḥēleq*) is an important word in Ecclesiastes and is to be contrasted with profit (*yitrôn*). One is to be satisfied with one's portion, which is a gift from God, whereas there is no real benefit *yitrôn*) in endless toil (*ʿāmāl*, e.g., 2:11). Now in 11:2, Qoheleth advises giving a portion to others. The phrase **to seven, yes to eight** is a Wisdom literature literary device known as a numerical saying (see comment on 4:8). It does not refer to a literal number but is indefinite. The examples often revolve around the number seven, which symbolizes completeness. If v 1 is taken as a reference to commercial ventures, then the **seven, yes to eight** would refer to diversifying investments in order to minimize losses, or to cultivating friendships that would be of financial benefit in a time of loss. However, elsewhere, Qoheleth is more concerned with advising against an orientation toward wealth, than he is in advising good investment strategies.

Qoheleth also reminds the reader of the reason for this generous activity—**for you do not know what disaster** (*rāʿâ*) **may come upon the land. You do not know** here is a recurring theme in Ecclesiastes. Qoheleth has elsewhere emphasized the limitations of human knowledge and wisdom, as opposed to the unlimited knowledge of God who sets the times for all events (ch 3). This lack of knowledge requires an attitude of humility and the enjoyment of the present moment. In this verse, it requires generosity.

Qoheleth links generosity with uncertainty of the future in this verse. The Hebrew word *rāʿâ* is usually translated "evil" but also includes natural or national calamity (e.g., Amos 6:3; Prov 1:33). If there were to be a famine or an invasion, those less fortunate would need the generosity of a wealthy benefactor, or those who have been helped in the past may be able to reciprocate. This possible calamity is the first clue that this unit may be about how to live with the prospect of war. Qoheleth will advise that life should be continued as usual rather than living in fear or suspending important activities like sowing seed (11:4, 10).

B. Knowledge Is Limited (11:3-6)

■ **3** Verse 3 relates two obvious constants in nature: if clouds are full, rain falls; and if a tree falls, it lies where it fell. Even if tree cutters controlled the place where the tree fell, the tree would still be difficult or impossible to move using ancient technology. The view that rain comes from clouds seems to be a progression in the biblical understanding of the scientific world. Elsewhere in the OT the universe is viewed as a watery chaos with the earth kept dry by a hard dome (or perhaps a flat barrier). Rain is possible because this dome has windows that are opened by God when it rains (e.g., Gen 7:11; but see Prov 25:14). Rain was considered a blessing and was not a metaphor for difficulties.

Humans cannot control rain, and they cannot change the place a tree has fallen. This is an expression of God's sovereignty, which Qoheleth has proclaimed elsewhere (in contrast to human lack of control; 7:13). The point

170

of this verse could be to remind readers that they have no control over future events, even the disaster of a possible invasion or war (11:2).

■ **4** Qoheleth conveys in v 4 the inability of humans to predict when wind will blow or rain will fall. Verse 4 warns that the farmer who worries about wind and rain will neither sow nor harvest. This is another metaphor for Qoheleth's advice to seize the moment at hand and not to worry overly about the future. Ahiqar wrote, "Work your fields in season, Perform every task. You will fill your belly, You will feed your household" (Matthews and Benjamin 2006, 307). In the light of the possibility of war, Qoheleth advises his readers to continue daily activities such as sowing seed, since they do not know when or whether there will be a disaster.

■ **5** Verse 5 places the lack of human knowledge and control in the context of the all-knowing, all-powerful God. Humans do not know which way the wind will blow, much less how breath comes to the bones in the womb of a pregnant woman (see 8:8; John 3:8). Ecclesiastes 11:5 seems to have a double meaning that sets up the reader in characteristic Qoheleth style. After stating the inability of humans to **know the path of the wind,** Qoheleth changes the subject to the bones in the womb of a pregnant woman. **Wind** in v 5 (*rûaḥ*) could also mean *breath* (see NRSV). Perhaps Qoheleth refers to the inability to know the path of the wind as well as the origin of human life. Both the way of the wind and the mystery of birth are unknown to humans, so both readings support the point being made in this verse.

The crucial lack of knowledge is now stated at the end of v 5. Humans do not know the work of God who does (works) everything. The sovereignty of God is once again stressed by Qoheleth. Humans do not control events or even know what God will do (see 3:11; 8:17; 9:12).

■ **6** In the final verse of this paragraph, Qoheleth gives some characteristic advice, **Sow your seed in the morning, and at evening let not your hands be idle** (11:6). At first glance this seems to advise an endless toil, but Qoheleth has already rejected toil (*ʿāmāl*). In the context of this unit, he is advising seizing the opportunity to act, instead of waiting for perfect circumstances (or waiting to see that there will be no war). In times of peace it is often greed that causes a person to demand the perfect circumstances that will insure the greatest harvest. Instead, Qoheleth advises taking action, but then leaving the results of that action in God's hands. Unlike God, humans do not know whether this or that will succeed or whether both will be good. There is great contentment in trusting the results to God.

C. Happiness in Youth (11:7-10)

■ **7** In v 7 Qoheleth connects **light** with sweetness (so the laborer's sleep, 5:12), and with seeing the sun. His characteristic phrase "under the sun" represents life on earth and if his advice to be content is followed (e.g., 9:7-10) then life will be sweet. Thus **light** is a metaphor for life and youth in this context (see 6:5; 7:11). Light often represents the presence and love of God in the OT (e.g., Ps 44:3). In Amos it represents salvation, that is, life, as the people expect the day of the Lord to bring salvation for themselves. But Amos tells them "it is darkness, not light" because the Israelites themselves will come under God's judgment (Amos 5:18 NRSV).

George Sandy on Light (1632)

How sweet is Light! How pleasant to behold,
The mounted Sun discend in beames of Gold!
Yet, though a Man live long; long in delight:
Let him remember that approching Night
Which shall in endlesse darknesse close his Eyes:
Then will he all, as vanitie, despise.
(In Christianson 2007, 221)

■ **8** Verse 8 suggests that light also represents peaceful times, as **days of darkness** (disaster, war) are coming (Amos 5:18; 2 Sam 22:29). Even without the threat of war, life does not last forever, and years of fulfillment may be followed by **days of darkness** (old age or suffering). But even the future is "vanity" (*hebel*), that is, short-lived and empty. A lifetime of fulfillment may last for **years,** but the darkness at the end of life is a matter of **days.** The darkness could also represent death, as the antithesis to life and light (Ginsburg 1861, 454, citing Ps 143:3; Job 10:21).

Pilgrim's Progress

Then I saw in my dream, that when they were got out of the wilderness, they presently saw a town before them, and the name of that town is Vanity; and at the town there is a fair kept, called Vanity Fair. It is kept all the year long. It beareth the name of Vanity Fair, because the town where it is kept is lighter than vanity, Psa. 62:9; and also because all that is there sold, or that cometh thither, is vanity; as is the saying of the wise, "All that cometh is vanity." Eccl. 11:8. (John Bunyan, 1678)

■ **9** Rejoicing is also the theme of v 9. This advice is addressed to a "young man" (*bāḥûr*), which is characteristic of Wisdom literature (although this word is not common). The book of Proverbs often uses the phrase "my son" to give advice to the younger generation (e.g., Prov 4:20). The rejoicing in Eccl 11:9 is specifically for young people who may be tempted to worry about the future to the extent that they cannot enjoy the present. This has been an important message throughout Ecclesiastes and this point is reiterated as the book draws to a close, possibly in the context of worries about a coming war (11:2, 8). Ankhsheshonq wrote, "Enjoy your body when you are young. Death comes to all" (in Matthews and Benjamin 2006, 311).

The advice continues, **Follow the ways of your heart and whatever your eyes see.** The heart is the seat of thinking and will as well as emotion in Hebrew thinking. This is advice to seek pleasure in life, but it is not an invitation to orient one's whole life around pleasure (Num 15:39 uses similar vocabulary to warn against disobedience to God's commands). There is also the balance that God will bring all actions to **judgment.** This judgment cannot be the final eschatological judgment of Christian thinking because Ecclesiastes has already rejected the concept of life after death (e.g., 9:1-6, although some interpreters read this unit as referring to a final cosmic eschatology). Qoheleth has also challenged the doctrine of retribution where righteousness is rewarded and wickedness is punished. He has seen too many examples where this did not take immediate effect (e.g., 7:15). Still he was unwilling to let go of this doctrine completely and still felt that somehow God's justice would have the final word. In his final words to young thinkers, Qoheleth now warns that enjoyment of life must be balanced by a healthy understanding that actions have consequences. God is still sovereign, and he will bring judgment. Krüger sees an application of judgment more specific to v 9, namely that God will judge more harshly those who have not enjoyed life to the full (2004, 197).

Francis Quarles on the Stock of Time (1638)

> Consume thy golden daies
> In slavish freedome; Let thy waies
>   Take best advantage of thy frolick mirth;
> Thy Stock of Time decaies;
>   And lavish plenty still foreruns a Dearth:
> The bird that's flowne may turne at last;
>   and painefull labour may repaire a wast;
> But paines nor price can call thy minits past.
> (In Christianson 2007, 222)

■ **10** This theme is continued in v 10. Contentment is stated negatively with the advice **banish anxiety from your heart.** The reason for this advice is stated: youth and vigor are vanity (*hebel,* **meaningless**) in the sense that they do not last long. The word for **vigor** (*šaḥărût*) is unique in the OT and ancient versions struggled to render it ("folly," "ignorance," "desire"). Other words from the same root mean "black" and "dawn." Since the context of 11:10 is youth, this could allude to the dawn of life, or black hair (as old age is designated by gray hair; Fox 1999, 319). Since youth is fleeting, it should not be wasted on worry about controlling the future (which is in God's hands). Whatever por-

173

tion God has given should be accepted with joy, even if there are worries about a coming war.

D. Remember Your Creator (12:1-7)

■ I Chapter 12 continues with advice to **Remember your Creator in the days of your youth.** The word *remember* in Hebrew (*zĕkōr*) is not only cognitive but also involves action. When God remembered the Israelites in Egypt, it was not that he had forgotten about them and did not know that they were in Egypt. Rather the time for decisive action had come. That is, he "remembered" his covenant with them (Exod 6:5; see Jer 31:34). Therefore, the youth addressed in ch 12 should remember God in the sense of serving God in every decision (the essence of Wisdom literature).

This advice may in some part be looking back at the royal autobiography of 1:12—2:26. In that setting the young king indulged in all kinds of pleasures but found no satisfaction. The answer to that opening scenario is found at the close of the book, **Remember your Creator** even when young. All throughout the book the call has been made to enjoy whatever God has given (e.g., 9:7). Youth is only wasted if it is spent striving for control or wealth (which cannot bring satisfaction). In this unit, a more pressing issue seems to be indicated, i.e., the possibility of a coming war, which is a likely meaning of the reference **days of trouble** (see 11:2, 8). Elsewhere the "day of trouble" refers to the destruction of a city (Jer 17:17-18; 51:2). The loss of **pleasure** is a feature of laments, which were invoked for cities that had been devastated by war (Lam 5:15; Barbour 2008).

This understanding is similar to Jewish interpretation recorded by Jerome, that resources should be enjoyed before the "time of captivity comes and they exchange youth for old age" (Kraus 2001, 194). This interpretation is allegorical but nevertheless reveals an understanding of vv 1-7 as an anticipation of war.

Other interpreters have taken the **days of trouble** and lack of **pleasure** to refer to death (Ogden 1987, 199) or old age (Gordis 1968, 341). This view of old age seems too negative for ancient Israel, which valued its elders and did not overemphasize youth in the manner of modern Western culture.

The presence of **your Creator** (*bôrĕʾêkā*) seems out of place to Crenshaw, who notes two proposed emendations: "your well" (*bĕʾērĕkā*) and "your pit" (*bôrĕkā*) (1987, 184; see Cohen 1946, 299). He favors the former as a metaphor for "wife" (Prov 5:15), which is consistent with Qoheleth's teaching in 9:9. The translation "pit" (as a metaphor for grave) would also be relevant here, as death and disaster are prominent in this unit. However, the word **Creator** is equally appropriate, as it suggests the gap between God's sovereignty and human knowledge of the future, also an important theme of this unit.

Qoheleth's choice of vocabulary was probably designed to call several meanings to mind.

■ **2** The images that follow in 12:2-6 are usually taken as metaphors for old age. They have been interpreted in a number of ways, and it is possible that the poetry here is meant to convey a double meaning. Qoheleth has used such a literary device earlier in the book (1:6, 8; 11:5). In the context of the threefold mention of coming disaster or darkness (11:2, 8; 12:1) it seems that these images could be referring to the conditions and results of war, which was a common reality in the Persian and Hellenistic periods.

Verse 2 portrays the darkening of the universal elements of sun, light, moon, and stars. The allegorizing interpretation of the Midrash saw in these images the darkening of the countenance, nose, forehead, and cheekbones. Wesley saw the face, cheeks, and eyes, while he interpreted the clouds as infirmities and griefs.

The sweetness of life, represented by light in 11:7, grows dim when the sun is darkened, which could be a metaphor for old age or death (Ginsburg 1861, 457). Darkness is sometimes a metaphor for the day of the Lord in the Prophets (Joel 2:10; Ezek 30:3; 32:7-8; Isa 13:9-10; Amos 5:18, 20; Zeph 1:15; Christianson 2007, 225). In this context it may be an image for war, even if the day of the Lord is not specifically meant. Fox recognizes the effect of the imagery to "evoke a vast catastrophe" but considers this to be a metaphor suggesting "a vision of individual death" (1999, 343). Instead of a metaphor it is likely that the main focus is an actual catastrophe and that Qoheleth is trying to warn his young readers that their lifestyle could be lost in a moment. Darkness is associated with death and Sheol and is the antithesis of life "under the sun" (1:3; see Isa 13:10; Amos 8:9). As such, it is important in city laments (Lam 3:2, 6; Barbour 2008). In Ecclesiastes, darkness can also refer to an unsatisfying life as experienced by the one who "eats in darkness" in 5:17.

What grows dark is **the sun and the light and the moon and the stars** (v 2). **Light** seems unnecessary here as the three cosmic light sources are named. Whybray sees here an example of hendiadys and suggests that the meaning "the bright stars" is intended (1989, 164). Provan observed that these four elements are the subject of creation in Gen 1 and so this verse represents an eschatological reversal of creation (2001, 213). The order that was established in Gen 1 is compromised in the chaos of war, such as the chaos that returned during the conflict with Pharaoh in Exod 7—11 (in the form of plagues).

The reference to clouds after rain is puzzling since clouds are usually associated with rain, and rain stops when clouds move away (Eccl 12:2). Qoheleth has already made a connection between clouds and rain (11:3). If the images point to old age, perhaps the point is that old age is like one rain storm after another. No sooner has one storm ended than the clouds return and another is imminent. Crenshaw suggests that the old person's vision has faded so much that the clouds appear to be there still, even though they have gone (glaucoma?) (1987, 185). It is possible that the reference is to the rainy season and the end of the rain means that war is more likely (2 Sam 11:1). The clouds are connected with darkness in this verse, and also in Isa 5:30; Ezek 32:7-8, and in the inscription from Tell Deir ʿAlla (Seow 1997, 353). Thus the clouds returning may represent a possible disaster (such as war).

■ **3** Verse 3 utilizes the metaphors **keepers of the house, strong men, grinders, those looking through the windows,** which the Midrash interpreted as the ribs, arms, stomach, teeth, and eyes. Wesley saw here reference to the hands, arms, legs, teeth, and eyes.

The **keepers of the house** could be servants (2 Sam 20:3, so Fox 1999, 323), but if the images are of war, which is probable, then these are the guards (perhaps of the dynasty or palace, **house**). **Tremble** (*yāzuʿû*), found more commonly in biblical Aramaic and postbiblical Hebrew, occurs only three times in the OT (12:3; Esth 5:9; Hab 2:7).

The reference to **strong men** stooping in v 3 has obvious connections with old age, and a man who had watched over his house in youth would tremble in old age, having lost the strength to protect his household. **Grinders** are literally the people grinding grain by turning millstones. **Cease** (*bāṭēlû*) is used only here in biblical Hebrew but appears in biblical Aramaic and postbiblical Hebrew. Ginsburg explains it as the cease of activities because of an approaching storm (v 2) (1861, 459). In Jer 25:10 the ceasing of the sound of grinding is a metaphor for a city in ruins (see also Jer 7:34; 16:9; 33:10-11). This is a key indicator of the possibility that these images refer to wartime. After the ravages of war, the usual sounds of normal activities (such as grinding grain) have ceased. Houses are abandoned and the lamps (**those looking through the windows**; literally, *the ones seeing in the windows*) are not replenished with oil and eventually go out (Jer 25:10 also has lamps extinguished; see also Rev 18:22-23; Luke 17:33-36).

The range of people mentioned in v 3 is characteristic of city laments that often portray the comprehensive nature of the crisis by identifying victims who represent different social groups. For example, Lam 5:11-14 names women, virgins, princes, elders, old men, and young men (Barbour 2008).

Francis Fawkes on Old Age (1761)

Ere yet the grinding of the teeth is o'er,
and the dim eyes behold the sun no more;
Ere yet the pallid lips forget to speak,
The gums are toothless, and the voice is weak;
Restless he rises when the lark he hears
Yet sweetest music fails to charm his ears.

. . .

Ere broke the golden bowl that holds the brain,
Ere broke the pitcher at the fountful heart,
Or life's wheel shiver'd, and the soul depart.
Then shall the dust to native earth be given,
The soul shall soar sublime, and wing its way to heaven.
(In Christianson 2007, 230)

■ **4** The Midrash interpreted the images in v 4 allegorically. The **doors to the street** were seen as the orifices of a person, and the rising up with **birds** as a fear of bandits when the birds are heard. Wesley understood the **doors** as the senses, mouth, and lips, and waking with the **birds** as the result of the insomnia of old age.

As an old person loses mobility, the effort of leaving the house becomes greater so that **the doors to the street are closed** and hearing begins to fail so that **the sound of grinding fades.** Sleep can also become fitful in old age so that **men rise up at the sound of birds,** that is, at the slightest sound (this contradicts the failing hearing), or they wake up as early as the birds. Ginsberg took the whole verse in the context of lost hearing so that "the voice of the bird becomes faint, and all the strains of music die away" (1951, 101).

Ginsburg's literal interpretation sees the doors closed because of the storm, and the birds rising up (not the men) in their prestorm flurry of activity and commotion (1861, 460). Jerome saw these as the doors of the temple as part of his interpretation of this passage as a picture of the destruction of Jerusalem. The **sound of birds,** then, refers to the temple singers who fall silent as a result of the crisis (Kraus 2001, 194).

The dual form of **doors** is a major clue that a city is in view here, not a house. Berger sees this city as "a symbol of human order (perhaps reason?)" that is falling into destruction (2001, 146 n9). But Qoheleth is also positive about the possibilities of order (although limited). Fox sees a village or estate engaged in a funeral procession (1999, 337). He claims that doors are closed during a funeral, presumably the doors of the houses. This does not fit well with the dual form of **doors,** and it is unlikely that a village would have gates. If it did, they would be open so the funeral procession could pass through them to the gravesite. It is likely that Qoheleth is not using the city as a symbol but is literally anticipating the destruction of a city because of the possibility of war. City gates would be closed for security in times of war, and the prophets spoke of deserted houses and towns being "shut up" (Isa 24:10; Jer 13:19).

Street (*šûq*) is a rare word in the OT (occurring only in 12:4, 5; Prov 7:8; and Song 3:2). Perhaps it is used in the sense of "market," as in a street market (so the Arabic cognate of *šûq*). The market doors or gates would be closed during wartime. Nehemiah closed the city gates to prevent vendors from selling goods on the Sabbath (Neh 13:19, where the city gates are also called **doors**).

If wartime images are intended, then the **sound of birds** may arouse men who are sleeping lightly because they are watching for the enemy. Singing would also be suspended because of the distress, hence the *daughters of song are brought low* (**but all their songs grow faint,** i.e., female singers; see Song 3:5 where "Daughters of Jerusalem" means "women of Jerusalem"). The vocabulary for **grow faint** ("lowered") is also used for humbling the land because of idolatry (Isa 2:8-9; 5:13-15; 29:4; Barbour 2008).

■ **5** Verse 5 conveys the idea of fear of heights and danger in the streets. The Midrash relates this fear to weakness and poor vision. This interpretation also relates **almond** blossoms to the spinal column, the **grasshopper** to the swelled ankles of old age, and the **desire** to sexual desire. Wesley saw in this verse reference to the fear of stumbling in old age, gray hair (almond blossoms), inability to carry burdens (grasshopper), and a loss of desire for food. The word **desire** (*hāʾăbiyyônâ*) is unique in the OT but the meaning "caperberry" is attested in postbiblical Hebrew and this is how the ancient translations understood it. The caperberry was a stimulant of the appetite, and the Midrash connected it with sexual desire.

Soon, death comes and **man goes to his eternal home.** Qoheleth has already argued, in line with the rest of the OT, that there is no meaningful life after death. **His eternal home** is therefore merely the grave, which is a place of no return. The literal translation is *house of his eternity* (*bêt ʿōlāmô*), which does not occur elsewhere in the Bible but was a common concept in nonbiblical sources (Healey 2001, 174). Youngblood translates the phrase as "dark house," referring also to the grave (1986, 408).

A literal interpretation of this verse yields images of spring when the rainy season comes to an end and the crops begin to ripen. This is the usual season for war. **Almond** trees blossom (before the wet season is over), the **grasshopper** is full and heavy and can hardly move, and the caperberry bursts. Ginsburg saw the terror in v 5 as fear of the gathering storm in the **heights** (sky) (1861, 461). He also translated **the almond tree blossoms** . . . as "the almond shall be despised, and the locust shall be loathed," as concern for the coming storm would overshadow any desire for delicacies. The caperberry (**desire**) would also be one of these delicacies. The verse closes with death imminent and the mourners already in the streets ready for the funeral.

With wartime imagery in view the heights would be the city walls that, when ascended, would reveal the attacking enemy (Deut 3:5); or the surrounding hills (Isa 30:25) for the same reason. Fox suggests that **heights** is to be understood as an epithet for God (Job 22:12) (1999, 327). Perhaps the meaning is fear of the high king, that is, the conquering emperor (Eccl 5:8).

The reference to **streets** is probably to be connected with references to the streets and squares of the city in laments (Lam 2:11, 12, 19; 4:1, 5, 14, 18; Barbour 2008). If this is correct, then v 5 reflects the destruction left by war.

■ **6** Qoheleth continues his advice in v 6. The NIV connects **before the silver cord is severed** in v 6 with "before the days of trouble" in v 1 and supplies the words **remember him** (not in the MT). The relevance of **silver cord** and **golden bowl** are not obvious but are often explained as an oil lamp comprising a **golden bowl,** suspended by a **silver cord,** and when the cord snapped, the bowl fell and broke (Ginsburg 1861, 465). The Midrash interpreted the **cord** and **bowl** in v 6 as the spinal cord and skull, and the **pitcher** as the stomach. Wesley saw the marrow of the backbone and membranes of the brain, as well as veins (**pitcher**), arteries (**wheel**), and the ventricles of the heart (**spring and well**). These may be taken as metaphors for death, and since the objects are positive (precious metals, refreshing water), Gammie sees here an affirmation of the positive aspects of life (1989, 52). An extinguished lamp is a metaphor for death in Prov 13:9 and so is a severed cord in Greek mythology (Murphy 1992, 120). The reader should remember the Creator in youth and not wait until old age or even death. A broken **pitcher** and **wheel** cannot hold or draw water, which is necessary for life (the broken wheel may have led to the pitcher being dropped and broken; Lohfink 2003, 141, notes that wheels were used at wells in Palestine from the third century B.C.). So these, too, are considered metaphors for death.

Taken literally as pointing to a coming invasion, the reference to severed silver cord and broken golden bowl calls to mind plunder taken in war (Barbour 2008). The silver is not **severed,** but "distant" (*yirhaq, ketib*), that is, taken away to the land of the conqueror (the *lō'* does not negate the distance but is part of the expression meaning **before,** *'ad 'ăšer lō'*). The shattered **pitcher** and **wheel** (or "pot"; see Dahood 1952, 217) are part of the destruction of war and symbolize the lack of drinking water and other supplies in the wake of war (Lam 5:4). They also contribute to the overall tone of desolation as the functioning well was a meeting place in ancient cities. This desolation is a theme of city laments, such as Lamentations (1:1; 5:18; see Jer 9:10; Barbour 2008).

The word **cord** (*hebel*) is remarkably similar to *hebel* ("vanity") and perhaps is intended to bring to mind earlier verses that warned that silver (money) does not give lasting satisfaction (5:10). In this context it is easily lost. The word **cord** (*hebel*) can have many meanings, such as "cord," "territory," "band," "trap," "measuring line." Perhaps the most appropriate in this context is "portion" (Deut 32:9; BDB 286b), which has been an important theme in Ecclesiastes with different vocabulary (*heleq*, Eccl 2:10). The portion of silver could easily be lost as plunder in war, and so it should be enjoyed in the present.

■ 7 By simple observation, ancient Hebrews observed that human bodies decompose to dust. Working backward, they assumed dust to be the raw material of the human body. Thus, at death, **dust returns to the ground it came from.** This understanding is reflected in Gen 2:7 and 3:19 where God took some dust from the ground (ʾādāmâ) to make the first human (ʾādām). What made the inanimate ʾādām a "living being" is "the breath of life" that God breathed into the nostrils of the first human (Gen 2:7). Life is thus a gift from God. So, by simple logic, Qoheleth assumes that the life breath (**spirit,** rûah) returns to God who gave it, just as the corpse returns to dust where it originated. This is not a spirit or soul in the Greek (Platonic) sense where a personal entity can exist apart from the body. It is merely a recognition that God is the giver of life.

George Sandys on Death (1638)

Man must at length to his long home descend:
behold, the mourners at his gates attend.
Advise, before the Silver Cord growes slacke;
before the golden Boule asunder crack:
Before the Pitcher at the fountaine leake;
Or wasted Wheele besides the Cisterne breake.
Man, made of Earth, resolves into the same:
His Soule ascends to God, from whom it came.
O Restlesse Vanitie of Vanities!
(In Christianson 2007, 235)

FROM THE TEXT

Generosity

Ecclesiastes has not been a defender of the poor and oppressed, unlike the Prophets. The few references to oppression give more of the impression of a disinterested bystander (4:1; 5:8). But in an enigmatic metaphor of casting bread on water, Qoheleth advises generosity (11:1-2). There is no guarantee in this advice that God will be generous and multiply the reward for one's generosity. Any demonstration of generosity with selfish or profit motives would be designated meaningless (*hebel*) by Qoheleth.

Mystery of Retribution

According to standard retribution, one *does* know **what disaster may come upon the land** (11:2) because wickedness leads to disaster, and righteousness to blessing. But in the real world the future is less controlled; while trees may lie where they fall, wind and rain are less predictable. Knowledge of the future belongs only to God and worrying about it will lead to a loss of joy.

Enjoy Life

So life is to be enjoyed, not worried about or controlled. No doubt hard times will come in old age or in a national disaster, so fleeting youth should be enjoyed within the bounds of the fear of God, who will surely bring judgment (11:9). The popular philosophy of *"Carpe diem* (seize the day)" is nuanced by Qoheleth in the direction of "Accept the gift" (Davis 2000, 182).

Fear God

Life is to be lived and enjoyed in the fear of God and in full recognition of the possibility of hard times and the end of enjoyment of life ahead. In the meantime, Qoheleth urges his audience to live life to the fullest—engage in everyday work building life and relationships and doing things that bring joy to one's life—before **the days of trouble come** (12:1).

The advice to **Remember your Creator** is another form of advice to fear God, who may be unpredictable to a certain extent but nevertheless should be obeyed. This relationship with God should be lifelong and not be left until the trials of old age or untimely death, for "no man knows when his hour will come" (9:12).

XIV. PLEASING WORDS (THEME AND EPILOGUE) (12:8-14)

BEHIND THE TEXT

The final unit follows the complex themes of the book with a one-dimensional epilogue that seems to reflect standard wisdom theology more than the nuanced treatment in the rest of the book. Instead of the values and limitations of wisdom, wisdom is presented as only positive. Instead of the mystery of retribution, justice is presented as certain. The standard wisdom theme of fearing God is repeated, with the addition of an admonition to keep God's commandments, a theme that is not present anywhere else in Ecclesiastes.

While Qoheleth has been dialoguing with standard wisdom teaching throughout the book, the epilogue reflects that tradition in most traditional terms. It identifies Qoheleth as a wisdom teacher (ḥākām) who imparted knowledge (daʿat) and set out proverbs (or comparisons, měšālîm). The foundation of Wisdom literature, the fear of God (usually fear of Yahweh outside Ecclesiastes), is advised, along with keeping the commandments. And the standard wisdom doctrine of retribution is expressed unequivocally, **God will bring every deed into judgment** (12:14), even though Qoheleth has spent a good deal of the book trying to nuance this doctrine (while refusing to abandon it). It seems that the epilogue is the product of traditional wisdom teachers who wished to preserve the teachings of Qoheleth but who were in the end unconvinced by his perspective (see von Rad 1972, 238) or perhaps wished to prevent distortion by those who were not yet ready for this kind of nuance.

The genre of the final unit is reflection and instruction (see v 13). The numerical value of the Hebrew consonants in **Meaningless! Meaningless! . . . Everything is meaningless!** (*hbl hblym . . . hkl hbl*, v 8), is 216, which is the same as the number of verses up to this point (Wright 1980, 43). Verses 8-14 can be outlined as follows:

Theme: Vanity of Vanities (12:8)

The Value of Wisdom (12:9-12)

Fear of God, and Justice (12:13-14)

IN THE TEXT

A. Theme: Vanity of Vanities (12:8)

■ **8** The words of Qoheleth end in 12:8 with the characteristic saying, "**Meaningless! Meaningless!" says the Teacher. "Everything is meaningless!"** After reading the book of Ecclesiastes, the meaning of the Hebrew word *hebel* (meaningless) can better be determined. At times Qoheleth has used it to mean "meaningless, futile" (e.g., 4:7-8) but many other times it has meant "incomprehensible" (e.g., 8:10, 14) or "temporary" (e.g., 6:12). Life is difficult to understand (incomprehensible) because only God knows the whole picture. Life is also temporary, fleeting, ephemeral because only God lives forever. Humans walk the earth "under the sun" for a relatively short period, then they die with no meaningful future (according to OT theology). Since life is incomprehensible, temporary, and in some cases meaningless, all one can do is to accept the sovereignty of God, enjoy whatever God has given, and be content.

This verse forms an inclusio with 1:2 that is almost identical (in some manuscripts and the Targum it is identical). These two verses could have been composed by the author, as they use his vocabulary. However, this blanket phrase is not used in the body of the book, so it seems to be the work of an editor. The article is used with Qoheleth (*the* Teacher) only here in 12:8 (except 7:27, which may be a scribal error).

B. The Value of Wisdom (12:9-12)

■ **9** The first person has dominated Ecclesiastes apart from the first two verses and the epilogue (12:9-14). Many suggestions have been made concerning proposed additions to the book, but this editorial conclusion presents the clearest evidence of an addition as the book is presented as the work of a third party, and Qoheleth is discussed in the third person. It is possible that there is more than one editorial conclusion represented here, as three distinct thoughts are presented (vv 9-10, 11-12, 13-14).

The first is a statement about Qoheleth's wisdom and his activities as a wisdom teacher. It is very positive about Qoheleth and may have been written by one of his students (Murphy 1992, 125). The presentation from the point of view of Solomon in chs 1 and 2 is not reflected in this summary. Qoheleth is remembered as a wisdom teacher, not as a king. The adjective *ḥākām* (**wise**) can be used substantively in the technical sense of a professional wisdom teacher. Qoheleth was both wise and a wisdom teacher.

He **imparted knowledge to the people** and also **set in order many proverbs** (12:9). These are standard activities of a wisdom teacher, and the same could be said of Solomon. Ecclesiastes contains some proverbs, but unlike the book of Proverbs, it is not a collection of proverbs. At times Qoheleth challenged the proverbs he quoted, which is consistent with his rejection of the oversimplification of standard wisdom teaching. Qoheleth did make many comparisons, which is the literal meaning of **proverbs** (*měšālîm*).

One of the key themes of the book is profit or gain (*yitrôn, yōtēr*) and this vocabulary appears in v 9 (*yōtēr*, **Not only**). The beginning of the verse is literally *and profit/gain* (or, *in addition*) *which Qoheleth was a wisdom teacher.* Having pessimistically declared that there is no gain in life (e.g., 1:3), the book ends with a hint that Qoheleth's teaching perhaps does bring gain (see also 7:11).

■ **10** The following verse almost reads like a defense of Qoheleth in the face of criticism, perhaps for his contradictions or unorthodox views. His words are defended as being *pleasing* (**just the right words**), **upright and true** (v 10; see Ps 19:9; Prov 8:8). These two verses (9-10) would be an appropriate ending for the book, but there is more.

■ **11** Verses 11-12 make a general statement about the value of wisdom. This is consistent with other statements made in the book, but Qoheleth has also been quick to point out the limitations of wisdom. This editorial addition could be a counterbalance to these statements of the limitations of wisdom, or a defense of the value of Ecclesiastes despite unorthodox elements. Ultimately the sayings of wisdom teachers come from God (**one Shepherd,** Pss 23:1; 28:9), but they are not always easy to accept (kings were thought of as shepherds, so it is possible that Solomon is in mind here). They can be **like goads** prodding one on to better living, but they are also like **firmly embedded nails** (v 11), timeless truths that will not be displaced.

Three rare words occur in this verse. **Collected sayings** (*baʿălê ʾăsuppôt*) occurs nowhere else in the OT and means "assemblies of scholars" in postbiblical Hebrew (Whybray 1989, 172). **Goads** (*dārěbōnôt*) are the ancient equivalent of the cattle prod (sharpened sticks), and this word is unique but a related word means "sharp instrument" in 1 Sam 13:21. In a similar epilogue to the Egyptian document *Instruction of Ani* the "son" is urged to be like an animal and to listen and learn what to do (Seow 1997, 61). The word **Nails** (*maśměrôt*) is unique here but is found with an alternate spelling in Jer 10:4 and 2 Chr

3:9. According to Delitzsch, these are iron nails; there is another word for wooden tent stakes (*yātēd*, Judg 4:21) (1875, 435).

■ **12** Verse 12 uses the common Wisdom literature address **my son,** which is not used elsewhere in Ecclesiastes, although the tone of the book is addressed to youth and alternate vocabulary is used with the same meaning (*bāḥûr*, 11:9; 12:1; see Prov 1:8, 10, 15; 2:1; 3:1; 4:1, etc.). Unlike the first epilogue, which began in 12:9 and sounded like the words of a devoted student of Qoheleth, the use of **my son** gives the tone of another wisdom teacher adding his contribution.

There is a warning not to add anything to the words of the wise and yet these two verses (11-12) seem to be an addition. Is this editor failing to take his own advice? (see 3:14; Deut 4:2; 12:32; Jer 26:2; Sirach 18:6; Rev 22:18-19). It is unclear why there should be a negative portrayal of multiplying books or a warning against adding to wisdom sayings. One would expect a wisdom teacher to find study refreshing, and not wearying. In Ecclesiastes it is the fool who wearies himself with many words (5:3, 7; 6:11; 10:12-14). The word **study** (*lahag*) is unique and may be related to *hag* ("meditation") or *hāgâ* ("to study"). A similar Arabic word means "be devoted" (BDB 529).

Horace on Learning

Consult with care the learned page,
Inquire of every scienced sage,
How you may glide with gentle ease
Adown the current of your days.
(In Ginsburg 1861, 476)

C. Fear of God, and Justice (12:13-14)

■ **13** Despite the warning not to add anything to the sayings of the wise, vv 13-14 seem to be another addition. This is also somewhat consistent with the teaching of Qoheleth but may have been provided to ensure that the balance ended away from the more cynical pronouncements in the book.

The conclusion of the matter is literally *end of the matter/word/thing* (*sôp dābār*), which is a postbiblical idiom for "in conclusion, finally" (Ginsburg 1861, 477). To **fear God** is a standard wisdom teaching, reflected in Ecclesiastes six times (3:14; 5:7; 7:18; 8:12, 13; 12:13) and forming an inclusio in the structure of the book of Proverbs (1:7; 31:30).

Keeping God's **commandments** is not a common emphasis of Wisdom literature, although Job claims that he had not departed from God's commandments (Job 23:12). Other references to commandments in Job are to God commanding nature (Job 9:7; 36:32; 37:12, 15; 38:12; 39:27; see Prov 8:29). Commandments in Proverbs are usually given by parents or teachers

(Prov 2:1; 3:1; 4:4; 6:20, 23; 7:1, 2; see also 10:8; 13:13; 19:16). Keeping commandments has not been mentioned in Ecclesiastes at all, except in a similar injunction to obey the king (8:2, 5). The fear of God is shown as an analogy from fearing the king in Prov 24:21. Biblical Wisdom literature generally focuses more on the human condition than on the history of Israel. Proverbs, Job, Song of Songs, and Ecclesiastes do not mention the promises to Abraham, the exodus, the giving of the Law on Mount Sinai, or the wilderness period. The word *law* (*tôrâ*) is found three times in Proverbs (1:8; 6:20; 13:14) but is used in the general sense of "teaching" not in the technical sense of the law of Moses.

There is a strong connection between the fear of Yahweh and keeping his commandments (Deut 5:29; 6:2, 24; 8:6; 13:4; 1 Sam 12:14; 2 Kgs 17:34; Ps 112:1). Fear of God caused the midwives in Egypt to have no regard for the commandments of Pharaoh (Exod 1:17), and fear of the people was King Saul's excuse for not obeying Yahweh (1 Sam 15:24).

■ **14** Throughout Ecclesiastes, Qoheleth has been critical of the doctrine of retribution, while not giving up on it altogether. In the editorial addition of v 14, the validity of the doctrine is reiterated. God's **judgment** will prevail and should remain a motivation for righteousness, as even **hidden** deeds will be brought into judgment (see 11:9). The comprehensive nature of the judgment shows that this is divine judgment, for humans could not know **every hidden thing.** But it does not require a future eschatological judgment (against Ginsburg 1861, 478), as the divine judgment can still be brought in this life. Nevertheless, the NT does use this language for a future judgment (Rom 2:16; 1 Cor 4:5; 1 Tim 5:24-25).

Delitzsch on the Fear of God (1875)

The sentence, *eth-haelohim yĕra* ("fear God"), repeating itself from v 6, is the kernel and the star of the whole book, the highest moral demand which mitigates its pessimism and hallows its eudaemonism. (438)

FROM THE TEXT

Vanity (*hebel*)

The editorial theme of the book, "vanity of vanities" (NRSV) (**Meaningless! Meaningless!**), is repeated in v 8 as an inclusio. Thirty-eight times the word is used with different nuances, but only in 1:2 and 12:8 is the phrase "vanity of vanities" used, which suggests that this characterization of the book is too simplistic and extensive. All of life is not meaningless and absurd, as there is much to be enjoyed in life, and God is to be feared.

Fear of God

The fear of God is an important theme in Wisdom literature and is not lacking in the book of Ecclesiastes, despite questions about God's justice and timing. What is unique to this unit is the reference to keeping God's commandments. While obedience to the king (8:2) implies obedience to God, and conduct before God should be appropriate (5:1-2), the commandments as a specific code are not mentioned elsewhere in Ecclesiastes (or Proverbs); this indicates that this addition is more of a concern for the editor than it was for Qoheleth himself.

Value of Wisdom and Retribution

As a whole, the epilogue defends Qoheleth but also defends two key elements of wisdom teaching that he tried to nuance, namely wisdom and retribution. The value of each was retained by Qoheleth, but he apparently felt that his audience was ready to move away from the oversimplification inherent in the first lessons of the wisdom teachers. The wisdom teachers who preserved his writings apparently added this epilogue to be sure that his readers would not go too far in the other direction. The epilogue cautions us against the temptation to read the book simplistically without giving careful attention to Qoheleth's portrait of the complexities of life.

12:8-14

LAMENTATIONS

BIBLIOGRAPHY FOR LAMENTATIONS

Albrektson, Bertil. 1963. *Studies in the Text and Theology of the Book of Lamentations.* Lund: CWK Gleerup.

Assis, Elie. 2007. The Alphabetic Acrostic in the Book of Lamentations. *Catholic Biblical Quarterly* 69:710-24.

Bergant, Dianne. 2002. The Challenge of Hermeneutics: Lamentations 1:1-11: A Test Case. *Catholic Biblical Quarterly* 64:1-16.

_____. 2003. *Lamentations.* Abingdon Old Testament Commentaries. Nashville: Abingdon.

Berlin, Adele. 2002. *Lamentations: A Commentary.* Old Testament Library. Louisville, Ky.: Westminster/John Knox.

Bettan, Israel. 1950. *The Five Scrolls.* Cincinnati: Union of American Hebrew Congregations.

Bracke, John Martin. 2000. *Jeremiah 30-52 and Lamentations.* Louisville, Ky.: Westminster/John Knox.

Brady, Christian M. M. 2003. *The Rabbinic Targum of Lamentations: Vindicating God.* Leiden: Brill.

Browning, Elizabeth Barrett. 1844. *Sonnets from the Portuguese and Other Poems.* Garden City, N.Y.: Dolphin.

Bruce, F. F. 1988. *The Canon of Scripture.* Downers Grove, Ill.: InterVarsity.

Brueggemann, Walter. 1997. *Theology of the Old Testament: Testimony, Dispute, Advocacy.* Minneapolis: Fortress.

Calvin, John. 1563. *Commentaries on the Book of the Prophet Jeremiah and The Lamentations.* Vol. 5. Repr. Grand Rapids: Eerdmans, 1950.

Cohen, A., trans. 1983. *Midrash Rabbah: Lamentations.* London: Soncino.

Driver, Samuel Rolles. 1897. *An Introduction to the Literature of the Old Testament.* Repr. Cleveland: Meridian, 1956.

Goldman, Solomon. 1946. In A. Cohen (ed.). *The Five Megilloth.* London: Soncino.

Gottwald, Norman K. 1962. *Studies in the Book of Lamentations.* London: SCM Press.

Gray, C. Paul. 1966. The Lamentations of Jeremiah in *Beacon Bible Commentary.* Ed. A. F. Harper. Kansas City: Beacon Hill Press of Kansas City.

Gunkel, Hermann. 1933. *Introduction to Psalms: The Genres of the Religious Lyric of Israel.* Macon, Ga.: Mercer University Press, 1998 translation.

Hall, Bert Harold. 1969. The Book of Lamentations in the *Wesleyan Bible Commentary.* Ed. Charles W. Carter. Grand Rapids: Eerdmans.

Harrison, R. K. 1969. *Introduction to the Old Testament.* Grand Rapids: Eerdmans.

_____. 1973. *Jeremiah and Lamentations.* Tyndale Old Testament Commentaries. Leicester, England: Inter-Varsity.

Hillers, Delbert R. 1972. *Lamentations: A New Translation with Introduction and Commentary.* Anchor Bible. Garden City, N.Y.: Doubleday.

Huey, F. B. 1993. *Jeremiah, Lamentations.* New American Commentary. Nashville: Broadman.

Hutchins, Michael, ed. 2003. *Grzimek's Animal Life Encyclopedia.* Detroit: Thompson/Gale.

Keil, Carl Friedrich. 1873. *The Lamentations of Jeremiah.* Repr. Grand Rapids: Eerdmans, 1986.

King, Philip J., and Lawrence E. Stager. 2001. *Life in Biblical Israel.* Louisville, Ky.: Westminster/John Knox.

Lanahan, William F. 1974. The Speaking Voice in the Book of Lamentations. *Journal of Biblical Literature* 93:41-49.

Linafelt, Tod. 2001. The Refusal of a Conclusion in the Book of Lamentations. *Journal of Biblical Literature* 120/2:340-43.

Longman, Tremper. 2008. *Jeremiah, Lamentations.* New International Biblical Commentary. Peabody, Mass.: Hendrickson.

Matthews, Victor H., and Don C. Benjamin. 2006. *Old Testament Parallels: Laws and Stories from the Ancient Near East.* New York: Paulist.

McDaniel, Thomas F. 1968. The Alleged Sumerian Influence upon Lamentations. *Vetus Testamentum* 18:198-209.

Meek, Theophile J. 1956. The Book of Lamentations in *The Interpreter's Bible.* Vol. 6. Nashville: Abingdon-Cokesbury.

Middlemas, Jill. 2006. Did Second Isaiah Write Lamentations III? *Vetus Testamentum* 56:505-25.

Miller, C. W. 2002. The Book of Lamentations in Recent Research. *Currents in Biblical Research* 1/1:9-29.

Morse, Benjamin. 2003. The Lamentations Project: Biblical Mourning Through Modern Montage. *Journal for the Study of the Old Testament* 28/1:113-27.

O'Connor, Kathleen M. 2001. *The Book of Lamentations: Introduction, Commentary and Reflections.* The New Interpreter's Bible, vol. 6. Nashville: Abingdon Press.

_____. 2002. *Lamentations and the Tears of the World.* Maryknoll, N.Y.: Orbis.

Paul, Shalom. 2002. *Amos.* Hermeneia. Minneapolis: Fortress.

Peake, A. S. 1911. *Jeremiah and Lamentations.* Edinburgh: Jack.

Pritchard, James B. ed. 1969. *Ancient Near Eastern Texts Relating to the Old Testament.* Third Edition with Supplement. Princeton University Press.

Provan, Iain W. 1991. *Lamentations.* New Century Bible. Grand Rapids: Eerdmans.

Renkema, Johan. 1998. *Lamentations.* Historical Commentary on the Old Testament. Leuven: Peeters.

Roberts, Charles George Douglas. 1893. *Songs of the Common Day and Ave!* Toronto: W. Briggs.

Robertson, David. 1969. The Morphemes -y (-ī) and -w (-ō) in Biblical Hebrew. *Vetus Testamentum* 19/2:211-23.

Salters, R. B. 1994. *Jonah and Lamentations.* Old Testament Guides. Sheffield: JSOT Press.

Seow, C. L. 1985. A Textual Note on Lamentations 1:20. *Catholic Biblical Quarterly* 47/3:416-19.

Soggin, J. Alberto. 1989. *Introduction to the Old Testament.* Louisville, Ky.: Westminster/John Knox.

Underhill, Evelyn. 1946. *The Cloud of Unknowing.* Charleston, S.C.: Forgotten Books.

van Hecke, Pierre J. P. 2002. Lamentations 3,1-6: An Anti-Psalm 23. *Scandinavian Journal of the Old Testament* 16/2:264-82.

Varughese, Alex. 1992. Lamentations in the *Asbury Bible Commentary.* Ed. Eugene E. Carpenter and Wayne McCown. Grand Rapids: Zondervan.

von Rad, Gerhard. 1965. *Old Testament Theology,* vol. 2. *The Theology of Israel's Prophetic Traditions.* New York: Harper and Row.

Wenthe, Dean O. 2009. *Jeremiah, Lamentations.* Ancient Christian Commentary on Scripture. Downers Grove, Ill.: InterVarsity.

Westermann, Claus. 1981. *Praise and Lament in the Psalms.* Atlanta: John Knox.

Wood, Fred M., and Ross McLaren. 2006. *Jeremiah, Lamentations.* Holman Old Testament Commentary. Nashville: Holman.

Yigael Yadin. 1963. *The Art of Warfare in Biblical Lands: In the Light of Archaeological Study.* New York: McGraw-Hill.

INTRODUCTION TO LAMENTATIONS

The book of Lamentations is a collection of five psalms that lament the fall of Jerusalem. They are largely an expression of grief and contain very little information about the historical events that caused the suffering. Instead they provide details of desolation and shame, expressions of emotion, accusations against God, and sometimes hints of repentance and glimmers of hope. The poems assign sovereignty to God and accept the actions of the attacking army as the justified actions of God. The writing betrays a profound faith that God will revert to his truer self of faithfulness and love. The reader is invited to share in the horror of the experience and to wonder if God will bring an end to the suffering.

A. Authorship

The book of Lamentations, like most biblical books, is anonymous. The name of a biblical book can sometimes suggest authorship or a tradition of authority. This is the case with the book of Amos, which contains the preaching of Amos, or the Gospel of Luke, which is thought to be written by Luke. The name of the book of Lamentations is not a person's name and so does not help in this regard. It is a translation of the ancient rabbinical designation *qînôt* (via Latin and Greek). The older Hebrew name is *ʾēkâ* ("how"), following the Hebrew custom of naming books after the first word used (or a word near the beginning). While the name "Lamentations" does not suggest authorship, many Hebrew manuscripts add "of Jeremiah" or "of Jeremiah the prophet" (Hillers 1972, xvii).

The Septuagint further identifies the book with Jeremiah by means of an introductory sentence indicating that what follows is the lament of Jeremiah as he sat weeping over Jerusalem. Harrison suggests that this widely followed tradition resulted from a misunderstanding of 2 Chr 35:25, which states that Jeremiah's lament over King Josiah was recorded in "the lamentations" (*haqqînôt*). Apparently Josephus also identified this lament over Jeremiah with the fourth poem in the book of Lamentations. However, Lam 4 is about Jerusalem, not a king or other individual (Harrison 1969, 1069). The reference to the king in 4:20 must be to Zedekiah, the king at the time of the Babylonian conquest of 586 B.C. (Hillers 1972, xx).

Much scholarship has focused the study of authorship on the refutation of the traditional understanding of Jeremiah as author, beginning with H. von der Hardt in 1712 (Hillers 1972, xix). While there are similarities between Jeremiah and Lamentations in terms of style, there are also significant connections with other books (Ezekiel, Isa 40—66, Psalms), and important differences of theology between Jeremiah and Lamentations.

There is not enough information to be certain about the authorship of Lamentations, but interpreters have suggested an origin in prophetic or wisdom circles, a royal setting, or (the most popular suggestion) the temple singers (Miller 2002, 11). Authorship by Jeremiah is supported by Wood and McLaren (2006, 353); Keil (1873, 339-50); Hall (1969, 344); Gray (1966, 504); and Huey (1993, 443).

B. Date

Tradition has always held that Lamentations was written soon after the destruction of Jerusalem in 586 B.C. Modern scholarship is in agreement because the horrors of the catastrophe seem to be fresh in the author's mind. Also, while there is some glimmer of hope in the third poem, there is not the optimism that is found in later postexilic literature. This suggests that Lamentations was written closer to the fall of Jerusalem, and still during the exile.

This is not conclusive, however, because the poems could have been written later by a skilled poet who conveyed a sense of immediacy. This is the case with the Sumerian city-laments, which were written fifty years after the tragedy (Berlin 2002, 33).

C. Place of Origin

Scholars assume that Lamentations originated in Palestine because of the specificity of details that it provides and because of a lack of interest in those exiled to Babylon (Hillers 1972, xxiii). Provan warns that this cannot be conclusive either (1991, 11). Someone familiar with Palestine could have written about it from elsewhere.

D. Occasion

The fall of Jerusalem to the Babylonians in 586 B.C. was apparently the occasion that gave rise to the book of Lamentations, although the certainty of this has been challenged (Provan 1991, 12-13; Bergant 2003, 14; but see Salters 1994, 77-78). The Babylonians controlled Palestine after their defeat of the Assyrian capital Nineveh (612 B.C.) and the Assyrian army at Carchimesh (605 B.C.). Nebuchadnezzar then became king of Babylon and he besieged Jerusalem when King Jehoiakim refused to pay tribute. Jehoiakim died during the siege and his son Jehoiachin surrendered to Nebuchadnezzar three months later in 597 B.C. This saved Jerusalem from destruction, but only for ten years. The Babylonians took Jehoiachin and others to Babylon as captives and placed Zedekiah (Jehoiakim's brother) as a puppet king over Judah. About ten years later, Zedekiah rebelled against Nebuchadnezzar. This led to another Babylonian invasion of Judah and the destruction of the city in 586 B.C.

The tragedy of 586 B.C. meant great loss for the people of Judah who believed that God would always protect them and their city. They believed that a descendant of David would always rule in Jerusalem (2 Sam 7). They believed that the temple, as a representation of the dwelling of God, would never be destroyed (Jer 7; 26:9). The loss of king and temple meant a theological crisis. Also lost was language (Aramaic would replace Hebrew in exile), land (many people were deported to Babylon), and independence. The tragedy is recorded in 2 Kgs 25, Jer 52, and also in the *Babylonian Chronicle* (Pritchard 1969, 563-64; Matthews and Benjamin 2006, 195-97).

E. Purpose

Lamentations was written as an expression of grief for this community, which lost the temple and the land. Other biblical literature addresses the crisis in a variety of ways. Psalm 137 also expresses grief, Kings explains the exile as the result of sin (2 Kgs 24:3), and Isa 40—55 seeks to give comfort. Lamentations also has a theological purpose. It answers questions raised by the defeat of Jerusalem (Gottwald considers the theological issues to be primary; 1962, 48). Eventually Lamentations came to be used in liturgy to commemorate the destruction of Jerusalem.

F. Sociological and Cultural Issues

Mourning

The outward signs of mourning in ancient Israel were fasting, abstaining from sexual relations, lamenting, throwing dust or ashes in one's hair, tearing clothing, wearing sackcloth, and sitting on the ground. Sackcloth was the clothing of the sinner in Babylonian documents (Gunkel 1933, 126; see Pss 30:11; 35:13; Isa 58:5; Job 16:15). Rejoicing (the opposite of mourning) was associated with the sacrificial feasts (Deut 12:11-12; 27:7). This implies that mourning and loss of the sacrificial system go together (as do rejoicing and praise; Ps 34:1-2). Since it was believed that the dead cannot praise God (Ps 6:5), to be in mourning is like being in Sheol, the land of the dead (Lam 3:6). This demonstrates the distance from God that the mourner feels and experiences. The destruction of the temple makes this reality permanent. As long as there is no temple at which to praise God, the whole nation is in a state of mourning and cannot rejoice. Leaving for exile to another country reinforces this distance from God. The repeated calls for God to hear, see, remember, pay attention, and take back are pleas for the comfort of access to God. This comfort is not found in the book of Lamentations (Berlin 2002, 15-16).

Lamenting the City

Lamenting the fall of a great city is known from other cultures of the ancient Near East. Five documents are preserved that lament the fall of Ur, including *Lamentation over the Destruction of Ur* (Pritchard 1969, 455-63; Harrison 1969, 1065). There are also more recent documents (eighteenth to second century B.C.), which may provide a more relevant background for Lamentations (Longman 2008, 334).

G. Textual History and Composition

The Hebrew text of Lamentations is well preserved, and variations in the ancient Greek translation (Septuagint) do not seem to point to a different Hebrew text but rather to scribal errors of transmission of the Greek text (Harrison 1969, 1071). This means that the ancient versions are not as helpful as they could be when the Hebrew text is difficult; it also means that conjectural emendations are more common for Lamentations (Hillers 1972, xxxix). There are small fragments of Lamentations in the Dead Sea Scrolls, as well as fragments of poetry that quote Lamentations (Berlin 2002, 36). The full Hebrew text is found in the Leningrad Codex (A.D. 1008) but not in the older Aleppo Codex (ca. A.D. 930).

Unlike Ecclesiastes, the place of Lamentations in the canon was never disputed (Salters 1994, 69). In English Bibles Lamentations follows Jeremiah, but in the Hebrew Bible it is separated from the Prophets and is located in the Writings section (*kĕtûbîm*). It is also one of the five scrolls (*mĕgillôt*) that are read in synagogues on feast days (like Ecclesiastes). Lamentations is read on the 9th of Ab, which is the day commemorating the fall of Jerusalem. Some Christian liturgies include portions of Lamentations on Maundy Thursday, Good Friday, and Holy Saturday.

The liturgical use has determined the order in many published Hebrew Bibles today. The five scrolls are ordered according to their occurrence in the Jewish calendar (Song of Songs, Ruth, Lamentations, Ecclesiastes, Esther). The critical edition of the Hebrew Bible, however, follows the order in the Leningrad Codex (the oldest complete manuscript), which follows a perceived chronological order for the five scrolls (Ruth, Song of Songs, Ecclesiastes, Lamentations, and Esther) (Hillers 1972, xvii).

While elements of Lamentations may have had an independent history before being collected together or given their acrostic structure, the nature of this history cannot be discovered with certainty, and the book forms a coherent whole as it now stands (Provan 1991, 17; Hillers 1972, xxii).

H. Literary Features

I. Genre

Hermann Gunkel was the pioneer of genre analysis of the Psalms; his work remains relevant for Lamentations, which shares several stylistic features with the Psalms. The most common genre in the book of Psalms is the lament or complaint psalm. Lamentations 5 reflects the characteristics of this genre (partially). Gunkel admits that the other poems are mixed, although he categorizes chs 1, 2, and 4 as funeral songs and ch 3 as an individual lament (1933, 95, 121). Because the whole book laments a community disaster, even ch 3 really reflects the voice of the community (Gottwald 1962, 34; Soggin disagrees [1989, 459]).

The classic expressions of the funeral song are occasioned by the deaths of Saul and Abner (2 Sam 1:17-27; 3:33-34; see Amos 5:1-2). The essential elements are an announcement of death, an expression of grief, a call to mourn, and use of the word "how." The funeral song differs fundamentally from the lament in that the circumstances cannot be reversed when someone has died. In a lament, however, there is a petition for Yahweh to reverse the misfortune (Berlin 2002, 24).

The poems of Lamentations lack essential elements of the funeral song (e.g., announcement of death) and add elements foreign to this genre (e.g., appeal to Yahweh). Such significant modification of form has prompted Hillers to declare that form criticism is of relatively little help for interpreting Lamentations (1972, xxviii). Yet while the set form of funeral songs and laments do not apply to Lamentations (except ch 5), the imagery and elements of these genres can be related to Lamentations.

The same is true for city laments, which have many elements in common with Lamentations but not a rigid format on which Lamentations is dependent. Such elements include a list of deities who departed from their temples, use of the word "how," divine decree of the destruction, a description of the destruction, deities who have acted like enemies, and prayer for the deities to return (Longman 2008, 333; see also Bergant 2002, 8, 10).

Lamentations is a lament over a fallen city with elements of city lament, funeral song, and lament (community and individual). The eclectic nature of the book has led Morse to suggest the analogy of a photo montage as the genre of Lamentations. "Graphically and provocatively, Lamentations thrusts images of destruction before the viewer in relentless bursts" (2003, 115).

2. Linguistic Style

The linguistic style of Lamentations is typical of postexilic writing except that verbs are sometimes constructed from nouns (e.g., *yāʿib*, "becloud," 2:1); and homonyms are used in the same verse (e.g., *ʿôlal*, "to do" and "little child," 2:20; Berlin 2002, 3). Verb tenses can be difficult in Lamentations and the overall context is often important to determine the time of action. Lamentations 3:56-61 in particular seems to represent hope for the future, although the perfect verb is used (which is usually translated as past; Provan 1991, 81).

3. Literary Style

Acrostic Poems

Lamentations consists of four alphabetic acrostics plus a poem that has twenty-two verses (the number of letters in the Hebrew alphabet) but is not acrostic. Usually acrostic poems spell out a meaningful word or name in the first letters of each line (as in ancient Near Eastern literature; Hillers 1972, xxv). The acrostics of Lamentations merely spell out the alphabet, which has no meaning in itself.

Some critics are of the opinion that a rigid form stifles and even obscures content, while others see form as an important clue to the nature of the content, and inseparable from that content. Some see the alphabetic acrostic as a masterful achievement, while others see it as an elementary form requiring little skill to produce.

While acrostics may be relatively easy to reproduce (my children are regularly required to write them in school), the poems of Lamentations have not used the form slavishly. There is variation among the poems. Moreover, this form must have been employed for a specific purpose; otherwise, the form could even belittle the depth of grief that is being expressed in Lamentations.

Commentators have given some helpful suggestions as to the purpose of the acrostic in Lamentations. There is always the advantage that the acrostic style gives in memorization. Recall is prompted because the next line will begin with the next letter of the alphabet. Some think it adds beauty (Hillers 1972, xxvi). A more significant possibility is that the use of the entire alphabet suggests the fullness of grief experienced (Keil 1873, 337). This seems to have an analogy in the Talmud, which mentions "the people who fulfill the Torah from *aleph* to *taw*" (*Shabbath* 55a; Salters 1994, 90). For Gottwald this also means a complete emotional catharsis, as well as a total confession of sin, which would lead to hope (1962, 30). The most hopeful poem, then, has the most extensive acrostic (third poem). Harrison thought that it implies a limit to grief (1969, 1069). Only twenty-two verses of emotion can be voiced before the alphabet is spent, and life goes on.

Another helpful suggestion is that the acrostic attempts to bring order to the chaos of suffering (Berlin 2002, 5). The third poem is the most extensive acrostic with three lines per verse, each of the three lines beginning with the same letter of the alphabet. As such it represents the bravest attempt to bring order and hope. But the effort cannot be sustained and ch 4 offers a less ambitious acrostic (with only two lines per verse). Chapter 5 abandons the attempt altogether, and the book almost ends in despair (with no acrostic and only one line per verse).

Voices

An important element of the literary style of Lamentations is the use of different voices. There is an interchange between an omniscient narrator, the city of Jerusalem, and the "man" (*geber*) of ch 3. God does not speak in the book, despite the prayers that are recorded. Lanahan identifies five voices in Lamentations corresponding to the five chapters: reporter, Jerusalem, soldier, bourgeois, and choral voice (1974, 41-49).

Meter

In 1882, Karle Budde identified a characteristic meter in Lamentations that he noticed was present in other OT laments (Driver 1897, 429). He titled this the *qinah* ("lament") meter, and it is characterized by three accented syllables in the first half of a line and two in the second (or some combination where the second half is shorter than the first). Most OT poetry has a three/three pattern. Driver noted that this meter is suitable for laments because the shorter second half of the line "seems, as it were, to die away in it, and a plaintive, melancholy cadence is thus produced" (1897, 430). The book as a whole also seems to follow this pattern. The first three chapters have stanzas of three lines each. In the fourth chapter there are two lines in each stanza, and in the fifth, stanzas are made up of only one line. The lament is thus gradually choked out and dies away. Where verses in Lamentations deviate from this pattern, Budde suggested emendation. Modern scholarship is less confident about Budde's analysis, and scholars readily admit a lack of understanding of ancient Hebrew poetry conventions and offer a number of different theories to explain the variations (Hillers 1972, xxxiii).

Outline

I. How Deserted (1:1-22)
II. The Cloud of God's Anger (2:1-22)
III. I Am the Man (3:1-66)
IV. The Gold Has Lost Its Luster (4:1-22)
V. Remember, Yahweh (5:1-22)

Summary

The book of Lamentations begins with the word "How," expressing wonder at the fall of Jerusalem and the subsequent suffering of its people under postwar conditions. The first contrast with prewar prosperity is the lack of people. Joy has been replaced with weeping, friends have become enemies, and ample provision has turned to hunger. There is an admission of guilt (1:8) and a call for God to observe (and act upon) the present state of suffering (1:9, 20). No comforter is found to alleviate the suffering (1:16). The situation of suffering in ch 1 is followed in ch 2 with an emphasis on the ultimate cause of the plight: God's anger (2:1-10). The extent of the resulting pain is emphasized with images of weeping (2:11-18), and there is once again a call for God to observe (and act; 2:19-22). In ch 3 the acrostic form of the poems intensifies as every line begins with a specific letter of the alphabet, showing that the central poem is climactic. The description becomes personal with the reflection of a "man" who has seen affliction (3:1-20), but nevertheless holds on to a thread of hope based on God's faithfulness and love (3:21-36). There is a qualified admission of guilt and an affirmation of the sovereignty of God (3:37-54). This poem also ends in a plea for God to observe (and act; 3:55-66). With the fourth poem the book begins to wind down, and each letter of the alphabet receives only two lines instead of three. The once precious inhabitants of Jerusalem are now likened to worthless clay (4:1-9), the prophets and priests are condemned for their role in the city's demise (4:10-16), and the plea for God to see is replaced by a recognition that no help was forthcoming in the time of crisis (4:17-22). Nevertheless there is a faint hope that the exile will not be endless (4:22). The exhausted acrostic form is abandoned in the fifth poem and the twenty-two verses are further shortened to one line each. There is a call for God to remember (and act upon) the continued hardships and suffering (5:1-18) and to restore the city to its former relationship with God (5:19-22). But there is an expression of God's excruciating delay in such a restoration, and the book ends in the despair of the possibility that God's anger has no measure (5:20, 22).

I. Theological Themes

The loss of Jerusalem presented a major theological crisis for Israel and different biblical books negotiated this crisis in different ways. Even through the expression of grief, Lamentations provides theological explanation for the calamity. First, the author (and the community) interpret the fall of Jerusalem as a major disaster. The disaster was brought about not by divine impotence or indifference but as a discipline for rebellion. God had indeed been faithful to his part in the covenant, while the nation of Israel had failed to keep its commitments. This holds open the hope that blessing could be restored through renewed covenant faithfulness (3:21-24).

1. Suffering

Suffering is the major theme of the book. Every chapter catalogs the desertion, shame, and hunger suffered by the inhabitants of Jerusalem.

2. Sovereignty of God

The profound sense of the sovereignty of God leaves the ultimate cause for the suffering with him. He made Jerusalem suffer (1:5), he has drawn his bow against the city (2:4), he has purposed this disaster (2:17), and his word is law (3:37; Brady 2003, 89).

3. Suffering Is the Result of Sin

Jerusalem's sin provides the rationale as to why God would use his sovereignty against his own covenant partner (1:5; 2:14; 3:42; 5:7; 5:16).

4. Repentance

Jerusalem is right to cry out in lamentation over its circumstances, but repentance is also a needed response. This is not a strong theme in Lamentations, but there are some moves toward repentance (3:40).

5. Hope

Like repentance, hope is veiled in Lamentations, but it is to be found primarily in the character of God, rather than human repentance or other activity. His faithfulness is great, and his compassions are new every morning (3:21-26; 3:55-66; 4:21-22). Yet the book ends unsure whether hope or despair will have the last word (5:22).

COMMENTARY ON LAMENTATIONS

I. POEM ONE: HOW DESERTED (1:1-22)

BEHIND THE TEXT

The first poem in Lamentations sets the tone of a deserted city facing the hardships and humiliation of defeat. This chapter introduces the main themes of sin and pleading to God. The second poem (ch 2) will intensify these themes with a focus on God's anger.

Lamentations 1 was classified as a funeral song by Gunkel (1933, 95). The opening word, **How,** and the reversal of fortunes are consistent with this, but the city itself is not said to be dead and there is no invitation to join the mourning. There are several elements of the city lament in ch 1: the word **How** (1:1); finding no rest (1:3); cessation of celebrations (1:4); **fire** from heaven (1:13); spreading **a net** (1:13); the collapse of civic order and the deity as the cause of the disaster (1:5) (McDaniel 1968, 201-2; Bergant 2002, 11).

The acrostic poems of Lamentations are carefully composed and yet, apart from the alphabetic form, they do not have a clear outline of form or content (or the structure is frequently interrupted). The outlines of individual poems offered here are therefore very generalized. Chapter 1 can be outlined as follows:

How Deserted Lies the City (1:1-11)
Look at My Suffering! (1:12-22)

IN THE TEXT

In the ancient translations, v 1 is preceded by information about Jeremiah as the author of the book. There is no mention of this in the Hebrew manuscripts and no other direct evidence of authorship (see Authorship section in the Introduction).

A. How Deserted Lies the City (1:1-11)

■ **1** **Alef.** The first verse of the book of Lamentations gives the setting for the entire book, presumably the deserted city of Jerusalem following its destruction by Nebuchadnezzar in 586 B.C. The city has experienced major reversals in terms of size and honor. In Hebrew the opening word, **How,** begins with *alef,* the first letter of the Hebrew alphabet, and so this verse begins the acrostic structure that characterizes the first four chapters. Like many Hebrew books, the first word is the Hebrew name of the book (*'ēkâ*) and also begins the poems in chs 2 and 4 (and is used in 4:2). The same form and usage of this word is found elsewhere only in Isa 1:21 and Jer 48:17. In Isaiah it is also the city of Jerusalem, which is lamented (specifically the loss of justice), and in Jeremiah the exclamation is for the defeat of the neighboring nation Moab. The word can also be used as a question ("how?"). The few uses of *'ēkâ* as an exclamation are all in laments.

The word **deserted** is ironic because this word (*bādād*) can also have the figurative meaning of "security" in the sense of "freedom from attack" (Deut 33:28; Jer 49:31; BDB 94-95). Jerusalem felt secure under Yahweh's protection but is now isolated and alone.

A repetition of vocabulary in v 1 is obscured in translation; **once so full** and **once was great** are the same word in Hebrew (*rabbātî;* see 2:6, 20 for other examples of homonyms in the same verse). Both meanings are within the usual range of the word, although **great** (that is, "large") is less frequent (BDB 913). This choice of words allows repetition in the first two lines of v 1 (each verse has three lines). The form *rabbātî* used in both instances is unusual, and the final *yod* is thought to be an ancient genitive case ending (GKC §90*l*). The archaic form does not indicate an ancient text (like it might for archaic poetry such as that found in Judg 5) but must have been chosen for poetic reasons.

McDaniel suggests that the translation should be "lady, mistress" following the use of this root in cognate languages (Phoenician, Ugaritic, and Punic; cited by Provan 1991, 35). This would give a translation "the city was a mistress of people . . . a lady among the nations." Biblical use of the word, however, favors the traditional translation and emphasizes the contrast better, without losing the feminine imagery for Jerusalem (**widow, queen**).

The city of Jerusalem is compared to a **widow,** which implied very low status in ancient Israel. With no social welfare system, widows were left destitute unless they had adult sons or other family support. Along with disadvantaged classes, such as resident aliens and orphans, widows were too often subject to oppression (see Isa 10:1-2), and special laws were in force to protect them (Deut 10:17-19; 24:17-22; 27:19). Isaiah also compared conquered Jerusalem to a widow, but in that case the prophecy is one of renewal, and widowhood is to be left behind (Isa 54:4; King and Stager 2001, 53).

Bergant has noted the significance of the personification of Jerusalem as a woman (**widow, queen**) (2003, 28). The city walls enclose the population as a mother's womb encloses a child. But the city-mother is no longer full of children, bereft like a widow.

Isaiah 54:4-6

"Do not be afraid; you will not suffer shame.
Do not fear disgrace; you will not be humiliated.
You will forget the shame of your youth
and remember no more the reproach of your widowhood.
For your Maker is your husband—
the Lord Almighty is his name—
the Holy One of Israel is your Redeemer;
he is called the God of all the earth.
The Lord will call you back
as if you were a wife deserted and distressed in spirit—
a wife who married young,
only to be rejected," says your God.

The word for **queen** (*śārātî*) does not specifically denote a sovereign ruler, or the wife of a king. *Śārātî* is the feminine form of a more general word for a chief or ruler, regardless of lineage. In the feminine form it is used for women who are nobility or daughters of kings (1 Kgs 11:3; Esth 1:18; Judg 5:29; Isa 49:23).

From this high status as a ruler among the nations and cities, Jerusalem has fallen to the status of **slave.** This is not the usual word for slave (*'ebed*) but is a group of laborers (*maś*). Jerusalem was already a vassal of Babylon. Its situation is now worse with even less independence. The term is also applied to Israel's slavery in Egypt (Exod 1:11; see Deut 20:11; Isa 31:8).

■ **2 Bet.** Adding to the loneliness and shame of defeat, v 2 decries the lack of comforters for Jerusalem (see 1:2, 9, 16, 17, 21; Jer 31:15). The same vocabulary is used in Isa 40 to call for comforters for the people of defeated Jerusalem (see Isa 40:1; 49:13; 51:3, 12; 52:9).

Jerusalem's loneliness is intensified by the fact that her **lovers** and **friends** have become her betrayers and **enemies.** The word **lovers** perhaps refers to pagan deities (see Jer 2:25, 28, 33). Jerusalem sought **friends** (political allies) among the Assyrians during the days of King Ahaz, and apparently among the Egyptians during the days of Jeremiah. But these "friends" were not real friends as they were more concerned with their own interests. Isaiah portrayed trusting Egypt as leaning on a "splintered reed of a staff" (Isa 36:6). Jerusalem has entered into these relationships unwisely and found her **friends** and **lovers** treacherous associates who cannot comfort her. The theme of treacherous friends is common in laments (e.g., Ps 38:11; Provan 1991, 13, 37). The word **enemies** occurs frequently in the book (1:2, 5, 9, 16, 21; 2:3, 4, 5, 7, 16, 17, 22; 3:46, 52; 4:12). The similar sound of the Hebrew words for **lovers** (*ʾōhēb*) and **enemies** (*ʾōyēb*) emphasizes the reversal of Jerusalem's experience. The people of Jerusalem are suffering the consequence of their failure to trust in God for their security and welfare. They rejected God and now they are being rejected by the nations they trusted.

■ **3 Gimel.** The Hebrew of v 3 reads literally as follows: *Judah was exiled from affliction and harsh labor.* The Targum took this to mean that exile came *because* (*min*) Jerusalem oppressed orphans (Brady 2003, 33-34). But elsewhere the verb *exile* followed by *min* means "exiled out of" (1 Sam 4:21-22; Ezek 12:3; Mic 1:16; Berlin 2002, 45). This suggests that the exile followed the suffering and leads to the translation **After affliction and harsh labor, Judah has gone into exile.** The last phrase exaggerates the situation for effect as only a portion of the population was deported (Provan 1991, 14, 38).

Judah **dwells among the nations** reiterates the condition of the exile of the nation. Moreover, in her condition of exile, **she finds no resting place.** This is a reversal of the promised rest in the land (Deut 12:9; Ps 95:11). The precise meaning of the last line (**All who pursue her have overtaken her in the midst of her distress**) is not clear. The word **distress** (*mĕṣārim*) comes from a verb that can mean "cramped, narrow" (Bergant 2003, 32). The reading in the New Jerusalem Bible, "her persecutors all overtake her where there is no way out," conveys the idea of Judah in a dangerous condition. **Distress** (*mĕṣārim*) also sounds like the Hebrew for "Egypt" (*miṣrayim*), which could be intended to recall the slavery in Egypt (Berlin 2002, 51). Goldman suggested that the reference is not to Babylonian exile, but to those who retreated to Egypt at that time (1946, 71).

The Deserted City by C. G. A. Roberts (1893)

There lies a little city leagues away.
    Its wharves the green sea washes all day long.
    Its busy, sun-bright wharves with sailors' song
And clamour of trade ring loud the live-long day.
Into the happy harbour hastening, gay
    With press of snowy canvas, tall ships throng.
    The peopled streets to blithe-eyed Peace belong.
Glad housed beneath these crowding roofs of grey.

'Twas long ago this city prospered so,
    For yesterday a woman died therein.
Since when the wharves are idle fallen, I know,
    And in the streets is hushed the pleasant din;
    The thronging ships have been, the songs have been;—
Since yesterday it is so long ago.

■ **4 Dalet.** Verse 4 continues the desolate and abandoned condition of Jerusalem. **The roads to Zion mourn** because of the lack of pilgrims coming to the feasts in Jerusalem. The book of Exodus required attendance at three feasts every year: the Feast of Unleavened Bread (or Passover) celebrating the beginning of the barley harvest and the commemoration of the exodus from Egypt; the Feast of Harvest (or Weeks) marking the end of the wheat harvest and later connected with the giving of the Ten Commandments; and the Feast of Ingathering (or Tabernacles), which marked the end of the fruit harvest and commemorated the time in the wilderness (Exod 23:14-17). Lamentations so far has not identified sin as the cause of the disaster, but the Targum charged that the roads to Zion were empty precisely because the people had not kept the pilgrim festivals (Brady 2003, 35-36). Jerusalem is called by the poetic name **Zion,** which is technically the stronghold of the Jebusites and which David captured and renamed "the City of David" (2 Sam 5:7; 1 Kgs 8:1).

In a walled city like Jerusalem, the gates were a meeting place. The destruction of Jerusalem brought an end to such gathering of people in the **gateways** and they remained as **desolate** places. The **priests groan** because they have lost their work and livelihood with the destruction of the temple and the cessation of worship (see Joel 1:9). The **maidens** of Jerusalem grieve because the destruction of the city meant an end of festivities, song, and dance in the streets of Jerusalem (see Jer 31:13). The Septuagint has the maidens dragged away, which may reflect the general displacement of the population or may have in mind the frequent treatment of women as plunder in the ancient world. The city itself, personified as a woman, is in **bitter anguish,** because of the loss of population and destruction and devastation all around the city.

■ **5 He.** Verse 5 continues the lament on the reversal of fortunes. Jerusalem is ruled by its **enemies** who are now **at ease.** The word **foe** occurs at the beginning and end of v 5, "linguistically surrounding and capturing Zion and her suffering children just as the foes surround the city" (O'Connor 2002, 21). Foes becoming **masters** (lit., *head*) echoes the covenant curse in Deut 28:44 (see 28:13), which warns of aliens becoming the head and Israel the tail if the nation fails to live in faithful relation to Yahweh. Lamentations 1:5 acknowledges the reality that Jerusalem's present condition is the work of Yahweh even though Babylon is the political agent that destroyed Jerusalem. This type of theological interpretation of historical events is common in the Bible. Though the immediate causes of an event may be clearly known, the biblical tradition often recognizes God as the ultimate cause. For example, in the prologue section of the book of Job, readers are first introduced to the role of the Satan in Job's suffering, but then the narrative identifies the Sabeteans, lightning, the Chaldeans, a mighty wind, and illness as the immediate causes. However, Job claims that God is the one who gives and takes away his blessings (Job 1:21). In the case of the destruction of Jerusalem, there is a connection between the historical and theological realities. It was the same rebellious spirit of the people of Judah, which led to both their rejection of Yahweh and their refusal to submit to Babylon (which brought the retaliation of the Babylonians). If they had a healthy relationship with God, their international relationships would also have been very different.

Verse 5 also makes clear the reason for Yahweh bringing grief to Jerusalem. This condition is the consequence of **her many sins** (*pĕšāʿêhā*). The OT often uses the word *pešaʿ* for political rebellion (e.g., 1 Kgs 12:19). This admission of guilt and culpability by the lamenting community also implies its recognition that it is experiencing discipline from God rather than punishment or retribution (see Ambrose in Wenthe 2009, 290). God was not trying to get back at them, but to get them back. The destruction of Jerusalem and exile was part of this discipline.

Annals of Ashurbanipal, Rassam Cylinder

Famine broke out among them and they ate the flesh of their children against their hunger. Ashur, Sin, Shamash, Adad, Bel, Nebo, the Ishtar of Nineveh—the Queen of Kidmuri—the Ishtar of Arbela, Ninurta, Nergal (and) Nusku (thus) inflicted quickly upon them (all) the curses written (down) in their sworn agreements. . . . Whenever the inhabitants of Arabia asked each other: "On account of what have these calamities befallen Arabia?" (they answered themselves:) "Because we did not keep the solemn oaths (sworn by) Ashur, because we offended the friendliness of Ashurbanipal, the king, beloved by Ellil!" (Pritchard 1969, 300)

■ **6 Waw.** Verse 6 portrays Jerusalem as a city that has lost its **splendor** and likens it to a **deer** fleeing from hunters. The Septuagint, assuming a different vocalization, translated **deer** (*ʾayyālîm*) as "rams" (*ʾêlîm*), giving the image of sheep before a drover, rather than deer before a hunter. The translation **Daughter of Zion** is misleading because it gives the impression that a subset of Jerusalem is in view, when in fact it is a term of endearment signifying the population of Jerusalem as a whole (Hillers 1972, xxxviii). The phrase (or a variation) is used twenty times in the book, sixteen times in Jeremiah, and about ten times elsewhere (Berlin 2002, 10). It may originate from the ancient Near Eastern idea of a patron goddess of the city (O'Connor 2002, 14, citing Dobbs-Allsopp). The Targum preferred the translation "congregation of Israel" (*kĕnesset*; Brady 2003, 84). **Princes** (*śar*) is not specifically the sons of the king, but a general term for leaders or rulers.

■ **7 Zayin.** In the midst of **affliction and wandering** Jerusalem **remembers all the treasures** she once had in the past. The remembrance of the past prompts Jerusalem to lament over the loss of her treasures. The word **affliction** is often used in connection with a sojourner or foreigner (*gēr*), representing the poor and disenfranchised in the land (e.g., Lev 19:10). However, if the consonants have been mistakenly transposed, the correct root could be *yārad*, "to go down," which is found in the form of a noun *môrād* (i.e., the consonants *mwrd* instead of *mrwd*). This word usually means a slope or a descending road (e.g., Jer 48:5). This would make the reference in Lam 1:7 to Jerusalem's **affliction** and fall or descent from honor (or the descent of the population as they leave the city). Verse 9 uses the same root to refer to the fall of Jerusalem. **Wandering** (*mĕrûdĕhā*) in v 7 is rare and of uncertain meaning. Some ancient versions render it "rebel" while the Septuagint offers "rejection, thrusting away." The RSV emends the consonants to translate as "bitterness." The translation **wandering** assumes the root *rûd*, which, if correct, could imply the **wandering** or traveling of Jerusalem's residents into exile.

Peake suggested that the line **all the treasures that were hers in days of old** is probably an addition to the text (1911, 305). Verse 7 has four lines, while other verses in the book have three lines each, which suggests that one of these four lines may have been added by a scribe. The phrase **days of old** uses the root meaning "in front of" (*qedem*) reflecting the Hebrew conception that one backs into the future. This is logical as the past is known, but the future is not. English usage parallels this, as the word "before" refers not only to the past but also to what is in front. Lamentations ends with uncertainty about what the future may hold.

The second part of v 7 reiterates the abandoned condition of Jerusalem's population. No one came to rescue or help the people when the enemy invaded the land. Jerusalem's humiliation included the laughter of Judah's neighboring nations and historic enemies (see Obad 11-13). The word for **destruction** (*mišbatehā*) is used only here in the OT. Ancient versions translate the word as "settlement, dwelling" or "deportation, captivity." Dead Sea Scrolls have "her ruins" (*mšbrh*). A translation such as "demise" would be appropriate.

■ **8 Khet.** Verse 8 acknowledges the grievous sin of Jerusalem (**Jerusalem has sinned greatly**). Jerusalem's sins have made the holy city an unclean place. The Hebrew word for **unclean** (*lĕnîdâ*) is used only here in the OT and could be understood in three ways. The first is the sense "wander" (assuming the root *nwd* with the Dead Sea Scrolls), which fits well as a consequence of sin (as Cain was sent to Nod, the land of wandering; Gen 4:12-16). The second is "derision" (from the same root), which fits well with the following line where people **despise** Zion. The third is an emendation giving the translation **unclean,** which fits well with the following verse. All three readings are helpful as the argument progresses (Berlin 2002, 54).

Verse 8 continues the theme of Jerusalem's humiliation. Once Jerusalem held a place of honor among the nations; now she is a despised and naked city. **Nakedness** conveys the idea of great shame and humiliation. It is also an image of being conquered and led into slavery (Isa 47:3; Jer 13:26; Nah 3:5). Verse 8 ends with the portrait of Jerusalem groaning because of rejection, humiliation, and loss of honor among the nations.

■ **9 Tet.** Verse 9 continues the theme of Jerusalem's uncleanness. **Her filthiness clung to her skirts** (*ṭum'ātāh bĕšûlêhā*) conveys the idea that Jerusalem has become an unclean place through idolatry and foreign alliances. The word **skirts** (*bĕšûlêhā*) here refers to the hem or lower part of the robe (Exod 28:33). **Filthiness** (*ṭum'ātāh*) often refers to ritual impurities such as menstruation (Brady 2003, 76). Here it refers to promiscuity (Berlin 2002, 54).

Verse 9 ends with Jerusalem's appeal to Yahweh to pay attention to its affliction. The first person form, **my affliction** (*'ānĕyî*), is unusual in a poem that has a third person perspective, speaking *about* Jerusalem and its fate. Hence the editors of BHS suggest reading "her affliction." But the first person form gives a personal force to the outcry to Yahweh, and the Hebrew text makes sense in its current form. The prayer for Yahweh to **look** on Jerusalem's **affliction** conveys hope; in the past Yahweh had seen Israel's affliction when the people were slaves in Egypt and saved them from their affliction (Exod 3:7). The appeal also conveys trust in Yahweh's power to save his people from their affliction.

■ **10 Yod.** Verse 10 decries the entry of foreigners into the temple to plunder its treasures. Temples were a common location of wealth, and invaders would always carry golden vessels away. Later the book of Daniel condemned Belshazzar for irreverently using these holy vessels as drinking cups in his banquet (Dan 5:2-3). The repeated occurrence of such events (e.g., illegal temple entry in 597, 586, and 167 B.C.) has prompted Provan to challenge the usual interpretation of the 586 B.C. fall of Jerusalem as the occasion of Lamentations (1991, 13). Those who were **forbidden to enter your assembly** are apparently the Ammonites and Moabites of Deut 23:3 and, by extension, the Babylonians.

■ **11 Kaf.** Verse 11 documents the shortage of food during the siege of the city. During such times, people traded their hoarded material possessions to buy food and to **keep themselves alive.** Wealth is of no other value to someone who is starving (see Matt 16:26). There is another call in this verse for Yahweh to **look** and **consider** (*wĕhabbîṭâ*) the plight of Jerusalem (see 1:9).

B. Look at My Suffering! (1:12-22)

■ **12 Lamed.** Verse 12 asks, **Is it nothing to you?** as none of the hypothetical observers offer any comfort (see vv 2, 9, etc.). Provan renders this question as "Is it not for you?" implying that Jerusalem's suffering is to help others avoid the consequences of disobedience (1991, 48). This can only be a peripheral purpose of the suffering, however, and the line could be a wish, "May it never happen to you" (Harrison 1973, 210), or more likely just a statement, "It is not for you (to be concerned about)" (see Albrektson 1963, 68-69). Passersby are more likely to mock than to comfort, and this is a common feature in laments (e.g., Ps 89:41). Obadiah condemned neighboring Edom for rejoicing at the misfortune of Judah and failing to help (Obad 12).

The second part of v 12 indicates the greatness of Jerusalem's suffering; it cannot be compared to any other people's suffering. It is great and without comparison because it is brought upon Jerusalem by Yahweh's **fierce anger.** Nevertheless, Jerusalem should seek comfort from Yahweh (v 11). God's anger is mentioned eleven times in Lamentations. **The day of his fierce anger** seems to connect with the "day of Yahweh," a common prediction of disaster in the Prophets.

The Day of Yahweh

The concept of the day of Yahweh apparently arose from the miracles of the past wars of conquest in which Yahweh delivered Israel from its enemies. Israel's popular tradition expected Yahweh to intervene and save Israel from future enemy invasions. Amos took this expectation of judgment for foreign nations and applied it to the northern kingdom of Israel (Amos 5:20). Israel apparently had its day of Yahweh when Samaria was destroyed in 722 B.C. The day of Yahweh was applied to Judah as a future event (Isa 22:5), and then as a past event (Lam 1:12; 2:22; Ezek 34:12). After the fall of Jerusalem the terminology was still employed for future events, often with cosmological significance (Joel 1:15—2:11).

■ **13 Mem.** Verse 13 describes the tragedy as actions that Yahweh sent or carried out to make Jerusalem a desolate place. **Fire sent from on high** is the usual way to describe lightning or volcanic eruption in the OT (Gen 19:24; Exod 9:23-24). The destruction of Jerusalem did not occur through either of these, but invaders often used fire to bring about complete destruction of a city. This was the case for Jerusalem, as for Hazor in the conquest of Joshua (Josh 11:11). Amos promised fire from Yahweh for all eight nations in his opening prophecy, which condemned not only foreign nations but also Judah and especially the northern kingdom of Israel. Although the literal fire that destroyed Jerusalem may have been set by the Babylonians, Yahweh is credited as the ultimate cause of the destruction.

Spreading of a **net** is another metaphor that the author uses to describe Yahweh's action on Jerusalem. This metaphor is also used by Ezekiel (12:13; 17:20; 19:8; 32:3) and Hosea (5:1; 7:12). In the Psalms, God rescues from the net (25:15; 31:4), but here Yahweh's action causes destruction, desolation, and fainting.

■ **14 Nun.** Verse 14 describes the sin of Jerusalem as **bound into a yoke** (*niśqad ʿōl*). This phrase is found only here in the OT; some Hebrew manuscripts (and Septuagint) have *niśqad ʿal*, that is, "watch is kept upon." Either Yahweh bound the sins of Judah into a yoke that Judah must bear (see e.g., Lev 19:8) or Yahweh has been watching their sins and has placed them upon the **neck** of Judah. Both readings yield the same meaning. The weight of Judah's sin is too great and its **strength** has failed. Neither can it stand or arise against the enemy, which is bringing God's punishment. A yoke is elsewhere a metaphor for servitude (e.g., Jer 27:8).

■ **15 Samek.** Verse 15 portrays Jerusalem as a city being trampled by a foreign army at the summons of Yahweh. The word **rejected** is only used four times in the OT (Job 28:16, 19; Ps 119:118). God rejects the effectiveness of Jerusalem's defenses (**all the warriors in my midst**), and sends **against** the city an **army** (lit., *assembly*) to crush the young soldiers of Jerusalem. The **winepress** (*gat*) is literally the stone pit where harvested grapes were trampled with bare feet to squeeze the juice out. In this verse it is metaphorical for the judgment of God trampling the people of Judah until blood flowed like red grape juice (see also Joel 3:13). **The Virgin Daughter of Judah** is not a subset of Judah but a metaphor for Judah as a whole (see comment on 1:6).

■ **16 Ayin.** Verse 16 revisits the theme of no comforter (1:2, 9), and the expression of grief takes the form of weeping. The Hebrew behind **overflow with tears** (*yōrĕdâ mayim*) is unusual because *yārad* ("to go down") is usually an intransitive verb (it does not take a direct object) but here it has the object "water" (lit., *my eye my eye goes down water*. The double occurrence of "my eye" adds emphasis, although it is missing from some manuscripts and may be an addition. There is no one to comfort or restore the spirit of Jerusalem. Jerusalem stands in need of both emotional comfort and physical survival in the aftermath of the destruction of the city in 586 B.C. The lament **My children are destitute** shows the natural parental concern for children, as it is more difficult to see the children suffer than to suffer oneself. This highlights the depth of desperation when the city was under siege and was later taken over by the enemy. The victory of the enemy over Jerusalem is another reason for the intense grief expressed in this verse.

Grief by Elizabeth Barrett Browning (1844)

> I tell you, hopeless grief is passionless;
> That only men incredulous of despair,
> Half-taught in anguish, through the midnight air
> Beat upward to God's throne in loud access
> Of shrieking and reproach. Full desertness,
> In souls as countries, lieth silent-bare
> Under the blanching, vertical eye-glare
> Of the absolute Heavens. Deep-hearted man, express
> Grief for thy Dead in silence like to death—
> Most like a monumental statue set
> In everlasting watch and moveless woe
> Till itself crumble to the dust beneath.
> Touch it; the marble eyelids are not wet:
> If it could weep, it could arise and go.

1:16-18

■ **17** Pe. The portrait of Jerusalem (**Zion**) in v 17 is that of a woman with hands stretched out and calling for help and comfort. This stretching out of hands (*pērĕśâ*) to seek comfort is necessary because of the stretching out of the enemy's hand in conquest (1:10, "laid hands") and the stretching out of a net (1:13, "spread a net"). Hands were also stretched out (raised) during prayer (Isa 1:15; Jer 4:31). Using different vocabulary (*nāṭāh*) God elsewhere stretched out his hand in judgment (Isa 5:25) and stretched out his arm to save (Deut 4:34).

Yahweh was credited with the destruction of Jerusalem earlier in the poem (1:5, 14), but in v 17 he is said to have "commanded" (**decreed**, *ṣiwwâ*) **for Jacob that his neighbors become his foes.** There is a sense in which this command comes because Judah has disobeyed the command God gave his people (this connection is explicit in the NIV translation of 1:18, but "command" is not in the Hebrew text of that verse). It is by Yahweh's decree that Jerusalem, the once holy place of Yahweh, has become an **unclean** place in the world (see v 8).

■ **18** Tsade. The first part of v 18 is a declaration of Yahweh's righteousness and Judah's confession of sin. Judah has not been righteous, but **The LORD is** righteous (*ṣaddîq*), or in the right (see 2 Chr 12:6; Dan 9:14; Neh 9:33). He has done the right thing in the covenant relationship while Judah has not. Not only has Judah neglected its relationship with God, but its prophets and priests have shed "the blood of the righteous" (4:13).

Ṣaddîq (Righteous)

The root word for **righteous** is used outside the Bible in the sense of a status or behavior that conforms to a standard. In the Bible, this standard may be the Law or some other standard related to a relationship. For example, Jacob was righteous when he dealt honestly with Laban over the division of the flock (Gen 30:33). Judah failed to be righteous when he did not allow Tamar to marry his son (Gen 38:26). Being in the right or doing the right thing applies also to the Law, which is set in a covenant relationship between God and Israel. God's righteousness is seen in his faithfulness to the covenant (Ps 9:4-5) (NIDOTTE 3:744-69).

Verses 9 and 11 called on the Lord to see the affliction of Jerusalem, but here in v 18 it is the **peoples** who are called on to **Listen** and **look**. This is a request to look on with pity, though Judah was more likely to receive the contempt of surrounding nations (see v 7). The Targum takes **I rebelled against his command** as a statement by King Josiah who was not commanded to fight Pharaoh Neco (at whose hand he met his death in 609 B.C.). Thus the Targum considers Josiah's sin to have contributed to the fall of Jerusalem, and Lamentations to contain Jeremiah's laments on this (2 Chr 35:25; Brady 2003, 39-40). The statement that **maidens have gone into exile** apparently contradicts the assertion of 1:4 that maidens are still in the city grieving (although the Septuagint has "dragged away" in v 4). Likewise, the **young men** sent into exile in this verse were already said to be "crushed" in v 15.

■ **19 Qof.** Verse 19 conveys the betrayal of Jerusalem by her allies. **I called to my allies but they betrayed me** is poetic justice for Judah's betrayal of covenant with Yahweh. Neighboring countries could hardly have come to Jerusalem's defense against the mighty Babylonian empire and all had treaties with Babylon that would have precluded any treaty with Judah. Judah also had such a treaty but attracted the wrath of Babylon by refusing to pay the tribute (which was one of the terms of the treaty). So Judah decries the betrayal of others even though it has betrayed both God and Babylon. The Hebrew word for **allies** is literally *lovers* (*lame'ahăbay*); this could mean other gods or inappropriate relationships with other nations. Yahweh should have been Judah's "lover," not other gods or nations (see 1:2).

The **priests** and **elders** should have been people of high standing in the community, and the last ones to starve in the crisis of siege. But things were so bad that even they could not find enough bread to eat. There is an apparent contradiction here with 1:4, which speaks of the priests groaning, not perishing. This is the first notice that conditions were bad enough that they resulted in death (see v 11).

■ **20 Resh.** Yahweh is again called upon to see the distress of Judah in v 20 (see vv 9, 11). The word **distressed** is the same as the word used for "enemy" in 1:5, 7, 10, and 17 (*sar*). Judah's distress is on account of her enemy, Babylon. The phrase **I am in torment within** is literally *my inwards are in tumult* (*mēʿay ḥŏmarmārû*). The word for tumult or **torment** (*ḥŏmarmārû*) is used elsewhere for boiling, or waters foaming up. In Hebrew thinking, bodily organs including the heart represent the seat of emotion, although the heart is often considered the organ of thinking and willpower (the function of the brain was not understood). The words *inwards* and **heart** together stress the totality of the distress.

I have been most rebellious suggests another confession. The word **rebellious** (*mārâ*) is similar to "bitter" (*mārar*), which seems to fit the context better (see the Septuagint). There is some ambiguity in the phrase **Outside, the sword bereaves; inside, there is only death.** Literally the words speak of the "street" (*miḥûṣ*) and the "house" (*babbayit*). More accurately, the sword was outside the city gates, while inside the famine was claiming lives (Jer 14:18; Ezek 7:15). Metaphorically, there was physical danger (outside), while psychologically the strain of siege was claiming all courage and even the will to live (inside).

■ **21 Sin and Shin.** Verse 21 returns to the theme of the lack of comforters. The order of the Hebrew alphabet allows this poem to follow up the call to "see" in v 20, with the call to "hear" in v 21. This assumes an imperative force for "hear" along with the ancient Greek and Syriac versions. The Hebrew text has the indicative "they heard," which also makes sense. This first poem has both cries to Yahweh to notice Judah's distress, and statements about what the onlooking nations were doing (failing to help or comfort). And so the lament is repeated, **there is no one to comfort me.** Verse 21 continues **All my enemies have heard of my distress.** The word used for **distress** (*rāʿātî*) is also used for evil or wickedness. The surrounding nations would have heard of Judah's distress but must also have known of their evil actions, specifically their rebellion against Babylon, and perhaps even the cry of Judah's own prophets announcing Judah's rebellion against Yahweh.

The last line of v 21 mentions **the day you have announced,** which must be the day of Yahweh that the prophets announced (see comment on 1:12). Verse 21 ends with the wish that the nations would become like Judah in the experience of Yahweh's judgment. This divine justice will be the source of comfort to Judah, which at the present time exists without comfort from anyone. **So they may become like me** goes naturally with the following verse, which calls for judgment on the nations.

■ **22 Taw.** The poem closes with a wish for the same fate to overtake the enemies of Judah. Prayer for God's judgment of one's enemies is frequently found in the lament psalms. In the prayer for vengeance in the lament psalms and in Lamentations, there is an implicit acknowledgment of God as the judge of all who practice evil. Jerusalem demands God's impartial judgment on her enemies in the same way he has brought judgment on Jerusalem. Many of the prophets pronounced oracles against foreign nations—not out of revenge but to bring justice, not only for crimes against Israel but also for crimes against other nations (Amos, Isaiah, Jeremiah, Ezekiel). The poem couples this call for justice with Judah's acknowledgment of guilt.

The lament closes with an expression of despair (**my groans are many and my heart is faint**) to motivate God to respond quickly to the crisis of Jerusalem. The depth of emotion expressed here has prompted interpreters to think that Lamentations was written soon after the disaster of 586 B.C. (see Introduction).

FROM THE TEXT

Suffering

Lamentations 1 introduces the sufferings of Jerusalem, which is the theme of the whole book. The city's suffering is superlative (v 12), it is the cause for unending tears (v 2), it is without comfort (v 21), and it is the result of sin (v 22). This expression of pain is a healthy response and invites the reader/hearer to participate in the sufferings, but it is not the only biblical response. Isaiah 40—55 calls for comforters (40:1; 49:13; 51:3, 12; 52:9), and the NT brings meaning to the sufferings of Christ and calls for contentment from his followers who also suffer (Rom 8:18; 2 Cor 1:5).

Justice

Lamentations laments the suffering of innocent women and children, and yet attributes the suffering to sin (v 22). This explanation for evil breaks down if punishment is to be commensurate with the crime (Bergant 2003, 72). Jerusalem's fall resulted from Zedekiah's rebellion against the Babylonian overlords. This decision had an impact on all in his kingdom, soldier and bystander, innocent and guilty. Sometimes it is appropriate to attribute suffering to sin (whether one's own or someone else's), and sometimes it is not. The NT calls us to alleviate the sufferings of others through practical means and to look ahead to a judgment day when justice will be done.

Complaining to God

Complaining to God seems as unnatural for a Christian as it seems natural for the OT believer. Lament psalms begin with complaint to God and are the largest category in the book of Psalms. Complaints in laments are meaningful expressions of suffering. Complaining to God is a profound act of faith and represents an expectation that God will act in the cause of justice. It is a step toward healing and restoration.

The various repeated and somewhat disjointed expressions of hurt and suffering in this chapter echo the indescribable and devastating human tragedies that we witness in the world today. We, too, hear in our world cries and complaints of those who suffer—the lonely and the abandoned, those who are hurt and traumatized by the tragic effects of poverty, violence, and war. The forsaken Jerusalem invites the church to see, hear, and enter into the contemporary world of suffering and thereby become a place where the brokenhearted and forsaken find healing and comfort.

II. POEM TWO: THE CLOUD OF GOD'S ANGER (2:1-22)

BEHIND THE TEXT

The first poem set the stage for the situation faced by Jerusalem; the second (ch 2) focuses on the cause: God's anger. The suffering is further described, and there is also a call for God to observe (and act). This poem contributes to a building crescendo that finds its climax in the third poem (ch 3).

Chapter 2 was classified as a funeral song by Gunkel but as in ch 1 there is no announcement of death or invitation to mourn, although the poem does begin with **how** (a common element of funeral songs) (1933, 95). It does share some features with city laments: the anger of the deity (e.g., 2:1, 22); the deity as an enemy (2:4-5); the deity abandoning the temple (2:7); the deity determining the destruction (2:8, 17); and the brickwork lamenting (2:8; McDaniel 1968, 203-5).

219

Literary devices in ch 2 include inclusio and catchwords (Bergant 2003, 56). The poem begins and ends with the anger of God (inclusio) thereby confirming the theme that is emphasized through repetition of the vocabulary of anger. There are catchwords linking most verses, for example, the word **Lord** links vv 1-2; the word **Jacob,** vv 2-3; the word **fire,** vv 3-4; the word **enemy,** vv 4-5. This device (called concatenation) is also used in Amos 1—2 (Paul 2002, 60). Chapter 2 can be outlined as follows:

The Cloud of God's Anger (2:1-12)

What Can I Say for You? (2:13-19)

Look, O LORD! (2:20-22)

IN THE TEXT

A. The Cloud of God's Anger (2:1-12)

■ 1 **Alef.** Verse 1 signals the anger of God as an important theme in ch 2. The first word is **How,** like chs 1 and 4. This supplies the first letter of the Hebrew alphabet (*alef*) for the acrostic format. The lament begins with the image of the **Daughter of Zion** covered with a cloud—the cloud of Yahweh's anger. The phrase **covered . . . with the cloud** is the only occurrence of the verbal form of **cloud** in the Hebrew Bible (*yāʿîb*). Usually clouds that are associated with God are positive, but not here (Exod 19:9; 34:5; 1 Kgs 8:10-11). The execution and the outcome of God's anger are stated in the rest of v 1. God's anger is mentioned eleven times in Lamentations, including six occurrences in ch 2. In his anger, God has **hurled down the splendor of Israel,** just as Babylon and Tyre were cast down from high places (Isa 14:12; Ezek 28:17). God's anger is further manifested in his lack of remembrance of his footstool. His **footstool** is Jerusalem (or perhaps the ark of the covenant). This is a positive designation in this case (it can be negative, see Ps 110:1). In Isa 66:1, heaven is described as God's throne, and the earth his footstool. The ark of the covenant is God's footstool in 1 Chr 28:2. God **has not remembered** Zion implies that he has remembered her sins. What is at work now is not God's compassion, forgiveness, and mercy, but anger brought about by the remembrance of sins. The verb **remembered** (*zākar*) involves not only recalling something but also acting on it.

■ 2 **Bet.** Verse 2 continues to describe the humiliation of Judah. The entire kingdom with all of its princes, dwellings, and strongholds has been **swallowed up** by God in his anger without showing any pity to the people of Judah. The **dwellings** (or pastures) stand in contrast to the **strongholds** (Ps 23:2; Amos 1:2; Keil 1873, 383). All is destroyed. The vocabulary of anger is expanded in this verse with the word **wrath** (*bĕʿebrātô*, also 3:1). **Swallowed up** (*billaʿ*) is a key word in ch 2 (2:5, 8, 16; see Jonah 1:17).

■ **3 Gimmel.** The portrayal of God's anger is intensified in v 3 with the phrase **fierce anger** (lit., *burning anger;* see 1:12). **Every horn** is a reference to all the symbols of strength. A bull is greatly disadvantaged if it has no horns. The strength of Israel is completely gone; v 17 uses the same imagery to show the increase of the enemy's strength (see 2:17; 1 Sam 2:10; Ps 112:9; also Ps 75:4-5; Jer 48:25). The Midrash applied the metaphor of horns to ten entities in Israel: Abraham, Isaac, Joseph, Moses, Torah, the priesthood, Levites, prophecy, temple, and Israel (Brady 2003, 99).

Two Bulls in Te Kowhai

Ellesmere Royal Highness ("Roydon") was the dominant male on the Bennett family farm, and he kept order in the bull paddock. As he aged, a new bull, Ellesmere Rotokauri Lad ("Buddy"), was added to the mix. As Buddy matured he grew big and strong and began to challenge the dominant bull and even human authority, a situation that could have led to a fatality. To level the playing field, a veterinarian was called in to cut off Buddy's horns. After the operation he strutted up to Roydon with his menacing challenge, unaware that his horns were gone. Roydon stood his ground and Buddy tried to hook him with his horns, but nothing connected. He moved a little closer, and closer again until his raw wounds banged into Roydon's head. Buddy immediately pulled back in pain. Order had been reestablished in the bull paddock.

God also made Israel weak by withdrawing his **right hand.** The **right hand** (*yĕmînô*) of God represents his power, which he used to protect Israel in the past (Exod 15:6; Ps 10:12). At a critical time when Babylon invaded Judah, God withdrew **his right hand** and allowed the enemy to prevail. The nation is suffering because of God's anger as well as his lack of help and support. Verse 3 ends with the comparison of God's anger with a burning fire that consumes everything in its path. The prophets often used **fire** as a metaphor of destruction (e.g., Amos 1:4); enemy nations often used fire in the ancient times to destroy cities they attacked (e.g., Ai, Josh 8:19). The metaphor of **flaming fire** (*kĕʾēš lehābâ*) here intensifies the image of destruction.

■ **4 Dalet.** The lament portrays God as an armed **enemy** who is on the path of destruction. The term **enemy,** mentioned six times in Lamentations up to this point for the destroyer nation, is here used for God (*ʾôyēb,* also 2:5). God is also described with the synonym **foe** (*kĕṣār*), used seven times up to this point for the invaders. The covenant relationship means that God should be a friend but, because Judah has broken the covenant, God has become an enemy. God is like a warrior getting his **bow** ready for battle. This image is used in Psalms (7:12; 77:17; 144:6) and in ancient Near Eastern art (Bergant 2003, 60). To preserve the function of the bow, it was not **strung** until it was ready for use in hunting or battle. God is about to use this weapon against Jerusalem, as he

2:3-4

has **strung his bow.** Verse 4 ends with the repetition of God pouring out **his wrath like fire on the tent of the Daughter of Zion** (using a new word for anger, lit., *heat, ḥămātô*).

■ **5** He. Verse 5 again emphasizes God's reversed role (see v 2). There is a play on the words **mourning and lamentation,** which have a similar sound (*taʾăniyyâ wāʾăniyyâ*). "Mourning and moaning" is an appropriate English translation to portray this wordplay (Meek 1956, 18).

■ **6** Waw. Verse 6 describes the destruction of the temple and its surroundings (**his dwelling** and **his place of meeting**) as if it were a **garden.** It is not clear what the phrase **like a garden** means here. A garden or park may be overgrown, or it may be well kept. Perhaps the imagery here is that of destroying an overgrown garden. The Septuagint has "like a vine" (*kĕgepen*) instead of **garden** (*kaggan*), which could refer to the spreading nature of grapevines (so the building is spread out and destroyed), or it could refer to a grapevine that has been pruned. The destruction of the temple meant the end of the celebration of the **appointed feasts** and **Sabbaths.** One of the **appointed feasts** was Sukkoth, the Feast of Tabernacles (or Booths), which came at the end of the summer harvests. Farmers lived in temporary booths or huts in the vineyards and olive groves during harvesttimes to protect the harvest from birds and thieves. These also served as a memorial of the nomadic tent dwelling days in the wilderness before entering Canaan. The word translated **dwelling** (*śukkô*) seems to be a variant of the word used for these huts and the name of the feast (Isa 1:8; Job 27:18). *Sōk* is used for God's dwelling in Ps 27:5; 76:2. Instead of protecting **his dwelling** and **his place of meeting** (*môʿădô*), God allowed it to be destroyed as if it were one of these temporary shelters (Bergant 2003, 62). The outcome was the disruption of worship and celebration of the festivals that God himself ordained. The destruction of Jerusalem and the temple is a sign of God's rejection of **both king and priest,** the custodians of the palace and the temple. The **fierce anger** of God has brought the demise of Judah's social, religious, and political life.

■ **7** Zayin. Verse 7 continues the theme of the destruction of the temple. The enemies are in possession of **the altar** that God has **rejected.** They have taken control of the **sanctuary** he has **abandoned.** The phrase **he has handed over to the enemy** shows God's active involvement in the tragic event of 586 B.C. What the people now hear in the temple are not shouts of rejoicing and celebration but the shouts of victory by the enemy as if it were festival time (Keil 1873, 389). The Targum shows a glimmer of hope here by interpreting **the day of an appointed feast** as Passover. The Targum seems to imply that God would deliver his people again, as he had done in the exodus when the first Passover was celebrated (also 2:22; Brady 2003, 126).

■8 **Khet.** Verse 8 shifts attention to the walls and ramparts around Jerusalem that were destroyed by God in his determination to tear down the protection of the city. Two metaphors are used. One is the image of Yahweh measuring the city as a surveyor would before a demolition project (see also Amos 7:7-8, 17). The other is a personification of the **ramparts and walls,** which lamented because they were unable to protect Jerusalem and were torn down by the Babylonians. In Jer 31:39 the measuring line is a metaphor for restoration, not destruction (also Zech 1:16). The complaint here also is that God has not withheld **his hand from destroying** Jerusalem. He has accomplished this by giving the city into the hand of its enemies (1:7; 2:4, 7; 5:8). The hand of Yahweh should have protected Jerusalem, but "he has withdrawn his right hand" of protection (see v 3). This allowed the enemy to spread out its hand of conquest (1:10).

■9 **Tet.** Metaphors for destruction continue in v 9. Jerusalem's **gates have sunk into the ground** and so are no longer able to exclude the enemy. The bar that holds the wooden gates shut has also been **broken and destroyed** (see Amos 1:5, where a broken gate bar is used as a metaphor for conquest). The broken gates and bars indicate a city that is vulnerable and open to destruction by the invading army. Verse 9 also portrays the existence of the city without political leadership, without the Law, and without visions from God. The enemy invasion has brought about the exile of political leadership (**king** and **princes**), the end of national life under the guidance of the Law (**the law is no more**), and the end of revelation from God (**prophets no longer find visions from the LORD**). The leadership has been **exiled among the nations.** The **law** (*tôrâ*) refers to God's instructions for life in his land (Deut 28:36). **The law is no more** most likely means that the Law has lost its effectiveness and Judah no longer benefits from the covenant. The written law was ignored and God's spoken word through the **prophets** also ceased. The loss of these meant an end to Judah's secure life in the land.

■10 **Yod.** The book of Lamentations opens with the city sitting alone like a widow. Here in v 10 **the elders** of the city **sit on the ground in silence.** Sitting **on the ground in silence** is a display of grief and sorrow (see Job 2:13). In their grief and sorrow, the elders of the city have no words of comfort for their people; they have no words of guidance. **Dust** and **sackcloth** are accoutrements of mourning and represent the opposite of treating the head with olive oil and wearing softer clothing (Josh 7:6; Ezek 27:30-31; Job 2:12-13). The young women of the city also participate in the demonstration of grief, bowing their **heads** in shame and humiliation (see Isa 58:5; Job 10:15; Ps 3:3).

■11 **Kaf.** Verse 11 switches to the first person. The expression of grief is so great that the eyes can no longer weep. This is the first open expression of emotion from the narrator. The phrase **I am in torment within** (*my inwards*

223

churn) is repeated from 1:20. **My heart** (*my liver*) **is poured out on the ground** expresses the intensity of pain and grief. Elsewhere inwards are spilled on the ground in a literal sense when someone is stabbed (2 Sam 20:10), but here the liver is spilled on the ground as a metaphor for grief. The word for *liver* is literally *heavy* (*kābēd*), as the liver was considered the heaviest organ, and it is related to the word "glory, honor." There is not only emotional distress expressed in this verse but also the loss of glory and honor. Verse 10 has already conveyed the idea of Jerusalem bowing its head in shame. The rest of v 11 states the reason for the pain and grief of the poet: the destruction of **my people** and **children and infants faint in the streets of the city.** The narrator lives in the world of pain; he not only witnesses pain but also experiences it in his own life.

■ **12 Lamed.** The plight of children and infants was introduced in v 11, and now v 12 documents their suffering and confusion as they cry out to **their mothers,** saying, **"Where is bread and wine?"** Bread and wine represent the basic source of nourishment that sustains life. The poet paints a vivid picture of the children's lives ebbing away **in their mothers' arms.** The portrait of children dying in the arms of their mothers evokes a great deal of sympathy for the dying children and their helpless mothers who are devastated by their inability to keep their children alive (see O'Connor 2002, 37). The dying children in this verse, according to O'Connor, represent the future of the nation (2002, 1041). The narrator laments in this verse because he sees no hope for the future of the nation.

B. What Can I Say for You? (2:13-19)

■ **13 Mem.** In v 13 the narrator speaks directly to Jerusalem and expresses his inability to offer any comfort. He has no words to comfort this unparalleled suffering. Jerusalem's **wound is as deep as the sea.** Verse 13 ends with the unanswered question **Who can heal you?** God is the healer of Israel (Exod 15:26), and comfort and healing must come from him.

■ **14 Nun.** Prophets like Jeremiah exposed the sin of Jerusalem, but v 14 attacks false **prophets** who gave visions that were **false and worthless** and **misleading.** Jeremiah encountered false prophets such as Hananiah who predicted the exile would only last two years (Jer 2:8; 5:31; 14:13-14; 23:11; 28:3). He complained that Hananiah's message carried the burden of proof because the sin of the people called for war, not peace. The poet reminds Jerusalem that these prophets have failed to expose the sins of Jerusalem and thus **to ward off your captivity** (or "restore your fortunes," see NRSV). **Expose your sin** is literally *uncover* (*gillû*); the root form of this verb also means to go into captivity. Because the prophets failed to *uncover* (*glh*) the sins of Jerusalem, the city had been "exiled" (*glh*) to Babylon (1:3; 4:22). The alternate translation, "restore your fortunes" (NRSV), implies a delay in the restoration of the fortunes of Judah because of the false prophets (Provan 1991, 74).

■ **15 Samek.** The desolate city Jerusalem is the object of mocking, ridicule, and hostility. The roads to Jerusalem that should have been filled with joyful pilgrims attending the annual feasts are empty (1:4) except for those who happen to be passing by. These passersby, to whom Jerusalem appealed for comfort (1:12-16), mock the lost reputation of the city that was once **the perfection of beauty, the joy of the whole earth.** Clapping hands, shaking heads, and scoffing (*šārqû*) are expressions that convey hostility (Provan 1991, 74). The tragic reversal of Jerusalem's fortune evokes no compassion and comfort but only ridicule and mocking from her former allies and friends.

■ **16 Pe.** Verse 16 records the scoffing of Jerusalem's enemies. Gnashing (grinding) of teeth may express mockery (Ps 35:16) or hostility (Ps 112:10; Job 16:9; Provan 1991, 75). The enemies of Jerusalem claim that they have **swallowed her up;** this is what the Lord has done to Jerusalem (see v 2). The enemies have waited for the day of Jerusalem's destruction, and now they rejoice in it.

The alphabetic order of the acrostic shifts at this point (*pe ayin* instead of *ayin pe*; also in chs 3 and 4); this has prompted scholars to suggest scribal error, an alternate order, or a poetic technique to mimic the shift in Jerusalem's status in the world, from its former place of honor to its current place of humiliation (O'Connor 2002, 40).

■ **17 Ayin.** The sovereignty of God is conveyed clearly in v 17. The destruction of Jerusalem shows that **he has fulfilled his word, which he decreed long ago.** Jeremiah had recently prophesied the destruction of Jerusalem, but early pronouncements came from Micah in the eighth century B.C. Deuteronomy and 1 Kings also laid out consequences for disobedience to covenant. Eighth-century threats did not materialize as Hezekiah followed Isaiah's advice and averted the Assyrian crisis in 701 B.C. (the northern kingdom did not escape). This demonstrates the conditional nature of the **word, which he decreed long ago.**

■ **18 Tsade.** Once the list of those unable to help (prophets, passersby, enemies) is finished (vv 14-17), the focus changes to prayer for God's help (v 18). Other entities cannot help because the wound has come from God (v 17), and only he can now heal. The third person of **hearts of the people** interrupts the direct address to Zion. The sense of **wall of the Daughter of Zion** is puzzling, and some translations leave out **wall.** Verse 18 implies that God who abandoned Jerusalem may respond again in mercy when he sees the intense grief, conveyed in the expression **tears flow like a river.** The people must weep **day and night** as Jeremiah wept for his people (Jer 9:1).

■ **19 Qof.** Verse 19 continues the call for prayer. The **watches of the night** are the three time periods marking the passing of the night (Judg 7:19; 1 Sam

11:11). Hands had mocked the fate of Jerusalem in v 15, and now v 19 calls for hands to be raised in the common posture of praise and prayer. Instead of tears like a river (v 18), there should be prayers poured out from the **heart like water.** The prayer is for relief for the children who suffer from hunger in **every street.** The Targum interprets this as a call to repentance and to spend nights studying the Jewish writings (Brady 2003, 56). The final line of v 19 is sometimes deleted (unnecessarily) by scholars because it makes this verse longer than the others (see also 1:7).

C. Look, O Lord! (2:20-22)

■**20 Resh.** The speaker changes at v 20, but the theme of God's anger continues. In v 19 the narrator called for prayer, which Zion does in vv 20-22 but without any confession or even request for relief. There is simply a call for God to **Look** and **consider** (Bergant 2003, 78). Asking God to **look** is the same as asking him to act. When Yahweh acted on Hagar's behalf she named him "the God who sees" (Gen 16:13). What follows is an accusation of God, one of the elements of lament (Pss 22:1; 42:9; 88:14). God is blamed for the disaster and even for the actions of mothers who are driven to unthinkable acts. The rhetorical questions in v 20 call for the answer "no." Women should not **eat their offspring,** and **priest and prophet** should not **be killed.** King Ahab tore his robes when he discovered that babies were being eaten when Samaria was under siege (2 Kgs 6:28-30) although O'Connor thinks that there may not be a literal occurrence in Lam 2:20, but a notice that the covenant curses of Deut 28:53 are coming to pass (see also Jer 19:9; Lam 4:10) (2002, 42). The questions in 2:20 reflect the extreme conditions of siege. A city under siege from an enemy would have the supply lines cut, sometimes for years, resulting in severe famine and starvation.

■**21 Sin and Shin.** Verse 21 returns to the theme of vv 5-8 and links the present conditions of death and destruction to God's anger. No one in the city is exempt from his wrath: old and young, male and female. They **lie together in the dust of the streets** without a proper burial.

■**22 Taw.** Chapter 2 closes with a return to the theme of a **feast day.** Jerusalem complains that God who summons to the celebration on a feast day has summoned against the city **terrors on every side** (see Jer 6:25; 20:4-5, 10). This means fear instead of joy, sorrow instead of celebration, death instead of life, and despair instead of hope. Pilgrims should be coming to the feasts in Jerusalem, but instead the roads are empty (Lam 1:4) and mockers line the roads (2:15). All around the city, what the people see is the terrifying and destroying actions of the enemy. No one escapes from or survives **the day of the Lord's anger.**

The Anger of God

The anger of God is an unpopular theme in contemporary Christianity, where the focus is predominantly on God's love, mercy, and grace. But Lam 2 repeatedly accuses God of anger and uses a varied vocabulary to do so ("swallowed up, torn down, brought . . . down . . . in dishonor, cut off every horn, withdrawn his right hand, burned, consumes"; Wood and McLaren 2006, 364). Love and hate are less personal in Hebrew and have more to do with appropriate responses in a relationship. But the word "anger" shows God's personal and emotional involvement in his action. These accusations help bring the situation clearly into focus, but perhaps they also expose God's actions as a departure from his truest self. The people of Judah admit wrongdoing and recognize the anger of God in their suffering. But God's anger is not irrational. The poet later affirms that God "does not willingly bring affliction" (3:33).

The anger of God and the accusations against God (2:20-22) do not destroy relationship with God. These accusations flow out of a depth of pain and suffering but do not accuse God of unfaithfulness. It is the people who have been unfaithful, and when other avenues of comfort fail, they turn to God for comfort and healing.

2:1-22

III. POEM THREE: I AM THE MAN (3:1-66)

BEHIND THE TEXT

The book of Lamentations reaches a climax in ch 3 with a very personal and intense portrayal of suffering, but also a beautiful confession of God's love and goodness. Together with God's sovereignty this is great cause for hope and the poem ends with an extended plea for God to act. The poems that follow (chs 4—5) descend from these heights to a more tempered hope, which betrays the underlying despair.

Gunkel classified ch 3 as a lament, although there is no invocation of God's name or vow of praise or sacrifice (1933, 95). There is prayer for help (vv 55-66) and expression of praise (vv 22-25). The elements of attack without cause (v 52) and determination of destruction by the deity (v 37) are common to the city laments (McDaniel 1968, 204, 206).

Chapter 3 is the only poem with a threefold acrostic structure. Each line in this third poem fits into the acrostic pattern so that there are three verses beginning with *alef*, three beginning with *bet*, and so forth. Assis identifies the reason for this as a signal that ch 3 contains the main message of the book (it is the most carefully thought out, as the detailed acrostic shows) (2007, 724). Chapter 3 can be outlined as follows:

I Have Seen Affliction (3:1-20)
Faithfulness, Hope, and Love (3:21-36)
We Have Sinned and Rebelled (3:37-54)
Hear My Plea! (3:55-66)

IN THE TEXT

A. I Have Seen Affliction (3:1-20)

■ **1-3 Alef.** The third poem begins with a first person account of the destruction of Jerusalem. The focus of vv 1-3 is on what God has done to the **man** (*geber*) who describes himself as one who **has seen affliction.** It is usually God who would see and act (1:9). In this case the seeing is focused on experiencing (Provan 1991, 4). The **man** may be the narrator or a typical inhabitant, but various interpreters have identified him as Jeremiah, Josiah, Jehoiachin, or Zedekiah (Bergant 2003, 82). Probably this man represents Israel just as Zion is personified in chs 1—2 and 4, specifically Israel in exile (there are also similarities with the suffering servant of Isaiah; Middlemas 2006, 523). The word for **man** (*geber*) comes from the root "to be strong, mighty" and is used for a strong man who defends women, children, and others who cannot defend themselves (e.g., Jer 41:16; BDB 149). This strong warrior now watches pathetically as he himself cannot even escape (Lam 3:7), let alone protect his own people. He does not even mention the sufferings of those he is charged to protect. His own suffering is overwhelming (Bergant 2003, 82-83).

Verse 1 uses the metaphor of a **rod** (*šēbeṭ*) to express the **wrath** of God. The rod is part of a shepherd's equipment, but kings saw themselves as shepherds of the people and the rod became stylized as a scepter (see Pss 45:6; 125:3). For the sheep, the rod is an article of comfort (Ps 23:4), but for the wild animal or enemy, it is a weapon to be feared (in Exod 21:20 it is used to beat slaves and in Prov 22:15 to discipline children). Jerusalem should have been comforted by the presence of God's rod, but instead it became an instrument of discipline against the city (see Isa 10:5). This and other elements leads van Hecke to describe 3:1-6 as an "anti-psalm 23" (2002, 264).

The man complains that God has **driven** him **away** and **made** him **walk in darkness** (v 2). The verb **he has driven** (*nāhag*) is used for the action of a shepherd (1 Sam 30:20) and also for God (Deut 4:27). The rod of God has been used to drive **away** so that instead of finding pasture and water (Ps 23:2), the divine Shepherd has sent Jerusalem to walk in darkness (see Amos 5:18; Ps 23:4). Light was the first element of God's creation in Gen 1 and as such represents God's order in the world, as opposed to the chaos of darkness in which Jerusalem must now walk. The wording **darkness rather than light** is identical to the prophecy of Amos 5:18, which warned that the day of Yahweh would be "darkness, not light," a warning that has now come true for Jerusalem, as it did for the northern kingdom of Israel in 722 B.C. (see Lam 1:12 for the day of Yahweh). Walking in the light is a positive metaphor in Ps 119:105 where the way is illumined by God's Word, the Word that Jerusalem has rejected and so must now walk in darkness, stumbling and without direction.

In v 3 the man complains that God has turned his hand against him **all day long.** Renkema relates this turning of the hand to the constant hand movements needed in driving a chariot, giving the impression of Yahweh "as a charioteer careering from side to side in hot pursuit of a prisoner" (see 1 Kgs 22:34; 2 Kgs 9:23) (1998, 355). Turning one's hand may be an idiom for a slap in the face (see Amos 1:8; Isa 1:25; Jer 6:9; Zech 13:7; Job 16:10; Ps 81:14; Paul 2002, 58).

■ **4-6 Bet.** The physical and emotional distress of the man is the focus of vv 4-6. God has made his **skin and . . . flesh grow old and has broken his bones** (v 4). The phrase **grow old** includes the idea of being worn out (*billâ*). **Broken** bones are appropriate for a city that is finally entered by the conquering army. These could be metaphors, however, as this kind of language is common in laments (Mic 3:1-3; Ps 38:3; Provan 1991, 85).

Verse 5 describes the siege of the man, not by the enemy army but by God. Jerusalem is a city besieged by **bitterness and hardship** due to the presence of the Babylonians.

God made the man "walk in darkness" (v 2) and also **dwell in darkness** (v 6). The imagery here is that of Sheol, the semiconscious place of the dead, since the comparison is made with those **long dead.** The vocabulary for **darkness** (*mahšāk*) here is rare, used only seven times in the OT, including Ps 143:3, which Renkema considers to be dependent on this verse (see Ps 88) (1998, 358).

■ **7-9 Gimmel.** The man focuses on his hardship as a captive in chains in vv 7-9. He is surrounded by a wall and **weighed . . . down with chains** so that he has no freedom of movement (v 7). The word for **weighed me down** is related to the word "glory," which the man has lost under the **chains** of servitude. Verse 8 indicates that God has not only shut the man within a wall but also shut out his **prayer.** He is severely restrained and confined, isolated and abandoned by God. Verse 9 continues the theme of the man's lack of freedom; God has **barred** his way with **blocks of stone** and made his path **crooked** so that he cannot escape from the prison in which he lives. Proverbs 3:6 promises straight paths for those who know Yahweh. The root word for **crooked** (ʿāwâ) is related to "iniquity" (ʿāwōn), one of the words for sin in the OT. What God has made good, people have twisted or perverted. That means that life will no longer have the ease of a smooth and straight path but will be difficult like a winding track. A crooked path is the natural consequence of a crooked life, a life outside right relationship with Yahweh.

■ **10-12 Dalet.** Verses 10-12 utilize the metaphor of an animal attack and hunting scene to relate Yahweh's attack on the man. **Bear** and **lion** are metaphors in v 10 that portray God as a predator lying in wait to attack and destroy his prey. The theme of animal attack is continued in v 11. God has **dragged** the man **from** his **path** and **left** him **without help.** There was no one to rescue Jerusalem from God's attack on the city. The word for **mangled** occurs only here in the OT, and the meaning is uncertain. Verse 12 describes the man as a target for God's arrows. The verb used in the phrase **He drew his bow** is the same root as "path" in v 11; this conveys the idea of an archer stepping on his bow in order to string it (see 2:4).

■ **13-15 He.** Verses 13-15 describe what God has done to the man to make his pain unbearable. Verse 13 continues the portrait of God as an archer who has **pierced** the **heart** (lit., *kidneys; bĕkilyôtāy*) of the man (see 1:20; Job 19:27; Prov 23:16). Bergant identifies four nuances of an arrow to the kidneys: it is interior, a deep wound; it strikes the center of life, a fatal blow; it strikes the seat of emotion, an emotional blow; and as the kidneys are in the back, it is a surprise blow from behind (2003, 85). In v 14, the man describes himself as the **laughingstock** of his own people **all day long.** It seems odd that Israelites would laugh at the suffering of their own, and some Hebrew manuscripts (and Syriac) render this "all peoples," which makes better sense (Provan 1991, 87; see also Jer 20:7). God has not only wounded and made the man a laughingstock of his people, but he has also filled him with "bitterness" (NRSV) and **gall** or ***wormwood*** (v 15). Wormwood represents bitterness or poison. Amos condemned his audience for turning justice into wormwood (Amos 6:12). The reference is to a plant known for a strong, bitter taste (see Lam 3:19; Deut 29:18; Jer 9:15; 23:15).

■ **16-18 Waw.** The man continues his complaint in vv 16-18. God overpowered him and made him suffer excruciating pain. Broken teeth and trampling in the dust provide vivid metaphors for suffering in v 16. The word for **broken** (*wayyagrēs*) is found only here and in Ps 119:20, and the word for **trampled** (*hikpîšanî*) is found only here in the OT. It is not clear what breaking teeth with gravel means. The reference could be to eating something unpleasant (Lam 3:15; Prov 20:17) or to humiliation (see Lam 3:29; Ps 72:9). Another possibility is that vv 15-16 portray the opposite of hospitality; a host offering unacceptable food, drink, and lodging (on gravel and dust; Provan 1991, 89, citing Kraus). Bergant suggests that the attacker seems to have pushed the man's "face down into the dirt, grinding his teeth into the gravel" (2003, 86). Calvin's suggestion that the reference is to grit or small pebbles hidden in food is consistent with the bitter herbs of the previous verse and also with ancient food processing practices, which were less efficient at keeping impurities out of the food (1563, 401; Harrison 1973, 224; Goldman 1946, 86). The Septuagint follows this by translating **trampled me in the dust** as "fed me with ashes." The mourner throwing dust/ashes/dirt on himself or herself could easily get some in the mouth, causing discomfort to the teeth. This verse gave rise to a custom of eating a small piece of bread sprinkled with ashes before the Ninth of Ab fast, which commemorated the fall of Jerusalem (Cohen 1983, 196).

The man not only suffers pain and humiliation but also is **deprived of peace** (v 17). The translation **I have been deprived of peace** in v 17 follows the passive form of the verb in the Syriac and Vulgate versions. The Hebrew verb is active: *you have rejected my soul from peace.* This is inconsistent with the context, which does not address God directly (Keil 1873, 410).

In v 18 the man laments the loss of his **splendor** (*nishi*), a word that is used elsewhere only for God (see 1 Sam 15:29; 1 Chr 29:11). He had hoped for good things from Yahweh, but his hope is vanished. He does not see the prospect of any good things coming from God.

■ **19-20 Zayin.** Verses 19-21 focus on what the man remembers or calls to mind. **I remember** could be taken as an imperative (as in Syriac and Vulgate), asking God to remember the man's condition. His painful memories include his **affliction** and **wandering.** He also remembers the **bitterness and the gall** (*laʿănâ wārōʾš*), which is a combination also found in v 15 and in Amos 6:12. These memories make the man dispirited and disheartened. The language of one's **soul** being **downcast** is frequently found in the Psalms (Pss 42:5, 6, 11; 43:5; 44:25).

B. Faithfulness, Hope, and Love (3:21-36)

■ **21 Zayin.** There is a turning point in this poem from the depths of despair in v 18 to a renewal of hope in v 21, which O'Connor calls "a lull during a violent storm" (2002, 44). This hope is detailed in the famous verses that follow. In the midst of his remembrance of his affliction, he also remembers **this**—the faithfulness of God celebrated in the following verses.

■ **22-24 Het.** The man focuses on his positive experiences with God in vv 22-24. In v 22, he places his hope on the **great love** (*ḥesed*) of Yahweh. The plural form of the noun (*ḥasdê*) conveys the demonstration of Yahweh's love through concrete acts of kindness (see 2 Chr 32:32). He reminds his audience that because of Yahweh's *ḥesed* they (**we**) are not totally destroyed (**consumed**).

Their salvation does not rest on their righteousness, or even repentance, but on the very character of God. This view of God as Savior is a reversal of the depiction of God as divine warrior elsewhere (1:5, 15, 17; 2:1, 2, 5, 7, 17; 4:11, 16; Middlemas 2006, 518). The man also affirms that Yahweh's **compassions** (*raḥămāyw*, v 22) **never fail.** The Hebrew word *rāḥămāyw* (which is related to "womb") conveys the idea of mercy and tenderness that mothers show to their children. In the midst of his afflictions and wanderings, the poet finds hope in the immensity of Yahweh's *ḥesed* and his unfailing mercy.

Ḥesed (Covenant Love)

The Hebrew word *ḥesed* is so rich that translators use multiple translations to convey its meaning. It has the basic meaning of loyalty, faithfulness, goodness, steadfast love, mercy, and love. This word is most frequently used for God's love and faithfulness, especially his loyalty and love to his covenant partner Israel. Yahweh's *ḥesed* defines the covenant relationship with Israel. He remains loyal to the covenant and in his commitment to love Israel even in the midst of Israel's sin and disobedience and breaking of the covenant. It is also used for loyalty and faithfulness in the relationship between humans, such as David's covenant with Jonathan (1 Sam 20:8). (NIDOTTE 2:211-18).

In v 23 the man affirms that Jerusalem, even in the midst of its affliction, continues to experience Yahweh's love and compassions in **new** and fresh ways **every morning.** This is evidence of the greatness of Yahweh's **faithfulness** (*'ĕmûnâ*) to Israel, his unfaithful covenant partner. **Great is your faithfulness** is "the joyous acclamation that comes out of the lips of the one whose heart has been pierced with arrows from God's quiver" (Varughese 1992, 680). The man who earlier complained about the loss of his earthly portion, now declares that **the LORD is my portion** (v 24). This declaration reflects the language of Num 18:20. In Israel the priests had no land of their own, but instead they had a special relationship with God (see also Deut 10:9; 32:9; Ps 16:5-6). This special relationship with God is more important to the man than a land inheritance. Verse 24 ends with the man's call to his audience to **wait** for the Lord using the vocabulary of hope also found in v 21 (*'ôḥîl*). Waiting in the OT involves expectancy and hope, displaying an active faith in God who has the power to turn mourning into joy, despair into hope, affliction into healing, and sorrow into comfort. Verses 22-24 are missing from the Septuagint, perhaps due to a scribal error because of the similarity of vv 21*b* and 24*b* (an error called homoioteleuton; BHQ).

■ **25-27** Tet. Verses 25-27 all begin with the word **good** (*ṭôb*), which has *tet* as the first letter in Hebrew. The focus of these verses is on the goodness of God. In the opinion of O'Connor, "Goodness requires repetition to become convincing" (2002, 51). **The LORD is good** is a fundamental affirmation of Israel's faith (Ps 100:5). The man begins with this affirmation and applies it to those who place their hope in Yahweh and wait for him with patience. This is the appropriate response to suffering and despair, because God is good. The first course of action is **to wait quietly** (v 26), which is an expression of hope and confidence. This attitude is in keeping with the suffering servant of Isa 53:7. What the community waits and hopes for is **the salvation of the Lord.** In the context of the Babylonian invasion, the salvation that Judah hopes for is military and political deliverance and restoration from the exile to its homeland. The OT concept of salvation is very concrete since ancient Israelites did not think of heaven as a place where people go (only God lives there). This salvation finally came when Persia overthrew Babylon and allowed Judah to return to its land in 538 B.C.

In v 27 the man urges the audience to **bear the yoke,** that is, Yahweh's discipline of suffering (Longman 2008, 369). In 1:14, the poet complains against the yoke of sin, or the burden and punishment of sin, that God has placed on Judah's neck.

■**28-30 Yod.** Verses 28-30 continue the appropriate response of a man who is suffering. He must **sit alone in silence.** This conveys the idea of self-imposed solitude and an end to resistance, complaint, and rebellion. Verse 28 echoes the language of 1:1 where the city "sits alone." Sitting alone here, however, is a display of hope and trust in God, and not of rejection and abandonment.

Let him bury his face in the dust (v 29) is a call for self-abasement and humility in the midst of suffering. This humility and patience is recommended because **there may yet be hope.** Although no one is entitled to God's grace, repentance is key to restoration of relationship with him.

Verse 30 conveys the thought of voluntary submission, acceptance of abuse and insult from others, and willingness to be filled with disgrace. The identity of the **one who would strike** is not clear; it could be the enemy (Babylon) or enemies in general.

Isaiah 50:4-8

The Sovereign Lord has given me an instructed tongue,
    to know the word that sustains the weary.
He wakens me morning by morning,
    wakens my ear to listen like one being taught.
The Sovereign Lord has opened my ears,
    and I have not been rebellious;
    I have not drawn back.
I offered my back to those who beat me,
    my cheeks to those who pulled out my beard;
I did not hide my face
    from mocking and spitting.

> Because the Sovereign Lord helps me,
> > I will not be disgraced.
> Therefore have I set my face like flint,
> > and I know I will not be put to shame.
> He who vindicates me is near.
> > Who then will bring charges against me?
> > Let us face each other!
> Who is my accuser?
> > Let him confront me!

■**31-33 Kaf.** Verses 31-33 continue the theme of hope. The man asserts that the suffering is short-term because people **are not cast off by the Lord forever** (v 31). God's ultimate will is not to cast his people off forever or to afflict them forever (see Ps 103:9; Exod 20:5), therefore, sinners have hope for forgiveness and restoration of relationship with God.

Verse 32 portrays God as the One who **brings grief,** but it also portrays him as the One who shows **compassion.** In v 23, the man affirmed the greatness of God's faithfulness. In v 32, he declares: **great is his unfailing love** (*hesed*). God's covenant loyalty has no end. Therefore, there is hope for Jerusalem.

The man who confesses his faith in God as the God of compassion, faithfulness, and covenant love now finds the suffering of Jerusalem as something that God did not willingly bring about (**he does not willingly bring affliction;** v 33). The **affliction** does not come *from his heart* (*millibô*, **willingly**). As typical of laments in the Psalms, the man moves from despair to hope, from doubt to faith and trust, in vv 1-33. We might also say that in the man's theological struggle between despair and hope, hope wins; in his struggle between doubt and faith, faith wins. But Lamentations will move from this climax in ch 3 to a more tempered position at the end of the book.

■**34-36 Lamed.** Verses 34-36 begin with a series of infinitives. All these infinitives represent oppressions of Jerusalem by its enemies: **To crush . . . all prisoners, to deny a man his rights . . . , to deprive a man of justice.** Verse 36 ends with the question: **would not the Lord see such things?** This implies that God who sees the injustice of the enemy will act to bring justice. This could also be read as a statement: "The Lord does not (or did not) see (or approve)." But the context of vv 34-36 suggests it is a question.

C. We Have Sinned and Rebelled (3:37-54)

■**37-39 Mem.** Verses 37-39 focus on the sovereign actions of God and turn the attention away from the oppressive actions of the enemies in vv 34-36. The calamities that came upon Jerusalem happened as decreed by God. God has the power to **speak** and make things **happen** (see Gen 1). The **Most High**

God is the source of **both calamities and good things** (v 38). In strict OT monotheism, the source of evil cannot be blamed on the devil. For the most part in the OT, calamity (*rāʿ*) ultimately comes from the hand of God. Amos asks, "When disaster (*rāʿ*) comes to a city, has not the LORD caused it?" (3:6). Lamentations 3:39 connects Jerusalem's calamities with her sin (*ḥāṭāʾ*). This is the first explicit mention of sin in this poem (see 1:22; 5:7; 5:16). Jerusalem's suffering is the result of sin and so complaint gives way to submission, which leads to hope.

■ **40-42 Nun.** Reflection and self-examination, and confession and repentance dominate vv 40-42. The first person plural in these verses indicates that the community is speaking here. Verse 40 begins with the community decision to **examine our ways and test them** and ends with an urgent decision to *return to Yahweh.* The Hebrew word for "repent" is literally *turn* or **return** (*šûb*); it is linked to the metaphor of life as a journey (on a way or road). **Return** reflects the recognition that the people have taken the wrong path and have made the decision to reorient their journey in order to follow the instructions of Yahweh.

Verse 41 is a call to the posture of prayer (of penitence and repentance, see v 42). In ancient Israel, prayer was conducted with **hands** raised (Pss 28:2; 63:4). The lifting of **hearts** implies sincerity on the part of the worshiping community. Genuine repentance is the issue here, not empty ritual. **We have sinned and rebelled** is the confession of the penitent community (v 42). No sin is specifically mentioned. Israel's covenant breaking involved both religious life (idolatry) and social and political life (social injustice and political alliances). Public acknowledgment of sin is the first and foremost requirement for the experience of forgiveness from God (see 2 Sam 12:13). Verse 42 ends with the reminder to God that he had not forgiven the community. This seems surprisingly bold coming from people who admit they **have sinned and rebelled,** but it reflects a long tradition of the OT that dares to call God to account for his lack of action (Pss 6:3; 10:1; 13:1-2; 22:1; 35:17; 43:2; 62:3; Isa 45:15; 49:14; Brueggemann 1997, 319-22, 333). The call to repentance in v 40 is thus somewhat nullified by v 42, which does admit guilt but seems less concerned with accepting responsibility and more concerned with blaming God who has **not forgiven.**

■ **43-45 Samek.** The man complains directly to God (**You**) in vv 43-45. Verse 43 accuses God of covering the community with his **anger** and pursuing it. God's anger is an important theme in ch 2. The verb **covered yourself** is not reflexive in Hebrew and could be translated *covered us with anger,* taking the pronominal suffix from **pursued us** (Hillers 1972, 59). Despite the vocabulary of God's love, compassions, and faithfulness earlier in the chapter (vv 22-23), the man now accuses God of showing no **pity** (*ḥāmal*).

The man complains that God **covered** himself **with a cloud** to block the **prayer** of the community that is the object of his anger (v 44). God has turned a deaf ear to the prayer of his people and made their prayer ineffective. The covering with anger (v 43) and the cloud (v 44) recall the cloud of anger from 2:1.

The Cloud of Unknowing (14th c. A.D.)

This darkness and this cloud is, howsoever thou dost, betwixt thee and thy God, and letteth thee that thou mayest neither see Him clearly by light of understanding in thy reason, nor feel Him in sweetness of love in thine affection. (Underhill 1946, 19)

The man continues his accusation of God in v 45. God has made Jerusalem **scum** (*sĕḥî*) and **refuse** in the world. The word *sĕḥî* is used only here in the OT and seems to come from the verb *sāḥah*, "to scrape" (Ezek 26:4). Israel was once God's treasured possession, a holy nation, and a kingdom of priests (Exod 19:5-6). The present condition of Jerusalem shows a total reversal in God's attitude toward his people and his city.

■ **46-48** Pe. Two letters of the alphabet are reversed at this point in the acrostic (*ayin* should come before *pe*). God's contempt toward Jerusalem is the reason why the enemies treat Jerusalem with disdain (v 46; also 1:7-8; 2:15-16; 3:14). Verse 46 describes the enemies with their mouths opened wide against the people of Jerusalem. This imagery probably conveys the idea of the enemies mocking Jerusalem with loud and contemptuous words. Verse 47 continues the description of Jerusalem's suffering. The word pairs, **terror and pitfalls** (*pahad wāpahat*) and **ruin and destruction** (*haššē't wĕhaššāber*), have similar sounds in Hebrew. This helps to convey the intensity of suffering. The singular voice of the man returns in v 48. **Streams of tears flow from** his **eyes** on account of the destruction of his **people**. Suffering here is personal; the man is heartbroken because of the brokenness of his people.

■ **49-51** Ayin. The crying in vv 49-50 has a purpose beyond the expression of grief; its primary objective is to attract God's attention. The **eyes** of the man will cry until God's eyes are opened to the suffering. It is assumed that God will act when he **sees** (see 1:9, 11, 20; 2:20). The man will let tears flow until God **looks down from heaven and sees** the suffering of his people (v 50). The man is grieved by what he sees in the city, particularly the suffering of **all the women of** the **city** (v 51).

■ **52-54** Tsade. Verses 52-54 continue the description of the dangerous conditions in which the man finds himself because of God's anger. Verse 10 portrays God like a bear or lion pursuing the man, and in v 52 the man likens himself to **a bird** being **hunted** by its enemies **without cause** (*ḥinnām*). The enemies have thrown him in a pit and tried to kill him by throwing stones at him (v 53).

Throwing someone into **a pit** was a common punishment or imprisonment in the OT. Joseph and Jeremiah were both thrown into pits (*bôr*; Gen 37:22; Jer 38:6). The pit also symbolized the grave or Sheol (e.g., Isa 14:15). Someone who was stuck in a cistern or pit could be in danger of **waters** closing in, which means an imminent death (v 54; see Jonah 2, which relates the prophet's experience of water swirling about him). Verse 54 conveys the near-death experience of the nation; the danger of being **cut off** from the land of the living.

D. Hear My Plea! (3:55-66)

■ **55-57** Qof. Verses 55-57 introduce another transition in ch 3 and signal the conclusion of the poem on a positive note. These verses utilize the letter *qof* at the beginning of each verse to emphasize the man's calling on God (*qārā'tî* in v 55), God hearing the man's voice (*qôlî* in v 56), and God's response of hearing and drawing near to the man (*qārabtā* in v 57). God heard and responded to the prayer he made **from the depths of the pit.** The phrase **You heard my plea** in v 56 should be taken as an imperative (*hear my voice*), which is consistent with the next line, **Do not close your ears.** The NIV resolves this difficulty by taking the second line as a direct quotation of words that were spoken in the past. This plea seeks to reverse the situation of ineffective prayer described in v 44. Verse 57 reports God's response to the prayer of man. This response, **"Do not fear,"** is a common initial announcement by divine messengers (e.g., Gen 15:1; Judg 6:23). This announcement conveys the message that God has already heard the appeal and that salvation is on its way. These words are the only direct speech attributed to God in the entire book.

■ **58-60** Resh. The man begins with acknowledgment that the Lord **took up his case** (*rîb*, v 58). The phrase **you took up my case** reflects the courtroom setting; Israel's prophets often announced Yahweh's case against Israel (e.g., Isa 3:13). Here *rîb* means the complaint of the man who was faced with the danger of being cut off from the land of the living (vv 52-54). God saved the man from death when he intervened as the defender and judge of the man as well as his redeemer (v 58). The metaphor of redemption comes from the concept of the "kinsman-redeemer" (*gō'ēl*). Israel's family law required the next of kin to purchase the freedom of a family member from slavery by paying off a debt or to recover the forfeited property of a kinsman. This custom is illustrated in Ruth 4:4-6 and Jer 32:6-12. Israel regarded God as the redeemer (*gō'ēl*) of his people (Isa 54:5).

Verses 59 and 60 begin with the word *rā'îtâ* (**you have seen**), which emphasizes God as the God who sees the wrong done to the man and the depth of vengeance and plots against his life by his enemies. These verses affirm Israel's faith that the God who hears is also the God who sees. Hagar, the first person in the Bible to name God, declared, "You are the God who sees me"

(Gen 16:13). The call for God to **uphold** the man's **cause** (*mišpāṭ*) emphasizes the role of God as the divine judge who corrects the wrong done and maintains justice in the world. Jerusalem had withheld justice from the oppressed but now calls for justice against the foreign oppressors. This cry for justice comes from a repentant community (see 3:40-42) that trusts in God's covenant loyalty and faithfulness (vv 21-24).

■**61-63 Sin and Shin.** Verses 61-63 acknowledge that God heard and saw the **insults** and **plots against** the man by his enemies. Verse 62 emphasizes the ever-present reality of these insults in the whispering and muttering of enemies **all day long.** The constant nature of the insults is further emphasized in v 63. Enemies have even made mocking songs to insult the man (and to entertain themselves) whether they are sitting or standing (that is, in all activities of life).

■**64-66 Tav.** The poem ends with a call for vengeance and retaliation (vv 64-66). The man makes an urgent appeal to God as defender, judge, and re-deemer of his people to bring his judgment on the enemies and **pay them back what they deserve** (v 64). Their punishment should match the crimes they have committed. Their sins should be returned (*šûb*, **pay them back**) to them in kind.

Verse 65 calls for a **veil** and a **curse** over the enemies' **hearts.** The word **veil** (*mĕginnat*) occurs only here in the OT. It may be a hard covering like a "shield" (*māgēn*). The word **curse** (*ta'ălātkā*) is also found only here in the OT. The ancient versions suggest "weariness, hardship" (*tĕ'ālâ*). Both fit the context (Provan 1991, 109). The man concludes his appeal to God with a call for the destruction of the enemy (v 66). The enemies have pursued him, now it is their turn to be pursued by an angry God. When the enemy is totally de-stroyed, then there will be a future for the man, and for Jerusalem.

FROM THE TEXT

God's Faithfulness

The lofty statement, **Great is your faithfulness** (v 23), overshadows the complaints hurled against God in this great poem, which is a mixture of angry lament, doubt, hope, and call for vengeance. This assertion of faith reveals intense hope for the healing and restoration of the suffering community. How-ever, the poem also reveals that this is not a steady hope; it "comes and goes" because of the intensity of suffering (O'Connor 2001, 1057). Nonetheless, the poem ends with hope in God's rescue of the suffering community (vv 55-63). The present reality of suffering does not compel the community to abandon its faith in God. Its experience with God in the past, his past actions of mercy and forgiveness, compassion and grace, and love and loyalty become the lens through which the community sees and evaluates its present conditions of affliction and suffering. The covenant God who acted on their behalf in the midst of their affliction will once again come to rescue them from their enemies. The children of God's wrath find the greatness of God's covenant love and faithfulness as the source of their salvation. The elder John reminds his readers: "How great is the love the Father has lavished on us, that we should be called children of God! And that is what we are!" (1 John 3:1). Paul reminds us (who are "objects of [God's] wrath") that what makes our salvation possible for us is the "great love" that God has for us, which he has lavished on us while "we were dead in transgressions" (Eph 2:3-5).

Revenge

The community that is confident in God's covenant loyalty and faithfulness calls on God to take revenge and retaliate against its enemies (vv 58-66). This prayer and other similar prayers in the OT seem to contradict the love commandment in the Sermon on the Mount (Matt 5:44). However, (1) the prayer for vengeance is not against one's personal enemies, but those who are enemies of the covenant people of God; (2) the community that complains and calls for retaliation does not take matters into its own hands; (3) the call for revenge in reality is an acknowledgment that God is the sovereign judge and that he will in the end bring justice to his people. The community thus leaves the matter of justice and judgment with God. In the end, the enemies of Jerusalem are the enemies of God, and the community is confident in God's judgment of his enemies (see 2 Tim 4:14-15). Our contemporary hearing of this call for vengeance in Lamentations should be balanced with Jesus' summons to love and pray for our enemies, and with a pursuit of the most excellent way of 1 Cor 13.

IV. POEM FOUR: THE GOLD HAS LOST ITS LUSTER (4:1-22)

BEHIND THE TEXT

The fourth poem descends from the intensity of hope and petition in ch 3 to descriptions of dishonor and despair, failing even to call on God for help, but lamenting the lack of help in the time of crisis. The final chapter will follow this trajectory further toward the hopelessness of despair.

Gunkel classified ch 4 as a funeral song, but while it includes the expression **how,** there is no announcement of death or call for mourning (1933, 95). The element of the anger of the deity (4:11) is present in city laments (McDaniel 1968, 202-3). Chapter 4 can be outlined as follows:

Gold Is Treated like Clay (4:1-9)

Prophets and Priests Shed Blood (4:10-16)

We Looked in Vain for Help (4:17-22)

243

A. Gold Is Treated like Clay (4:1-9)

■ I Alef. The fourth poem begins with *ʾēkâ* (**how**), the title of the book and of the first and second poems. The imagery of **gold** becoming **dull** and **gems** being **scattered** in the **street** is intriguing because gold does not tarnish and no one throws gems in the street. The temple immediately comes to mind because it contained so much gold and *holy stones* (*ʾabnê-qōdeš*, **sacred gems**), but Lamentations never mentions the temple; its focus instead is on the suffering of the people. The parallel line, **fine gold has become dull** represents an emendation of the text (*šānâ*, "changed," for *šānāʾ*, meaning "unknown"). A better emendation is to take the gold in line 1 as despised (emending *yūʿām* to *yūʿāb*) and the gold in line 2 as hated (emending *yišneʾ* to *yiśśānēʾ*) (Hillers 1972, 75). This fits the context better as the **gold** and **sacred gems** (representing the people of Judah) are hated and discarded. Their true worth is not appreciated.

■ 2 Bet. Verse 2 makes the meaning of v 1 clear. The gold and gems of v 1 represent the people of **Zion,** highly treasured by God (Exod 19:5), but now considered as worthless as **pots of clay** to the conquering army. The repeated reference to gold in vv 1-2 shows how much God valued the people (using three words for gold). Jerusalem and its inhabitants were once beautiful, sacred, and precious to God; to the invading army they have become dull, common, and worthless.

■ 3 Gimel. Verses 3-5 describe the conditions of the city under siege. Nursing mothers are compared unfavorably with jackals, which, although despised animals, still suckle their young. Jackals are associated with desolation in Jer 9:11. The imagery sheds light on the description of the condition of the people of Jerusalem—they have become **heartless like ostriches in the desert.** Ostriches are known to discard eggs from their clutch when they have too many, although the Hebrew vocabulary for ostrich in this verse is uncertain (Hutchins 2003, 8:101).

■ 4 Dalet. Verse 4 describes the pitiful state of starving children and the selfishness of the adults who refuse to share their food with children who are dying of hunger and thirst. The people of Jerusalem have lost even natural instincts such as caring for infants and dying children.

■ 5 He. Verse 5 notes that **those who once ate delicacies are destitute in the streets.** The opulence of the wealthy in former times is irrelevant in times of siege. The wealthy were nurtured in **purple** garments (which were very expensive), but they now live in uncomfortable and insecure conditions. War and siege do not treat the wealthy with favor; they, like everyone else in the city, **lie on ash heaps** and share with the rest of the population suffering and indignity.

■ **6 Waw.** Verse 6 compares the fate of Jerusalem to that of **Sodom,** referring back to the destruction of Sodom and Gomorrah in the time of Abraham (Gen 19). Although Sodom was completely annihilated and only Lot and his family escaped, the fate of Jerusalem is said to be worse. Jerusalem was also destroyed, but many did survive the siege. Things were worse for the inhabitants of Jerusalem because of the eighteen months of deprivation (Jer 39:1; 52:12). Sodom, on the other hand, **was overthrown in a moment** and did not face the prolonged suffering.

The word **punishment** is literally *sin* (*ʿāwōn*), with the meaning of punishment or the result of sin (see 1 Sam 28:10; Zech 14:19). The phrase **without a hand turned to help her** conveys the idea that no one came to the rescue of Sodom. Jerusalem's offense is worse than that of Sodom because it has violated covenant obligations.

■ **7-8 Zayin and Khet.** Verses 7-8 compare the **princes** or "rulers" (*nāzîr*, lit., *consecrated ones*) of Jerusalem with the rulers of Sodom. Before the judgment on the city, they were like **snow, milk, rubies, sapphires;** they were healthy and well-groomed people who were used to the luxuries of life. The judgment has made their snow-white bodies darker than soot and they have become unrecognizable figures in the streets with shriveled skin **as dry as a stick.** The reference to **snow** and **milk** seems to refer to the whiter skin of the ruling class that was protected from the sun (see Song 1:5-6). Perhaps **rubies** and **sapphires** refers to another form of skin treatment for the wealthy, or hairstyles (see Song 5:11). This description of the reversal of beauty and the appearance of the rulers highlights the despicable condition of Jerusalem's elite and the sudden reversal of their wealth and glory.

■ **9 Tet.** Verse 9 continues the focus on the prolonged suffering of Jerusalem during the Babylonian siege. Those who died with the strike of a sword are considered **better off** (and luckier than) than those who suffered extreme conditions of hunger and starvation during the siege.

B. Prophets and Priests Shed Blood (4:10-16)

■ **10 Yod.** Verse 10 returns to the theme of 4:3-4 and describes the desperation of hunger that led besieged mothers to cook **their own children** for **food** (see 2:20). These were **compassionate women** who were crazed by their hunger. The Hebrew wordplay here is powerful; these women are **compassionate** (*raḥămāniyôt*), which emphasizes the fact that their young ones came from their "womb" (*reḥem*), the seat of their compassion where unborn children find comfort and security. The portrait of mothers cooking their children with their own hands projects the image of unthinkable cruelty and loss of any motherly feeling and affection during the days of siege.

■ **11 Kaf.** Verse 11 departs from the description of siege and begins reflection on the theological cause of the disaster. The disaster came from Yahweh who gave **full vent to his wrath** and **anger,** starting a **fire** that went to the very **foundations** of Jerusalem (see 2:3-4). The word translated **given full vent** (*kālah*) is literally *be complete, at an end* (BDB 477a). Although this verse expresses the full extent of Yahweh's wrath, it also implies that his anger is coming to an end. The sending of fire is a common announcement of judgment in Amos 1, especially against the foreign nations.

■ **12 Lamed.** Verse 12 represents the popular Zion theology of the time, which held that Jerusalem could not be destroyed (Pss 46:5; 48:8). This theology is put in the minds of the **kings** and inhabitants of the world who reportedly find it incredulous that **enemies** could **enter the gates of Jerusalem** as conquerors. In reality, Assyria (in 701 B.C.) and Babylon (in 586 B.C.) did believe they could enter the city. While the failure of the Assyrians in 701 B.C. must have fueled the view of invincibility on the part of Jerusalem's residents, the conquest by Babylon showed that the belief was unfounded. Jeremiah had voiced this unthinkable possibility in his famous Temple Sermon, which attracted condemnation from the priests, prophets, and people of Jerusalem (Jer 26:8; see 7:1-15).

■ **13 Mem.** Verse 13 now places the blame for the disaster on the **prophets** and **priests,** presumably the false prophets and not prophets like Jeremiah who warned against the **sins** and **iniquities** that led to God's withdrawal of protection. The shed **blood of the righteous** is not necessarily an accusation of direct violence on the part of prophets and priests but a condemnation of participation in a corrupt system that robbed poor people of their family land holdings and thus of their livelihoods.

■ **14 Nun.** Verses 14-16 continue the condemnation of prophets and priests (or perhaps people; Hillers 1972, 90). They are **like men who are blind.** Blindness can be a metaphor for distress or lack of divine guidance (see Deut 28:29; Isa 59:10; Zeph 1:17; Isa 42:18-20; Provan 1991, 118). Prophets or priests should see visions but do not (see Mic 3:5-7). They have fallen from their position of respect and honor and have become as unclean as common murderers whose garments are stained **with blood.**

■ **15 Samek.** The cry of a leper is **unclean!** as a warning for healthy people to avoid contamination (see Lev 13:45-46). The unclean prophets and priests do not know of their own disease, or do not admit it, so the cry **unclean!** comes from others who add, **"Away! Away! Don't touch us!"** Even **people among the nations** who have not received the Law realize there is something wrong and shun them.

■ **16 Ayin.** The loss of honor by the priests is made explicit in v 16 and the change is credited to the action of Yahweh who **has scattered them.** The prophets are not mentioned in this verse. Instead the elders are placed in the same category as the priests. They receive **no favor** from God.

C. We Looked in Vain for Help (4:17-22)

■ **17** Pe. Verse 17 shifts focus away from prophets and priests to the fate of the people who now speak for themselves (4:17-20). In 2:11 the poet's eyes failed from weeping; now the people say: **our eyes failed, looking in vain for help** (v 17). This is apparently an allusion to military aid from Egypt, which never materialized (Jer 37:7; Isa 36:6; Hillers 1972, 91). The Egyptians had a vested interest in keeping Palestine as a neutral buffer zone between them and the empires of Mesopotamia, but their actions in protecting this interest did not necessarily involve defending Jerusalem at all costs. It was the Egyptian army that killed King Josiah in 609 B.C. just twenty-three years before Babylon destroyed Jerusalem. The nation in mind could be Edom (not Egypt), which is the only nation mentioned in ch 4 (vv 21-22, Edom refused to help; Provan 1991, 121). Watch **towers** were a common feature of ancient cities and fields as surveillance depended primarily on the naked eye. The people of Jerusalem watched from their towers for help to come from others; it did not come because Jerusalem was looking for help from the wrong sources.

Psalm 46:1-4

God is our refuge and strength,
an ever-present help in trouble.
Therefore we will not fear, though the earth give way
and the mountains fall into the heart of the sea,
though its waters roar and foam
and the mountains quake with their surging. *Selah*
There is a river whose streams make glad the city of God,
the holy place where the Most High dwells.

■ **18** Tsade. Verse 18 portrays the condition of constant watch over the city and the movement of the people within the city by the enemy forces. The citizens had no freedom to walk in their own streets. This signaled the coming of the end of their freedom and the end of the city's existence.

■ **19** Qof. Verse 19 describes the enemy as **swifter than eagles** chasing their prey **over the mountains,** and as thieves ambushing desert travelers from their hideout. The citizens of Jerusalem had no prospect of escape from the enemy forces that surrounded the city.

■ **20** Resh. Even the king **was caught in their traps** (v 20). He is identified as **our very life breath** and the **LORD's anointed** (*měšîaḥ*). The title "anointed one" usually applies to a Davidic king. The title **life breath** was a common Egyptian title for pharaohs (Bergman 2003, 121). Zedekiah was the king when Jerusalem was destroyed in 586 B.C. and he must be the one in mind here. The Targum, however, connected this reference to Josiah (d. 609 B.C.) presumably because of the reference in 2 Chr 35:25 to Jeremiah's laments over Josiah (Brady 2003, 42-43). The Zion theology expressed in 4:12 focused on the indestructibility of Jerusalem. In v 20 the focus is on the false sense of security that came with having a descendant of David ruling in Jerusalem. This ideology and false sense of security come from an oversimplification of the promises given to David in 2 Sam 7:16, "your throne will be established forever."

■ **21 Sin and Shin.** The last two verses of ch 4 are a warning to the nation of Edom, presumably for mocking Jerusalem during its distress (see Ps 137:7). The book of Obadiah is also dedicated to this theme. This reflects the ancient enmity between the Edomites (descended from Esau, see Gen 36) and the Israelites (descended from Jacob). Though Jacob and Esau reportedly reconciled their differences and were reunited (see Gen 33), their descendants lived in constant conflict with each other in their long history (see Num 20:14-21). Lamentations 4:21 ends with a word about the anticipated suffering of Edom; Edom must drink from **the cup** of God's wrath (see Jer 25:15-29).

■ **22 Tav.** Verse 22 continues the prediction of ill for Edom but includes an element of hope for Jerusalem: **your punishment will end; he will not prolong your exile.** The two nations will exchange their places; the Daughter of Edom from her pride and glory to shame and judgment and the Daughter of Zion from her place of shame and judgment to restoration and return to her home. Yahweh's comfort comes to Jerusalem through his announcement of the end of her own days of punishment. The fourth poem ends with this great anticipation of a new future for Jerusalem.

FROM THE TEXT

Hope

The clearest glimmer of hope in the book comes at the end of ch 4. Looking back on history we can see how long the exile lasted and what the circumstances were after the return. Those living in that period had no idea how long it would last or what would happen. But the few hopeful words at the end of this poem anticipate a total reversal of all that the community had to endure during its siege by the Babylonian army. The lamenting community declared that suffering would come to an end and hoped hopes for a future that did not yet exist. In a few words it imagined a world without pain and suffering, a world where children will not starve and die of hunger and thirst, a world where adults will protect and care for their children, and a world with faithful political and religious leaders. This hope comes at the end of a full disclosure of the tragic conditions that made life a bitter experience for the community. Suffering and lamenting about intolerable human conditions energized the community to become hopeful. The hope we find at the end of this poem is not unlike the hope the church finds in the narrative of Jesus' death and resurrection. The church declares in the resurrection faith not only the agony of the cross and the pain of death but also hope for all who suffer in conditions that are intolerable, conditions that prevent the flourishing of human life because of the tragic effects of sin.

V. POEM FIVE: REMEMBER, YAHWEH (5:1-22)

BEHIND THE TEXT

Hope is abandoned altogether in the final poem (ch 5), which has much less to say. While it does call on God for restoration, it closes with an admission of the nagging possibility that God's anger will never end. The lofty (although qualified) hope of ch 3 and the ray of hope in ch 4 have been replaced with doubt, if not despair.

Gunkel classified ch 5 as a lament (1933, 95). It is the clearest example of a lament in Lamentations with the invocation of God's name (5:1), statement of present need (5:2-20), prayer for help (5:21-22), and expression of praise (5:19). Missing elements are the reasons why God should help, and the vow to praise or sacrifice once God has helped. Even though this is the clearest example of a lament psalm in Lamentations, Westermann called it "a transformation of the form" (1981, 174). Chapter 5 also has elements common to the city laments: musical instruments cease (5:14) and there is a plea for restoration (5:21; McDaniel 1968, 206).

The acrostic structure that dominates the book is abandoned for the last poem, although there are twenty-two verses (the number of letters in the alphabet). These verses only have one line each (contrast three lines each for chs 1—3, and two lines each for ch 4). Apparently exhaustion is setting in and the lament is winding down. Assis explains the lack of acrostic structure by identifying ch 5 as a prayer (not a lament), an application of the more structured theological message of chs 1—4 (2007, 724). A spontaneous, heartfelt prayer would not have a carefully designed structure. Chapter 5 can be outlined as follows:

Remember, O LORD! (5:1-18)

Restore us, O LORD! (5:19-22)

IN THE TEXT

A. Remember, O LORD! (5:1-18)

■ I Poem 5 does not begin with *'ēkâ* ("how") like chs 1, 2, and 4. Instead, the opening word is **remember,** a call for God to intervene (see Ps 74:18, 22). The verb **remember** (*zĕkōr*) is more than calling something to mind. It is a call to act on the basis of the knowledge of Jerusalem's suffering. The same goes for the other imperatives in this verse, **look, and see,** which are calls for God to "see to it"; not just to notice, but to take notice and take action. God's action could lead to the end of the **disgrace** that came from the destruction of Jerusalem.

■ 2 Verse 2 laments that **Our inheritance has been turned over to aliens.** The word **inheritance** calls to mind the allocation of land in the book of Joshua (chs 13—19) and emphasizes the land as a gift from God (see Num 26:53; Deut 4:38). This gift has been taken by force by Babylonian aggression. **Aliens** and **foreigners** now possess the native land of the Israelites. The community that has lost its land implicitly appeals to God to restore his gift.

■ 3 A common target of compassion in the OT law are the marginalized members (or nonmembers) of society, usually named as **orphans, fatherless, widows,** and foreigners/sojourners (e.g., Exod 22:22; Deut 10:18). In v 3 the people announce that they **have become orphans and fatherless.** Technically an orphan has no father or mother, but in ancient Israel, the loss of a father or other male protector was more socially and economically devastating. A man could provide for his children if their mother died, but a woman may have no means of support if her husband died. Verse 3 continues to emphasize the situation of mothers who are no longer able to provide for their families. They are **like widows;** like the city of Jerusalem that was once so great and independent (see 1:1).

■ **4** The image of a people without homeland rights continues in v 4; they have lost their properties and possessions, their wells and their trees. Now they must buy the basic necessities of **water** and (fire) **wood** from those who have taken the land away from them.

■ **5** In v 5, the people describe themselves as fleeing to escape their enemies. The phrase **those who pursue us are at our heels** is literally *on our necks we are pursued* (ʿal ṣawwāʾrēnû nirdāpĕnû). Several emendations have been suggested for this phrase. Provan makes sense of it as it stands by reading here a hunting metaphor (1991, 127). The reference is to a predator about to seize and break the neck. The people who are trying to escape the enemy are weary and find no **rest**. This is a reversal of the rest the people found in the Promised Land (Deut 12:10).

■ **6** Verse 6 continues the conditions of famine as bread was only available from the empires of Egypt and Assyria. **We submitted to Egypt and Assyria** conveys Judah's alliances with foreign political powers. Judah has made alliances with these nations for political support and strength in the past. Prophets often warned Judah against relying on Egypt and Assyria for military aid (Isa 7; 36:6; Jer 2:18).

■ **7** In v 7 the lamenting community confesses that the punishment it bears is the outcome of the sin of its ancestors who are now **no more. Punishment** of the children for the sins of the **fathers** seems blatantly unfair to the modern mind. But children do pay the consequences for their parents' sin. They live in the society that the former generation created and carry the advantages and disadvantages of the homelife that their parents provided. What is missing from v 7 is an admission of personal guilt from the generation in question. Ezekiel warned of the limitations of the proverb, "The fathers eat sour grapes, and the children's teeth are set on edge" (18:2). Instead Ezekiel's prophecy warned that "the person who sins is the one who will die" (18:4; see Jer 31:29). This is also a warning against the assumption that a sinner will avoid consequences because they will be borne by the next generation. The omission of guilt here is corrected in v 16 where sin is freely admitted (see 3:42).

■ **8** Verse 8 describes Judah's perspective of its social status. Those whose social status is equivalent to that of slaves are in places of authority over the people of Judah (see Eccl 10:7). The application of the label **slaves** here is not clear, but there is a reversal of appropriate roles. God's treasured people should be living in freedom and authority, but instead they are in subjugation.

■ **9** Verse 9 describes the perilous conditions in which the people live. **The sword in the desert** probably refers to an approaching army. Bergant suggests robbers outside the city (2003, 129). The people live under dangerous conditions, and they risk their lives to get bread. It is possible that the reference here is to the army that is camped outside the walls of the city, which makes it dangerous for the people to go out into their fields to grow grain for making bread. But this does not explain the reference to **the sword in the desert.** Another possibility is that the reference is to an enemy blockade of the desert road that made it dangerous for the people of Judah to go down to Egypt to buy food (see Provan 1991, 131).

■ **10** Verse 10 describes the high fever that accompanies illness caused by famine and starvation (**Our skin is hot as an oven**). The verb translated **hot** (*nikmārû*) only occurs three times in the OT (Gen 43:30; 1 Kgs 3:26; Hos 11:8). Hillers translates, "black as an oven" (following Septuagint and Syriac; 1972, 98).

■ **11** The people lament about the rape of their **women** in Jerusalem and their **virgins in the towns of Judah.** One of the harsh realities of war in the ancient world was rape and abuse of women by the invading army, which caused fear and dread of the invaders in the land. Inheritance rights and blood lines were compromised by rape and adultery, which made the Israelites even more sensitive to these crimes. "Rape defiled the integrity of the family itself" (Bergant 2003, 130).

■ **12** Verse 12 conveys the humiliation and suffering of those who were in positions of honor and authority. The **princes** or rulers were **hung** from their **hands,** and they were made helpless by the enemy. The enemy also disregarded the position of the **elders** in Judah and gave them none of the honor or respect they deserved.

■ **13** Verse 13 focuses on the slavery and forced labor imposed on the young people of Judah by the Babylonians. The enemy made the life of young people miserable by heavy labor at the **millstones** and by forcing them to carry **loads of wood** to meet the needs of the invading army.

■ **14** Verse 14 provides a contrast to times of peace when the city gate was a bustling venue for wisdom, commerce, and justice. Elders would sit there and witness transactions and pronounce judgments (Deut 21:19; 22:15). But in times of siege, **the elders are gone from the city gate,** and other festivities have ceased. There is no business as usual, only a desperate striving to survive.

■ **15** The city under siege remains without festivities that brought joy to the people. Instead of dancing, the people mourn. The people voice this loss in the hope that God will once again turn **mourning** into **dancing** (Ps 30:11).

■ **16** The people live without any honor in the world (**the crown has fallen from our head**); they no longer have their former glory (see Job 19:9; Jer 13:18). A crown symbolized festivity (Song 3:11) as well as sovereignty. Verse 16 may also be understood as a reference to the fall of King Zedekiah, the last king of Judah, and the killing of his sons by the Babylonians (2 Kgs 25:7). The admission **we have sinned** connects all this suffering with national sin. The community recognizes that its precarious life under enemy occupation is the result of sin against God.

■ **17** Judah's recognition that sin is the cause of the destruction of the city makes the **hearts** of the lamenting community **faint** and weakens their **eyes.** Faint heart and **dim** eyes convey the hopelessness, despair, and discouragement that the community experiences because of the destruction of the city. They do not see any future for the nation.

■ **18** Verse 18 contrasts the once thriving and cultivated land with the present reality of desolation. Zion, the city of God's dwelling where people assembled for worship and sounds of joy were heard in the streets, has become a desolate place, a place where **jackals** live.

B. Restore Us, O Lᴏʀᴅ! (5:19-22)

■ **19** The last four verses of ch 5 move back to the tone of v 1 with a direct address to God. The personal pronoun **You** is added for emphasis. The lamenting community begins its prayer with a confession of the enduring nature of God's sovereignty. This confession, **Your throne endures from generation to generation,** contrasts God's eternal kingship with the kingship of Zedekiah that ended with the Babylonian invasion. There is also an implicit message that the throne of Babylon will not last. The book of Daniel also emphasizes the temporary nature of all kingdoms except God's. Only Yahweh's throne will endure forever.

■ **20** Verse 20 explicitly returns to the theme of v 1, this time in the negative: **Why do you always forget us?** or *Why do you forget us forever?* (*lāmmâ lāneṣaḥ tiškāḥēnû*). This is a rhetorical question that is meant to spur God into action on behalf of repentant Judah. It is a statement of faith that God is real and powerful and cares.

■ **21** The request becomes explicit in v 21; the community asks God to **restore** (*šûb*) them to himself as his people. Restoration to the land of Israel is restoration to God because he made his earthly dwelling there. The people were powerless to return by their own initiative; their return to the land depended on God's willingness to return them to the land. The people also petition God to **renew** their **days** so that they may live and fellowship with God as in the former days—days before they suffered the tragedy of 586 B.C.

■ **22** The chapter and book end on a somewhat depressing note, prompting Jewish liturgy to go back to v 21 in order to end on a high note (Bettan 1950, 120). The possibility presented in v 22 is that God has **utterly rejected** his people, and is **angry** with them **beyond measure.** This possibility is entertained as a matter of emotional response, not as an enduring logical possibility. It cannot be that God will remain angry forever. His discipline can only last a matter of generations (Exod 20:5), but his mercy endures from generation to generation (see 3:22; 5:19). The community expresses hope, but it also expresses doubt. This verse also implies that without a favorable response from God, the community will continue in its desolate and abandoned state, a community that will be in lament forever. Its lament will end only when God responds mercifully to its appeal for restoration. The book ends without an answer from God; so the lament continues, but the community has placed its hope in the God whose "compassions never fail," and who is "good to those whose hope is in him" (3:22, 25). Despite that rousing climax in ch 3, the final word of the book reflects the continuing suffering of Jerusalem. "With thinning hope and flagging energy, the voices drift away" (O'Connor 2002, 79).

FROM THE TEXT

Complaint to God

Though the lamenting community expresses lofty (although muffled) declarations of hope in chs 3 and 4, it returns to a monologue of complaint directed toward God in ch 5. The community speaks directly to God. Although the book records no response from God, the community continues to address him in complaint. The book does not offer easy answers to the voice of suffering, but permits it to be heard in forceful language. It presents pain and suffering as powerful realities that human beings experience. However, the fact that the people direct their complaint to God also shows their tremendous confidence in God as the source of their hope. They also recognize that they are not entitled to God's grace, but they remain hopeful, like Job who declared, "Though he slay me, yet will I hope in him" (Job 13:15). And Jerusalem understands that God is the only viable option, just as the disciples responded when Jesus asked them if they would desert him: "Lord, to whom shall we go?" (John 6:68).

O'Connor from *The Tears of the World*

The voices of Lamentations urge readers to face suffering, to speak of it, to be dangerous proclaimers of the truths that nations, families, and individuals prefer to repress. They invite us to honor the pain muffled in our hearts, overlooked in our society, and crying for our attention in other parts of the world. In this way Lamentations can shelter the tears of the world. (2002, 95)